BLOODY DAWN

BLOODY DAWN

The Story of the Lawrence Massacre

THOMAS GOODRICH

THE KENT STATE UNIVERSITY PRESS
KENT, OHIO, AND LONDON, ENGLAND

© 1991 by The Kent State University Press, Kent, Ohio 44242
All rights reserved
Library of Congress Catalog Card Number 91–8638
ISBN 0–87338–442–3
ISBN 0–87338–476–8 (pbk.)
Manufactured in the United States of America

06 05 04 03 02 01   8 7 6 5 4

Library of Congress Cataloging-in-Publication Data
Goodrich, Th.
  Bloody dawn : the story of the Lawrence massacre / Thomas
Goodrich.
      p.   cm.
  Includes bibliographical references and index.
  ISBN 0–87338–442–3 (alk.) ∞
  ISBN 0–87338–476–8 (pbk : alk.) ∞
  1. Massacres—Kansas—Lawrence—History—19th century.
2. Lawrence (Kan.)—History.   3. Kansas—History—Civil War,
1861–1865.   4. Quantrill, William Clarke, 1837–1865.
E474.97.G66   1991
978.1'65—DC20   91–8638

British Library Cataloging-in-Publication data are available.

CONTENTS

BLOODY DAWN

I

OLD SCORES

On a bright Missouri morning in August 1863, nearly three hundred horsemen emerged from the timber along the Blackwater River. Onto the prairie they rode in military order, four abreast. Many of the men, those at front and rear, wore coats of Union blue, but most in the column did not. Some had been working fields the day before. They carried no flag.

When possible, hills were used to screen their movements, brush and creek bottoms as well. Later that day, however, a Federal scout from Warrensburg spotted the riders passing west, apparently toward the Kansas line, forty-five miles away. The scout rode back to report.

That evening the column skirted the town of Pleasant Hill, fifteen miles east of Kansas, and here it veered slightly, slanting southwest. Halts to water and graze were frequent, but short. Over one hundred Rebel recruits, weaving their way south to Arkansas, met the horsemen and agreed to join. Together the four hundred rode into the night.

By daylight, Thursday, August 20, the column left the prairie and entered the woods along the Grand River, four miles east of the Kansas line. Here a camp was made. Horses were unsaddled and tethered. Food was prepared, sleep taken. An additional fifty men rode in from downriver and joined the camp.

At approximately the same time, two companies of Union militia left Warrensburg and struck off in pursuit. The identity and nature of the column was yet a mystery, but a messenger was hurried west to spread the alarm.

By noon the temperature approached 100.[1]

The entire eastern border of Kansas is shared with only one state—Missouri. For seven suspenseful years the eyes of the nation had been locked on this border because it was here in 1854, after passage of the Kansas-Nebraska Bill, that the dramatic struggle between freedom and slavery began. For decades the annoying issue of slavery had been swept under the rug only to sift up again and again. But at length the showdown came and the stage was this border, a land not particularly beautiful or rich in itself, yet at the time, and to the parties concerned, it was the most valuable tract of sod on earth.

For the South it was simply a question of survival. To hold the line with the North in Congress, Kansas and all the territories west and south must embrace slavery. There were never any claims to Nebraska or the wild regions beyond, and it was well understood that these lands would go to the North. But above all Kansas had to be delivered to the South because, as one observer prophesied, "if Kansas is not made a slave state . . . there will never be another."[2] And even worse, others warned, should the new territory fall to the North it would be but a matter of time before Missouri too was lost, because with much of its slave population located in the western half of that state the Kansas line would pull like a magnet on runaways. But if there was deep concern among some Southerners, an air of confidence surrounded others, for it was Missouri's mere proximity to the territory with its settlers ready to swarm over the western border that gave the slave power its highest hope.

Nebraska for the North, Kansas for the South. Such, it seemed, would be the compromise. And for those who ignored the claims of the South, a warning: "Kansas must be a slave state or the Union will be dissolved."[3]

To a good many in the North, the idea of further compromise with slavery was unthinkable. The South had no rights to Kansas, political or otherwise, and this they were determined to enforce even if it did mean the breakup of the Union. Not only would Nebraska be free and all the country beyond, they insisted, but so too would Kansas and all the land lying west. "Not one inch further," was the cry; no "chains, shackles, Negro-whips, [or] blood-hounds on the beautiful plains of Kansas."[4]

Consequently, when the territory opened to settlement in 1854 and the two sides met, the results were as tragic as they were predictable. Much to the shock and anger of the South the North did not bow to slavery's bid on Kansas, and in an even more surprising development their immigrants came in far greater numbers than expected. Desperately, proslavers worked to stem the tide. Bluster and threats came first.

"God damn you," shouted one Southerner, "if you are ever caught here again you shall be strung up! Go to Nebraska, damn you! You have no right in Kansas!"[5]

Not cowed in the least, free-soilers held their ground. "With God, humanity, and Sharp's rifles on our side, we are prepared to meet any struggle," they replied defiantly.[6]

As the scales tipped hopelessly against them, Missourians grew violent. They marched to Kansas in mobs, "Border Ruffians" they were called, crossing the state line to enforce the territorial "laws"; chasing, jailing, even tar and feathering free-soilers and rafting them downriver. Murderous fanatics arose on both sides and each claimed divine sanction for his deeds.

On a dark, windy night in May 1856, John Brown led a small group of believers to Pottawatomie Creek and with musket and blade butchered five proslavery settlers. Thus was inaugurated civil war, and for the next several years death and destruction swept the prairie. By 1858, however, the outcome for the most part was settled. Although Brown's atrocity was repaid in kind when five free-staters were mowed down on the Marais des Cygnes in the spring of that year, this proved but the parting shot of a vanquished South. Northern immigration came on in a rush. Kansas would, after all, be free. And none understood this more clearly, nor acted upon it more readily, than slaves in adjoining Missouri.

"The long agony is over," sighed one of the victors. "The last act of the drama which opened in blood and was continued in violence has been enacted, and the curtain has fallen upon a happy consummation."[7]

And at the moment so it might have seemed. Yet those with a common degree of foresight plainly saw that the "drama" was not over; the curtain had been raised, not lowered. Kansas, the great experiment, proved a failure and solved nothing in the end. It did illustrate, however, what many had feared all along—that America as it existed in the middle of the nineteenth century, half free, half slave, could no longer abide with itself.

As the thunderhead that had boiled over this ill-fated land for the past seven years spread eastward, the border as a national arena was all but forgotten, forgotten, that is, by all save those who remained— the Missourians and Kansans. A legacy of hatred and violence had evolved which neither side could, which neither side would, forget.

At the beginning of the American Civil War, Kansas contained a population of roughly one hundred thousand strung almost entirely along the Missouri and Kansas, or Kaw, River valleys. And it was in part because of the recent territorial excitement that a shabby air of want lay heavy on the new land. Business and commerce had been crimped, building and public works were disrupted, crops went unattended while settlers had devoted a vast amount of time to politics and the struggle for freedom. Then nature added to the problem. From early 1859 to late 1860 a severe drought wracked the territory, ruining crops and causing widespread suffering and dismay. It was with much effort and no mean amount of Eastern philanthropy that the people were set back on the road to recovery. But complete recovery was slow in coming and by the spring of 1861 the young state remained impoverished.[8]

By contrast western Missouri was a bloom of prosperity. A solid, rooted society of forty years dwelled here on splendid farms and plantations, rich in cattle, horses, and mules, with black slaves hoeing fields of corn, tobacco, and hemp. Green-lawned courthouses surrounded by thriving, white-fenced towns dotted the countryside. Everything bespoke plenty. And even though the Missouri border was in many respects crude, rough, and unmistakably Western, it was like another world when compared to the land over the line.

To most Kansans, the contest of the fifties was proof enough that one needn't look for Dixie and treason in Virginia, South Carolina, or Mississippi—one need only gaze across the border. Shortly after the firing on Fort Sumter in April 1861, their convictions rang true when throughout western Missouri acts of disloyalty and sedition were daily occurrences. With their neighbor in virtual revolt, no further excuse was needed. To some Kansans, "Sumter" was the eagle's cry to march across the line and with firm hand and bayonet steel crush the rebellion and thus help preserve the Union. But for a larger flock of Kansans, "jayhawkers," as they came to be called, Sumter was the signal gun for open season on the pride and bounty of western Missouri. It was also a chance to settle some old scores.

Unlike the battlefields farther east, the western border for the most part was not a stage where vast armies acted out grand strategy or clashed in bloody conflict. The war in the West was instead a very personal war, a war among neighbors, a war of theft and arson, a war of midnight murder and torture—a vendetta.

No Kansan personified this brand of war more, nor had a greater hand in promoting it, than did one Charles Jennison. Actually, the outbreak of civil war simply lent an aura of legitimacy to a program Jennison had been pursuing all along. Characterized as cruel, heartless, cowardly, a "moral vagabond" by his detractors, to friends the

jockey-sized jayhawker was a mailed fist of retribution, punishing
Missouri for crimes past and present. Whatever the opinion, Jennison and his regiment became in fact the scourge and salt of western
Missouri during the first summer and winter of the war. One by one
the towns along the border fell victim to their forays. Stores were
looted, safes emptied, elegant homes gutted. Nor was the countryside spared. Night after night the skies over the border were aglow as
barns, cabins, and crops were set ablaze. Those hapless farmers
lucky enough to escape the torch watched powerless while the fruits
of their labor were hauled off in their own wagons. Herds of cattle,
horses, and sheep were likewise driven west. And wherever Jennison
and his men marched, despite President Abraham Lincoln's bid to
hold loyal slave owners to the Union, there followed in the wake
large crowds of blacks stepping gaily over to Kansas and freedom.
Masters who tried to recover their chattel were beaten or killed.[9]

Most Kansans praised Jennison's style of war. Abolitionists
thrilled to the irony of Missouri slaves, "contrabands," escaping
bondage under the banner of the same regiment in which John
Brown, Jr., served as captain. And newspaper editors, gloating over
the colonel's "victories," eagerly echoed his warning that "desolation will follow treason." Others smiled and found sport in the numerous tales, one of which claimed that Missouri mothers quieted
restless children simply by whispering the name "Jennison." From a
distance it did seem as if the jayhawkers were putting down the rebellion in Missouri single-handedly, and it was a certainty that
much of the plunder rolling into Kansas greatly enriched the state.

Across the border it was another matter. Among Missouri's hard-
pressed loyalists, Charles Jennison marching under the U.S. flag was
seen as a much more serious threat to peace and accord than all the
secessionists in the state combined. His brutal treatment of captured Rebels did little more than fire the will of those who escaped,
as did the terrible reports which stated that some even had their ears
"cropped" as a ghastly, living reminder to others.[10] Although his
crimes against Missourians were legion, opposition might have remained minimal had Jennison been more selective on whom he
preyed. But he was not. Consequently, many would-be Unionists and
the important neutral segment, formerly little more than fence-
sitters on the jayhawkers' approach, soon became active, violent enemies of the government on their passing.

Renowned artist and ironclad Unionist George Caleb Bingham
led the campaign, orating throughout his beloved Missouri, pounding Washington with the same message: "Jennison must be removed,

Jennison must be removed. His outrages in this state are so notorious that I no longer have sufficient brass . . . to defend the authorities of the government."[11] Largely through Bingham's efforts others were spurred to protest.

The problem might have been simple were Jennison's men the only Kansans on the border. But they were not alone. There was James Montgomery, a Bible-toting evangelist whose easy philosophy on war—to "keep the Missourians from our doors . . . give them something to do at home"—translated into men rebuilding what he and his raiders had destroyed and trying to recover goods they had stolen. Later there was also George Hoyt, a handsome, educated, "whole souled New England boy," leader of a group known as Red Legs because of their bright leather gaiters. Ostensibly organized to scout and defend the Kansas border, Hoyt's murderous gang was in fact engaged in a lucrative horse-stealing operation. Other jayhawkers banded together and joined the treasure hunt. Indeed, the sport of plundering western Missouri became so popular that, weather and crops permitting, even more Kansans slipped across the state line in twos and threes and jayhawked "on their own hook."[12]

There was also a rise in the number of men such as Marshall Cleveland, men who dropped the mask of patriotism altogether and randomly robbed and murdered on both sides of the line. "Like all other good institutions," lamented one Kansas editor on jayhawking, "it is liable to abuse." And as the "abuse" of Unionists in Kansas, as well as in Missouri, became more blatant each day, enthusiasm for jayhawking quickly vanished.[13]

A few of the sworn free-booters like Cleveland and his gang were driven off or killed. James Montgomery soon took his jayhawking skills to the swamps of Florida. And shortly even Jennison was leashed and jerked from the border. But all this came much too late to help Missouri. By the winter of 1861 the depredations of the Kansas jayhawkers had proven so thorough that the region was little better than a waste, inhabited by herds of hogs and cattle running wild through fields idle and overgrown with weeds. Homes still standing were rare. The entire countryside was a burned-out shell of its former self, and along with it many a grave had been added in a brief summer and winter of war. "If I had to sentence a man to solitude I should send him into one of the border counties of Missouri," wrote a Kansas soldier.[14]

Not all Missourians took it lying down, however. During the summer and autumn of 1861 a number of small raiding parties crossed into Kansas to pillage and burn. But these forays were by and large pathetic attempts at revenge, and when contrasted with the efficient rape of western Missouri they were of no consequence.[15] Kansans were hardly put out. What little anxiety they did feel was more than offset by the knowledge that their old territorial foe had been brought to its knees and its wealth redistributed west.

"Old scores are all settled," laughed one jayhawker, "and with a tolerable fair interest."[16]

But the war on the border was far from over. Although it did seem to end that winter, the fact that it had not became abundantly clear when a storm broke over Kansas in 1862. With the small Southern army under former governor Sterling Price driven from the state by superior Union forces, a few defiant Rebels—"bushwhackers"—chose to remain in Missouri, take to the woods, and continue the fight from there. As the struggle between the guerrillas and Federal soldiers progressed, the partisans not only hung on and survived but became daring as well. Many recent victims of Jennison and other jayhawkers took heart and joined until the bands grew considerably in strength and boldness. By late that summer, as one Kansas town after another was seized and plundered, those west of the line began to appreciate amply the trials Missourians had endured during the previous year.

At various times after 1861 it did seem to some hopeful observers as if the guerrilla war against Kansas had peaked and that Union arms were at last gaining the peace and security demanded. But then, and often preceded by weeks of quiet, the hammer would again fall. At length, angry Yankee commanders responded with a series of violent acts and measures. Unable to deal militarily with the bushwhackers themselves, they struck for the root of Rebel support—civilians. One such measure began in midsummer 1863.

With little warning friends and relatives of known or suspected guerrillas were located by squads of Federal soldiers, roughed up, arrested, then led off to detention at Kansas City. As the sweep progressed and the jails filled, accommodations soon became inadequate. Finally, toward the first of August, a small number of prisoners were lodged in a makeshift guardhouse at the edge of town. The inmates were treated well enough there, but the choice of buildings was unfortunate.

Prior to its use as a prison, authorities were cautioned that the brick structure was unfit for habitation. Originally but two floors high, it was only in afterthought that the burden of a third story was added. And with little or no planning, the rear of the place had been clumsily built over a ravine. As the days passed the steady deterioration of the building became quite evident to all. Thus, early on the morning of August 13 an inspector was called in. The officer examined the structure, took note of the definite signs of shifting—walls cracked, dust and mortar along the foundation—then turned in his report to superiors. This, however, prompted a further inspection of the building, which quickly but quietly overruled the verdict of the first; the structure was deemed safe and the issue was dropped. The prisoners remained.

Later that day, shortly after lunch, a soldier on the third floor of the jail heard a creaking sound; glancing up he saw the walls slowly separating from the ceiling. Swiftly the man dove to safety, shouting for everyone to jump. But there was no time. Within seconds the walls fell inward; moments later only dust and debris remained. A huge crowd gathered. Muffled cries and moans drifted up from the wreckage as rescue efforts began. Pulled from the rubble, bloody and broken, survivors became hysterical, screaming that the Federals were murderers, that the building had been a death trap. The crowd became angry and loud. With bayonets fixed, troops soon arrived. They were jeered and threatened by the mob.[17]

The following day, on the third page of the Unionist Kansas City newspaper, a small article under "Local Matters" made passing note of the incident:

> *Western Journal of Commerce*
> Kansas City, Mo. Aug. 14, 1863
>
> The large three story brick building . . . occupied for the last two weeks as a guard house, fell in yesterday afternoon. . . . There were in the building at the time, nine women prisoners, two children and one man: Four women were killed; the balance escaped without fatal injuries.

That day another woman did succumb to injuries and two others remained horribly crushed.[18]

Few Kansans heard the roar of these crashing bricks or the screams that soon followed, but in the deep, dark woods of western Missouri, the sounds were both terrible and utterly deafening.

2

THE DEAD MEN

Aubrey, Kansas, is situated on a swell of prairie several miles west of the state line. Except for a small hotel and a cluster of homes the sole attraction in Aubrey was the military. Capt. Joshua Pike commanded two companies of Kansas cavalry here, and for the defense of the state Pike's outfit held the most important post. From Aubrey the country could be seen for miles around, sloping gently to the tree-lined creeks beyond.

Captain Pike, "one of the best officers in the service," some people said, had proven to be just the man for the job—a steady performer.[1] Although important, it was a tedious, thankless assignment for the one hundred men quartered here. Barren, far from any large town, hot, dusty.

"Life at this station is very dull," a trooper wrote during the second week of August 1863. "Everything is quiet and but little of an exciting nature occurs to relieve the monotony."[2]

Then, late in the afternoon of the twentieth, a nervous farmer rode into Aubrey. An unusually large number of men, he revealed to Pike, had been encamped on the Grand, just east of the border. They were now moving up the river, he added, toward the state line and . . . toward Aubrey.[3]

Although born and bred in Missouri, Bill Anderson considered himself a Kansan. He'd spent five years there. Heeding the irresistible call of the West, Anderson's father had picked the family up one day in 1857 and then set it down again on the virgin plains of Kansas. The old man passed along the Santa Fe Road, ignoring the more populated, troubled eastern counties, opting for the peace and quiet and plentiful land of the Council Grove area. They were a hardworking, law-abiding family, the Andersons—the father and mother, the three brothers, the three sisters.[4] And the land of their adoption,

9

a wilderness of rolling prairie and endless sky, was in many ways similar to the old home in Missouri, two hundred miles away. There was an important difference, however: although they were Southerners, most of their new neighbors were not. When war came in 1861, the Andersons refused to take up arms against the South.

In early May 1862, a local judge accused the Andersons of horse stealing. Hard words were exchanged, tempers flared, and a short time later a showdown occurred between the elder Anderson and his accuser. When the shooting stopped and the smoke had finally cleared, Bill Anderson's father lay in a pool of blood, cold and still. In turn, the son delivered himself into custody, and although he was soon set free on bail, an angry mob snatched another man also charged with stealing horses and quickly hanged him. Young Anderson didn't linger near Council Grove long, and after abandoning the farm, he and his family fled to the border.

Two months later, accompanied by several others, Bill Anderson returned. The judge, at home with his wife and her brother, also ran a small grocery by the wayside; thus when a stranger came one night seeking whiskey, the Kansan grabbed his gun and led the way. Just as he was about to leave the cellar of his store, two shadowy figures stepped from the dark and opened fire. When the brother-in-law appeared, he too was shot and, along with the judge, was stuffed into the cellar. As the wounded men struggled desperately to escape, the store was set ablaze over their heads. Finally, after torching the other buildings and herding in the victims' horses, Anderson and his companions rode back up the trail to the woods of western Missouri.[5]

Following the Council Grove affair and his escape from Kansas, Bill Anderson did surprisingly little for the next twelve months. True, his father was gone—"murdered," Bill said—and this wound would remain deep and open. But the rest of his family was yet together and safe, and at the time there seemed no reason to suppose that they would not always be. He did fall in with the bushwhackers and was in a few small actions. But Anderson was not a leader of men; he was a follower. And it suited his tastes to keep things just that way. He was partial to the lighter side of life. He also favored a bottle now and again. Then, on July 31, 1863, Bill Anderson's world began to change.

On that night Anderson led a small band of bushwhackers on a raid through eastern Kansas. After murdering two men and burning several homes along the way, the marauders slipped up the Kaw Valley to a home in which the Anderson family was staying. Through-

BILL ANDERSON
(courtesy of the State Historical Society of Missouri, Columbia).

out the region the military roundup of guerrilla relatives was in progress, and it was for this reason that the Kansan had come—to hustle his family away to safety. And so, early next morning the mother and her children left with the eldest son. Crossing back to a point just over the state line, the family pulled up; here Anderson quietly hid them among a group of friends.

Whatever his hope, Anderson's plan was a failure. The effort postponed his family's arrest by only hours, for hardly had they settled when a squad of soldiers arrived and herded them off to Kansas City and to prison. Legend has it that two weeks later, on August 13, Bill Anderson began toting a silk cord with him wherever he went and that generally, no matter where his shadow fell after that day, a new knot or two was tied. That was the day the building collapsed, crippling one sister for life and crushing another to death.[6]

One of the Yankee officers who had helped run the Todds from town the year before reflected on the matter with a riding companion in early August 1863. The son, George, he concluded, was a "blood thirsty cuss." And it was true. Since his family's banishment from Kansas City Todd had lived up to that label, and he had every intention of living up to it even more.[7]

One dark morning in March 1863, near Sibley, Missouri, Todd and a gang of guerrillas forced a steamer to land as it was passing close to shore. The Rebels rushed aboard, rifled the clerk's safe, robbed the male passengers, and then compelled them to dump boxes of government supplies into the river. A further search of the boat turned up a handful of Yankee militiamen and eighty frightened blacks. Except for two who were shot and killed, the remaining Federals either escaped or were given paroles. As for the slaves, contrabands going west to resettlement and freedom, all were ordered ashore. The man in charge of finding homes for these bondsmen, their sponsor, was searched for several times but not found. With that the bushwhackers prepared to leave the boat. When asked by the edgy captain what he intended to do with the blacks, Todd didn't even have to think. "Blow their brains out!" came his simple reply. Although most wisely escaped earlier, nine of them had not, and as the boat's mate held the lantern Todd shot them dead, one after the other.[8]

Three months later, on a warm evening just before dusk, a company of Kansas cavalry entered the long, wooded lane south of Westport, Missouri. That day the weary outfit had ridden up over a dusty trail under a fierce sun. They planned to camp for the night at the

GEORGE TODD
(courtesy of the Carl W. Breihan Collection).

military post in Westport, and many of the men, with the captain's consent, had strapped their unwieldy carbines to the saddle. A short time before, another outfit had passed the same way.

When one mile from Westport, George Todd and sixty bush-whackers rose up from behind a stone wall and fired into the ranks. The Yankees toppled off in a row. Before the stunned survivors could free their guns, the guerrillas fired again, then charged. Panicked, the troopers broke and fled back down the lane followed by riderless horses and screaming Rebels. Later, when a relief column arrived, they found fourteen bodies sprawled in the road. Most were stripped clean of clothing, and many had numerous wounds. But all, it was noticed, had fatal shots to the head and heart—a little something extra, just to make sure.

The next morning a party of Federal scouts located a fresh trail. They followed it for several hours, then dismounted and entered a thick undergrowth. Moving softly, the squad approached to within a few yards of a clearing in which four men were discovered asleep. Someone made a slight noise and one of the figures rose up on an arm, rubbed his eyes, then fell back again with a hole blown through his chest. Two others were also killed, but although wounded, the fourth escaped.

Some days later, another group of scouts successfully ambushed a band of guerrillas, and in this fight the soldiers triumphantly announced that, indeed, George Todd was among the slain. Word spread rapidly and loyalists rejoiced.[9]

Few men in western Missouri commanded more respect than did Henry Younger of Harrisonville. Colonel Younger was a pleasant, likable man, honored and admired by all fortunate enough to have his acquaintance. For many years he had served as county magistrate, ruling with a firm but fair hand. Such was his popularity that he even sat several terms in the state legislature at Jefferson City. Younger was also extremely wealthy: his homes in the region were splendid showcases, and his land-holdings throughout the area were vast. Younger also owned numerous slaves. Although fiercely proud of his Southern heritage, when war came Henry Younger prayed for peace, held hard to the Union, and as a U.S. mail contractor carried on with his duties.

In late 1861, when the jayhawkers under Charles Jennison marched into Harrisonville flying the Stars and Stripes, they loaded Younger's possessions into wagons, threatened, bullied, and abused his helpless family, stole forty top horses, then marched out again. At that moment the old Missourian made an abrupt about-face and became an avowed secessionist.

The following summer Younger was returning home from a trip to Kansas City. Just south of Westport he was surrounded by a gang of Union militia, robbed of a large sum of money, murdered, then left bloating in the sun. Later the Younger mansion was burned to the ground and the mother and children forced out to face the winter.[10]

On a night in August 1863, Younger's oldest son, Coleman, led fifty raiders to Pleasant Hill, Missouri. Several loyalist homes were put to the torch, as were the dwellings of those who had recently sheltered a Kansas regiment. The next night the son returned and burned some more.[11]

Cole Younger didn't need a new reason to hate Kansas and fight the Yankees in his state, but on August 13, when the prison fell and killed a cousin, he got it nonetheless.

When Dick Yager returned to Missouri from the West, as foreman on one of his father's wagon trains, he found that Jennison had already been there. In a single night the Yagers' farm and lucrative freighting business were all but wiped out. The jayhawkers made off with thousands of dollars in furniture, horses, and slaves. If there was a glimmer of hope, the Yagers did manage to save a large herd of sheep and almost fifty head of fine stock. Even this spark sputtered out, however, when the Kansans returned a few days later to finish the job.[12]

Already a secessionist at heart, joining the Rebel forces was an easy step for Dick Yager to take. Fighting in a few engagements at first, falling on and looting the town of Gardner, Kansas, one night without firing a shot, Yager then led a daring raid to Diamond Springs, over one hundred miles deep into Kansas. Here, after murdering a storekeeper, he and two dozen men rode back toward Missouri, working along the Santa Fe Road, robbing and killing.[13]

Partly through his own words and partly through his son's actions, Yager's father was now rotting away in a dark cell of a St. Louis prison.[14]

At 6:00 P.M. on August 20, 1863, with the sun still blazing above the horizon, Bill Anderson, George Todd, Cole Younger, and Dick Yager, along with William Gregg, Frank James, and over four hundred others rode over the State Line Road and entered Kansas. Except for those in blue at front and rear, most wore tattered butternut or faded red shirts, patched trousers tucked inside well-worn boots, and sweat-stained, wide-brimmed hats. They carried only a minimum of food and supplies. Yet they also had with them an ample amount of black powder and lead. Some balanced carbines over saddle bows. Many more, however, had stuck in holsters, belts, or side bags up to eight revolvers apiece—Colt's big navy model, a .36 caliber cap and ball machine that left an "ugly looking wound" when fired into a man at close range.

Just over the line the column rode up a small lane leading west toward Spring Hill. Shielding them on the right was a diminishing row of trees along the headwaters of the Grand. To save strength in the terrific heat, horses were held to a fast walk, occasionally a trot, but never more. Still, a large cloud of dust rose in their wake. The first test was coming soon, just up the road.

"Make no attack unless fired upon," was the command.[15]

Some of the four hundred, such as Anderson and Younger, were kin to the dead girls at Kansas City. Most, such as Todd and Yager, were not. Many had little left in life to lose except that life, and a majority didn't consider this much to risk. Half were farmers, such as the ones who had joined that morning or the fresh-faced recruits who had come along for the ride. The other half—guerrillas like Anderson, Todd, Younger, and Yager—the other half, at this moment, were the most dangerous men on earth.

After hearing the farmer's story, Captain Pike ordered his men to saddle and mount. Before he left Aubrey, however, Pike quickly jotted out two messages—one to Coldwater Grove in the south, the other to Little Santa Fe in the north—warning these posts that 700 Rebels were on the state line. Riders were given the notes and sent on the double-quick.[16]

Pike then mounted and led his force south. After a short ride the captain halted, and as his men drew their carbines and revolvers, he formed a line of battle.[17] Above the trees of the Grand, a mile or so in the distance, a large cloud of dust could be seen. In a few minutes, as the brush gave way to open ground, the first of the invaders slipped into view, then more and more until the entire guerrilla force was passing to Pike's front—more such horsemen than he or his troops had ever seen before.

Suicide, the captain thought.

And thus, as the Rebels continued their progress west, Pike turned and led his company back to camp. Once there the nervous officer dispatched a second rider north, bearing the word that 800 bushwhackers were in the state and on the move. Pike then settled in at Aubrey, awaiting developments.[18]

JOSHUA PIKE
(courtesy of the Kansas State Historical Society).

3

THE "LIVE" MAN

At dusk, the courier from Joshua Pike reached the military camp at Coldwater Grove, thirteen miles southeast of Aubrey. Lt. Col. Charles Clark read the news of guerrillas on the Grand with growing apprehension. Acting promptly, Clark sent runners to outlying stations ordering all troops to rush forward immediately. The colonel then returned a hasty message north, cautioning Pike to "watch the enemy and report." With men and mounts fresh and ready, Clark held to his post, awaiting further word on the Rebel whereabouts.[1]

At approximately the same time, 8:00 P.M., Capt. Charles Coleman at Little Santa Fe, a dozen miles north of Aubrey, received Pike's first report. Fifteen minutes later the second dispatch arrived, stating in part that 800 guerrillas were in Kansas and moving west. Without hesitation Coleman sped a courier west to Olathe, warning of invasion, requesting that word be relayed inland as rapidly as possible. Another rider was sent north to the district headquarters at Kansas City.

By nine o'clock Coleman and eighty cavalrymen left camp, riding hard down the trail to Aubrey.[2]

In retrospect, the border war of 1861 must have seemed like light and carefree sport. Looking back on it all from the dark days of 1863, Kansans could be forgiven if in their hearts there was a longing for a return to those simpler ways of life; back to that joyous time of springtide war when, with flags and banners flapping, the jayhawkers had swooped across the state line to crush the rebellion for God and the Union and in the process pluck old Missouri clean for God and themselves. Like so many children loose in a farmer's orchard, the war had been more a wonderful game back then. And like children at the peak of their excitement and greed, few seemed mindful of another day or the ultimate consequences of their rash acts. But as always, a new day did finally arrive. And when it did, the "game," for all practical purposes, was up.

With the dawn of 1862, Kansans awoke to find vengeance-hungry Missourians crossing west of the line much as the jayhawkers had crossed eastward the year before. And thus with this sobering reality upon them, and with both sides of the border suddenly locked in a vicious little war, Kansans began to clamor for protection.

Various theories were tossed about as to which method of safe-guarding the state was best. When all was said and done, however, the answer was usually the same. With few exceptions Kansans agreed that the only sure way to gain relief from Missouri was sim-ply to seal it off by placing a permanent army along the border as one might place a fence—a fence of scouts, pickets, and patrols watching day and night, spreading alarm to the interior when a Rebel force did approach, then concentrating with overwhelming might to chase, corner, and finally, to destroy them. To the amazement and utter dis-gust of Kansans, however, no Federal commander viewed the prob-lem in quite the same light. The most effective way to gain security for Kansas, these officers argued, was by killing bushwhackers where they lived, in Missouri. When a new raid on Kansas demonstrated the weakness of this policy, the embarrassed officials tried to mute the outcry by rushing men to garrison the stricken communities. But then, when the furor had faded, the troops were quietly with-drawn, the same course was pursued, and the same results soon fol-lowed. Despairing of ever gaining relief, Kansans sometimes banded together and watched the line themselves. In the end, however, this also proved ineffective, because after the excitement had passed, farmers were always forced back on fields to work neglected crops.

The want of a reliable border defense would have been frustrat-ing enough. But then there was also an unfortunate run of mili-tary commanders, none of whom could quite measure up to the task. The latest, Brigadier General James Blunt, seemed at last, a man for the times. Physically awesome, aggressive, a Kansan himself, Blunt had earlier suggested that a system of signals and patrols be adopted along the border to warn of attack from Missouri.[3] Noth-ing of substance came of it, however, and Blunt was soon seen by many for what they felt he really was: a "holiday officer," a heavy-handed, political would-be whose harsh measures only fueled the hatred and will of the bushwhackers. His gala banquets and late-night revelries proved entertaining for some, and the former doctor's penchant for grand reviews was inspiring for others—but the death and destruction continued, the garrisons were again rushed in, and Kansas under Blunt was more vulnerable than ever.

"This method of protecting burned towns, dead bodies and destroyed private property, don't suit us," snapped an irate journalist. "Give us a *live* man to take charge of Kansas."[4]

Perhaps no family in Ohio was so prominent or so accustomed to power and success than were the Ewings of Lancaster. The patriarch, Senator Thomas Ewing, a master statesman with an ambition that fully mantled his giant frame, was a man honored and esteemed nationwide. And at the sunset of an illustrious career the father could with confidence pass along the family baton to any of seven children—which included a foster son, William Tecumseh Sherman—and expect each to add to the Ewing legacy.[5]

One of the children, Thomas, Jr., seemed especially promising. And like the grand old man whom he loved and admired, the son's horizons were as broad and boundless as they were bright with hope. In the late 1850s, with opportunity beckoning, the younger Ewing turned west and, with his brothers Hugh and "Cump" Sherman, cast his fate to Kansas Territory. Once settled, the three Ohioans opened a law and real estate office in Leavenworth.[6]

After weighing his many options, however, Thomas Ewing aligned with the free-state party, became active politically, cultivated friends, and watched while his star dramatically ascended. Soon, with lofty aims and, as he admitted, "big plans a foot," the son of Senator Ewing was a political force in his own right. As a result he was awarded the first chief justiceship of Kansas.[7]

This well-charted course didn't reckon on war, however. Already by the autumn of 1862 Cump was a major general and the other brother and former law partner, Hugh, was rising almost as spectacularly. Consequently, Thomas abandoned his lofty though lackluster position and began recruiting and organizing the Eleventh Kansas Cavalry. At its completion, the man with no prior military experience was in turn commissioned colonel of the regiment. Shortly thereafter, the Eleventh engaged Rebel forces in Arkansas, and in the resulting battle the regiment performed so well and the colonel conducted himself with such distinction that by spring 1863, less than seven months after his entrance into the service, Ewing was elevated to the rank of brigadier general.[8]

On the morning of June 16, 1863, three months after his latest promotion, Thomas Ewing, without "fuss or parade," entered his office at the finest hotel in Kansas City, the Pacific House, and assumed his duties as commander of the District of the Border.[9]

At first glance, the task might have seemed simple. On closer inspection, however, the thirty-three-year-old general found himself facing the greatest challenge of his young life. The District of the Border was a huge region encompassing most of settled Kansas and the two tiers of Missouri border counties lying roughly between the Osage and Missouri rivers. East of the state line existed a bitter and generally hostile populace just beginning to recover from the ravages of 1861. Guerrillas roamed the land almost at will and the Missouri farmer, through "fear or favor," was obliged to help them. Conversely, west of the line was Ewing's home and seat of ambition. Here the loyal people of Kansas resided, and even though the state was liberally laced with thieves, rogues, and scoundrels, all in the end were voters and all in the end demanded protection. Ewing well understood that by accepting the border command he inherited the old territorial battleground in which hatred—black, abiding hatred—had become a firmly rooted fact of life. The challenge was staggering. Much, perhaps the impossible, would be expected of him. And undoubtedly, should he stumble along the way and meet with a reverse or two, those who now waited so hopefully for miracles would quickly turn against him. But if the challenge was great, Ewing felt himself greater still and more than man enough for the job ahead.

Tall, broad-shouldered like his father, cool, confident—vain, some thought—Tom Ewing entered the hotel overlooking the big river and quietly took his post.

General Ewing's tenure began on a tragic note. The day following his arrival in Kansas City an extremely bloody ambush took place near Westport in which fourteen of his new command were slain. Federal scouts swiftly ran down and killed three of the attackers, however, then held to the track of the rest. In the next few days more and more bushwhackers were "put through" until stunned Kansans suddenly realized that not only had a new man stepped onto the scene but a new and rare energy had arrived as well. "Hurrah for Ewing," one editor cheered. "Put in the licks, General, the very biggest you can lay on, and all the people will say amen."[10]

A week later, before a crowd at Olathe, Ewing kept the excitement alive and exhibited his mettle by assuring Kansans that the recent success was no charade. "I hope soon to have troops enough on the Missouri side not only to prevent raids into Kansas, but also to drive out or exterminate every band of guerrillas now haunting that region. I will keep a thousand men in the saddle daily in pursuit of them and will redden with their blood every road and bridle path of the border."[11] Although admittedly he wasn't much of a speaker,

THOMAS EWING, JR.
(courtesy of the Kansas Collection, University of Kansas Libraries).

these were the very words Kansans needed so desperately to hear, and the general was applauded warmly.

Then Ewing turned to his chief concern—the defense of Kansas. From his headquarters at Kansas City in the north to beyond the banks of the Osage in the south, there ran a sixty-mile border open to any and all who cared to cross. The very nature of this border was manifest when the jayhawkers of 1861 crossed and recrossed and crossed again, a favor the bushwhackers returned in 1862. Much of the line for ten to twenty miles on either side was devastated, yet beyond, the interior of Kansas lay unscathed. This, at all costs, had to be saved. With less than four thousand men present for duty, from buglers to clerks, and with many needed actively in the field, the chore would be difficult.[12] Yet Ewing was not dismayed.

With Kansas City the anchor of the north, a series of stations was established along the border linking up respectively at Westport, Little Santa Fe, Aubrey, Harrisonville, Coldwater Grove, Rockville, and the Trading Post. With the exception of Westport and Harrisonville, each site was an insignificant speck on the map and hardly warranted such attention. But the value of each, as perceived by Ewing, was in its unique location. At approximately thirteen-mile intervals, from Westport to the Trading Post, a station was situated, thereby assuring that in any given crisis a camp would be within rapid supporting distance of another. Every day and every night mounted troops would leave these posts, patrol the border, communicate with men of the next station, scan the eastern horizon, then turn and ride back to their base. Over and over this procedure would repeat itself. And although this system—this virtual human wall— would greatly facilitate alerting other posts and towns to the rear, this was not its sole purpose. The border camps' importance rested also in their strength. Each of the seven stations contained a complement of over one hundred well-armed, well-mounted men. No guerrilla raiding party yet had ventured over the line in numbers sufficient to risk an engagement with or face pursuit by a force such as this.[13]

A program of this magnitude was expensive. Supply was ponderous and the tedium of camp crushed young spirits. Hundreds of men needed to hunt bushwhackers were thus held back. Despite the many drawbacks, the value of the guard was never doubted and, Ewing felt, for the defense of Kansas it was well worth the investment. And grateful Kansans could not have agreed more. To allay fears even further, the young general sent a small number of soldiers to garrison several border towns and issued arms and rations to the militias in the area.[14] Satisfied, Ewing turned his sights east once more, to Missouri and "those devils in the bush."

"One thing is certain," warned William T. Sherman, an officer who had his own problems with partisans, "there is a class of people, men, women, and children, who must be killed or banished before you can hope for peace and order."[15]

On this score the two brothers saw as one. So long as the families and friends of guerrillas remained, thought Ewing, there could be no hope of pacifying Missouri. For quite some time he had toyed with the notion of clearing these players from the board by exiling "several hundred of the worst" Rebels to the hills and brakes of Arkansas. With the most fanatical supporters out of the way and the country relatively quiet, Ewing believed he could then "offer terms" to those who remained.[16] Kansas would thereby gain greater security and in Missouri much of the fighting would end. Such was the plan and such was the course he now embarked upon. So certain was he that his immediate superior would countenance the plan that Ewing had already directed his troops to begin the roundup of families before a formal order of expulsion had been written.

During the first week of August 1863, Ewing's confidence in the border situation enabled him to leave his post at Kansas City and travel downriver to St. Louis. There he met with Maj. Gen. John Schofield and sought permission to carry through with the plan.

John Schofield was a plump, balding, undramatic sort of fellow without a trace of the pomp and flourish most men naturally looked for in a general. Nonetheless, to command the most delicate of all border states President Lincoln wanted none other.

Although quite aware of the valuable service he performed in Missouri, Schofield thoroughly despised the job and longed to join the great armies of the East. Since the beginning of the war, when he was caught between lectures as professor of physics at Washington University in St. Louis, Schofield had seen no assignment other than the West. After breathing the smoke of battle at Wilson's Creek in 1861 where he was "ever in the lead, foremost, coolest," Schofield for the most part sat at one uneventful desk job after another, albeit influential posts for which he was handsomely rewarded, but drab, inglorious, enervating posts as well.[17] Thus in the spring of 1863, when he was ordered to report for active duty in Tennessee, John Schofield was quick to go.

The transfer proved temporary, however, for in less than a month a surprised and travel-worn general found himself back in St. Louis and, by direction of the president, in charge of the Department of the Missouri. In the choice of commander Lincoln found a man, a fellow Illinoisan, who knew Missouri as did few others, and just as important to the president, Schofield was a political moderate with no strings attached.

"Exercise your own judgment," wrote Lincoln, "and do right for the public interest. . . . Let your military measures be strong enough to repel the invader and keep the peace, and not so strong as to unnecessarily harass and persecute the people. It is a difficult role, and so much greater will be the honor if you perform it well."[18]

Petulant and moody, resentful of the "promotion" that forced him back to the Missouri desk, Schofield, the West Pointer, would nonetheless stay and perform a soldier's duty as the president asked. At the same time he would never miss an excuse to escape Missouri and take the field. Lincoln's choice, although politically unpopular, was nevertheless a good one, for no matter how weak and bending John Schofield might appear outwardly, he was in fact inwardly a very strong man.

The Department of the Missouri was comprised of Kansas and Missouri and those parts of Arkansas and the Indian Nations held by Federal troops. To guard this huge area Schofield had some forty-three thousand men. In June 1863, however, the general sent nearly half the soldiers in his department downriver to reinforce U. S. Grant in his campaign against Vicksburg. Although Washington was heartily pleased with the move and Schofield himself was "willing to risk it," as he said, "in view of the vast importance of Grant's success," the risk left his department dangerously undermanned.[19] One way of making up the difference was by mustering into service tens of thousands of Missouri militiamen. Another was to cut back and eliminate needless assignments. Yet another way to ease the troop shortage and possibly cool the guerrilla war was by hearing suggestions such as Thomas Ewing now proposed.

The two men—one the scion of an important national politician, the other the son of a Baptist minister—discussed the plan of removal confidentially, of its necessity, scope, and value. While Ewing soon returned to Kansas City, Schofield held off on a decision, requiring several more days to weigh the merits of the move. Then on August 14, 1863, the St. Louis commander telegraphed his approval. Along with the approval, however, were certain stipulations: because of "expense and trouble" and the suffering of children, the people removed must be kept to a minimum—only those, wrote Schofield, of the "worst character." He also cautioned Ewing to be alert during the following weeks; because of the banishment of their relatives, guerrillas might in some form or another seek retaliation.[20]

And so Ewing signed into law General Orders, No. 10, the forced removal of bushwhacker families and friends and their exile from west Missouri. Throughout August his troops continued the sweep begun in July, herding scores of men, women, and children to prison prior to their passage downriver.

On into the weeks of August, Tom Ewing busied himself with the many affairs of his district. And with each passing day the general's faith in his ability to tame the border grew. Even before he assumed the difficult assignment in June, Ewing had already owned a veritable river of self-confidence—the result of a life unsullied by failure. And as of late, the shower of public acclaim and attention could not but help give the flow a mighty, swift rise. There was some criticism, however, political in nature mostly. A number of hard-shelled abolitionists hammered on Ewing's slavery stand, or as they said, the want of it. Others pointed to the renewed rumblings in the woods of western Missouri as proof that the new commander was no better than the rest. Even more were irate at the general's tough handling of the jayhawking problem and his declaration of martial law in Mayor Dan Anthony's Leavenworth, the well-known black market capital of the West. And some, with little else to carp about, just called Ewing "selfish."

But the overwhelming majority of loyal, honest men would hear none of it. They could plainly see all about them the results of an active policy conducted by a man of intelligence and energy, of the return to calm after a reign of terror and near anarchy. The reasons for the general's success were clear for any who cared to look. Brigandage along the border had been throttled by martial law in Leavenworth and was nearly at an end. Also, as soldiers became adept in brush tactics there was a sudden swing in the balance of fighting. At no point in the war was the morale of the troops higher, for after a series of "petty skirmishes and engagements" the Federals had come away with the decided advantage. Additionally, Ewing's spies had infiltrated the guerrilla ranks so thoroughly that it was felt no move by large bodies of Rebels could be made without the general soon learning of it. In the past few weeks alone a band of bushwhackers had been scattered by just such information.[21] There was, as Schofield predicted, a noticeable surge in guerrilla activity throughout western Missouri. But once again Ewing felt confident that the trouble could be contained until the completion of Order No. 10. And the order itself was progressing smoothly. Except for the incident at the prison in which the five women were killed, the transfer had come off without a hitch.

But undoubtedly, of all his many achievements, the source of Ewing's greatest satisfaction was the border guard and the protection he had given Kansas.

"No General in command of the District has . . . given so much peace to the border," rang one admirer.[22]

"Everything seems to have taken new life since Gen. Ewing came," echoed another.[23]

Indeed, Thomas Ewing could take pride in his labors, for in less than two months he had raised from raw material something that none of his predecessors, during the past two years, had been able to construct—he had rebuilt a solid sense of safety and security over the western border. In that same speech at Olathe, shortly after assuming command, Ewing had told Kansans: "I can assure you there is little at present to fear on this side of the border from guerrilla bands." What seemed true then seemed doubly so on August 20, 1863. In two short months the sweet breeze of peace and hope had come flowing over the line in waves unlike any time in the past, and since the onset of war Kansas had never experienced such tranquility. And in the minds of the people of that state, only one person could take the credit. Thankful Kansans, searching so long for that one general, that one "live" man, were convinced they now had found him.

"The terrible state of affairs," wrote one editor, expressing the mood of many, "is coming to an end. . . . *Ewing is the man.*"[24]

Near midnight on August 20, 1863, Capt. Charles Coleman and his company reached the camp at Aubrey. Probably no Federal officer on the border had adapted to the guerrilla war as well as Coleman; he seemed born to it. When he entered the woods of western Missouri he lived as the bushwhacker lived, fought by stealth and surprise as the bushwhacker did, and understood the tricks of the game and knew his dangerous adversary as well as any. His record and the roll of Rebel dead bore this out. Incontestably brave, clever, daring to a fault, Coleman's élan had caused near disaster three weeks before. Hunting guerrillas one hot, tension-filled night in July, the captain and his men came stealing up behind a large force presumed to be that of the foe. Actually, it was another Federal outfit on the same hunt with a band of Indians riding rearguard. Coleman charged, the Indians broke, and with wild screams and feathers flying the rest of the panic-stricken company was carried into the night. Fortunately, only one man was killed by the error, but Union troops were thereafter mindful when Charles Coleman was in the vicinity.[25]

Learning that Captain Pike had failed to send any warning west and that only one message had been relayed south to Lt. Col. Charles Clark, Coleman hastily sent a courier of his own to Clark, informing him that Kansas had been invaded. Then, with their forces combined, Coleman, Pike, and nearly two hundred troopers struck for the trail of the invaders.[26]

CHARLES COLEMAN
(courtesy of the Kansas State Historical Society).

At approximately the same time, twenty miles to the north, the second dispatch rider sent by Captain Coleman was entering the long, wooded lane south of Westport. The moon was down and the way north was black and frightening. Even though Kansas City and General Ewing's headquarters were only five miles away, the exhausted mount could not be held to more than a trot in the smothering heat. If out of curiosity the courier struck a match and read the message he carried, a practice not uncommon, then he would see that at 6:00 P.M. that day 800 guerrillas had crossed the state line just south of Aubrey. When last seen they were headed west. To any Kansas soldier, "west" meant one of three places: the first two, Olathe and Paola, both short hops from the border, were lately always alert, now continually defended by troops and militia; the unlikely third, fifty miles from the line and by far the largest of the three, was Lawrence.[27]

4

THE DARKEST HOUR

*T*he messenger sent west from Olathe stopped short when almost to Gardner. Here he was met and warned that a large
body of men had just passed through town riding down the Santa Fe
Road. Confused, afraid, alone, the trooper turned his horse and rode
back up the trail toward Olathe.[1]

At almost the same time, 12:30 A.M., August 21, a second message reached the Pacific House in Kansas City. Maj. Preston Plumb,
chief of staff, read the dispatch and quickly ordered what cavalry
there was in the town to saddle and prepare to move. Before he left
the major sent urgent notes of his own directing all available men in
the area to mount and strike for the south. Then, shortly after 1:00
A.M., Plumb and fifty troopers crossed the state line and raced down
the road to Olathe.

The commander of the border, Thomas Ewing, knew nothing of
all this. He had left his desk the day before and traveled upriver to
Leavenworth on what he claimed was official business. A telegraph
wire stretched between there and Kansas City, but it was no use trying to reach him because the office in Leavenworth closed at 11:00
P.M. "for want of . . . operators." They would not open again for another seven hours.[2]

At 9:00 P.M., January 29, 1861, the first news of statehood reached
the darkened streets of Lawrence. Word spread rapidly from house to
house until in a moment the sounds of celebration echoed from every corner of the snow-covered town. While church bells pealed,
while homes and shops were illuminated, while a cannon boomed
out one hundred salutes, men and women laughed and shouted,
danced and hugged, kissed and cried. They built huge bonfires, singing away the night, while toasts were lifted again and again.

It was an occasion the people would remember for as long as they lived. But wonderful though the news was, the celebration was more than merely a salute to statehood—much more. It was a paean of victory, a victory of freedom over slavery. For as the new state picked itself up and "moved to America," it moved not as a slave state, as everyone in the South had earlier predicted, but as a free state, as everyone in Lawrence had hoped and prayed. And if the people of Lawrence laughed a little harder, sang a little louder, and danced a bit longer than other folks in Kansas it was with good reason, because it was here, more than in any other place and more through their efforts than anyone else's, that the victory over slavery had finally been won.

But it had not been easy. *Ad astra per aspera* ran the new state motto—To the stars through difficulties. Although the stars had not quite been reached yet—indeed, they were hardly in sight—everyone celebrating in the streets of Lawrence, and throughout Kansas as well, would have agreed that the little New England colony by the banks of the Kaw had already passed through more than its share of difficulties.

Behind them now were the dark days of fear and uncertainty, the days of "bleeding Kansas" and the uphill struggle to rescue the territory from slavery. Gone were the awful, anxious, though blood-free days during the siege of Lawrence when men from the North and men from the South had for the first time, after years of vowing to do so, glared at one another down the sights of their guns. Gone too were the days when gangs of Missouri "Border Ruffians," drunk and swaggering, had bullied to the polls to ensure a proslavery government. Behind them also was that memorable day when free-staters, heeding a "higher law," had met in Lawrence to form their own government. And no more would the people hear those hideous taunts and curses when the men of Lawrence were called "white-livered abolitionists," "black-hearted Yorkers," "nigger heroes," and such and were warned to clear out or face death by lead, hemp, and fire.

"We shall have Kansas—we won't be cheated out of it," growled Southerners back then. "We are going to have Kansas if we wade to the knees in blood to get it."

But Lawrence was made of sterner stuff, and although they should have been, the citizens were not cowed in the least. Missourians were dared to come on and make a war of it, then jeered and spat upon as "drunken rif-raf," "white-trash," and "pukes."

And finally, for those singing and laughing in the streets this night, behind them was the time most remembered of all—the time when, after months of threats and vows, their town was at last invaded and sacked. Lawrence had always held a special place in Missouri hearts. Everyone knew this. Because it was peopled by the most troublesome free-staters in Kansas, and because it was the headquarters of the detested New England Emigrant Aid Society, slavers had always bristled to "burn out" the hated abolition nest and have an end of it. Thus when the golden opportunity presented itself one day in May of 1856, a mob of Border Ruffians eagerly swarmed into town. The free-soil leaders were quickly collared and jailed, the newspapers and hotel were destroyed, and then several homes were looted and another burned, just for good measure. Although none of the townsfolk were injured in the affair, it was one dismal day to recall nonetheless.

But looking back on it now, anyone could plainly see that, black cloud though it was, the sack of Lawrence had its silver lining as well. For no sooner had word of the outrage reached the East than a fierce cry of indignation went up. Where before there had been merely a trickle of help, now money, guns, and men—angry men— flooded into the territory, enough so that any further doubts about the outcome were quickly erased. Thus, even in its hour of apparent defeat, Lawrence had sown the seeds for freedom's victory and had, in the process, sealed the doom of the South. The irony: the people of Lawrence loved it.

Ad astra per aspera—although the phrase was hoisted for Kansas, nobody was fooled. The words were written at Lawrence, written in fire. It was here against odds that the war to end slavery was begun; it was here during the darkest days that the battle was continued; and finally it was here, fittingly, gloriously, triumphantly, that freedom was ultimately won. Those dancing and singing in the snowy streets of Lawrence this memorable eve knew this simple lesson in history, and now, all too clearly, all too painfully, Missouri knew it as well.

As everywhere throughout America, the spring of 1861 was a suspenseful, breathtaking time in Lawrence. Statehood . . . South Carolina . . . secession . . . it was a hissing fuse of events that finally exploded in one word—Sumter! President Lincoln's call for men to suppress the rebellion had no greater reception anywhere in the nation than in Lawrence, for here at last was the war all had waited for: the war to end human bondage. No longer was it simply a defense of freedom in the territory, but a direct assault on treason and slavery in Missouri. It was also a time of thrill and high pageantry.

Lawrence men, "Old '56 Boys," eagerly rushed to arms and formed companies overnight. Behind them, teenagers banded together into the Union Cadets and behind them still, noisy children marched with paper hats and wooden swords. The ladies of Lawrence bestirred themselves with patriotic committees and the sewing of flags and tunics. Troops from the interior, bound for the border, were "almost constantly" tramping up flag-bedecked Massachusetts Street, and with band music blaring, each green outfit received a hero's welcome. Daily the small city armory filled as guns, powder, and bayonets arrived.[3]

"The martial spirit of the people is fully aroused," huzzahed Hovey Lowman, editor of the *Lawrence Journal*. "All around the eye meets the gleam of the freshly burnished Sharp's rifle, and the ear catches the significant click of the newly oiled revolver."[4]

Then, one night in early May, Lawrence was thrown into a commotion reminiscent of the territorial days when Missourians were reportedly on the march to seize the city and its armory. The scare was brief, however, and by morning everyone was ready "to welcome invaders to 'hospitable graves.'" In fact, the emergency only added spice to the wonderful war mood as well as confidence in the town's preparedness.

"We invite any number of Border Ruffians to visit any part of our State," goaded the *Journal*. "The nearer they come to Lawrence the better!" Nevertheless, scouts were sent ranging and the militia found new call to quicken its step.[5]

"Fight for fun," trumpeted John Speer of the *Lawrence Republican* as more troops arrived in the city.[6] And following them hundreds more from outlying counties came down the valley, bivouacked for a night or two, then pushed east, all the while giving the town the thump and boom of an important military post. The Lawrence Guards, with Ens. Joshua Pike, joined the parade as did other city companies. And a great many had the supreme satisfaction of marching and camping among their old foes at Kansas City and Westport, never missing an opportunity to exhibit their patriotism and, "in every possible way," their contempt.[7] Other local adventurers dashed off in their dust to "spread terror," free slaves, and lay claim to Missouri loot.

Then in late July 1861, when the camps had cleared and when an unusually calm and lonesome mood settled upon the town, a second rumor of an impending raid came. Excited citizens once more rushed to arms, and over a hundred militiamen rallied from the country. In the end, however, the report proved just as unfounded as before. Still, apprehension was duly aroused. Coming as it did on the heels of the Union debacle at Bull Run and the continued Rebel resistance in Missouri, men soon realized that the war would not be over in a few months as predicted. Sidewalk idlers speculated that a dozen or so daring horsemen could steal into Lawrence some night, burn a portion of the town, then escape across the border unmolested.

Even though several new militia companies were rapidly formed, the scare passed, and by late autumn the war again seemed far away. In fact, looking back over the year, most all of Lawrence would agree that 1861 had been a memorable, enjoyable time generally, a time when all the world seemed hued in red, white, and blue, or, as everyone had prayed for in January, a "year of peace and plenty." War had raged to the east and wild rumors had caused some excitement, but slight was the effect in Lawrence as men, women, and children sat down to roast turkey and oyster pie and enjoyed Thanksgiving "in true New England style." But while others held seasonal parties and crowded around warm firesides, a few individuals watched events taking shape on the border. What they saw worried them. Because of the unbridled rampage of Jennison and other jayhawkers, thousands of Missourians were going hungry and homeless this winter. Some felt the punishment only fit the crime and quietly reveled in its execution. But the chilling question still arose: "How long before Lawrence may expect a return visit? Home guards drill! drill! drill!"[8]

The following spring, 1862, a fresh wave of troops flooded up the Kaw Valley bound for duty in New Mexico. "Lawrence . . . citizens seem as much pleased to gaze on a military display as when the first squad of soldiers passed through her streets," noted the *Journal*.[9] This benign attitude soon began to crack, however, then crumble. Unlike previous troops these newcomers were ill-mannered and rowdy and chafed at the thought of service in the desert Southwest. During the day there were fistfights, drunkenness, and shootings, and at night there was singing and howling when most of the town was abed. Theft became more commonplace. Consequently, soldiers were kept from the city as much as possible and not allowed to enter at all after sundown.[10]

Troops weren't the only visitors to enliven Lawrence during the early years of the war; there were also slaves by the hundreds. Some

Missouri runaways crossed the line and went no further than their first step on free soil, settling for good in Wyandotte, Leavenworth, and Atchison. But more, it was observed, "as they break their fetters . . . strike for the center of abolition." And that center, as everyone white and black knew, was Lawrence.[11]

From the earliest days bondsmen looked upon Lawrence as the "city of freedom." Unlike other states where runaways were forced to flee—Illinois, for instance, considered a bill to punish any black crossing its border with a fine, imprisonment, and thirty-nine lashes—Negroes here were greeted with open arms. In ten days during the winter over one hundred entered the town; on another day twenty-seven more followed; and on another day still jayhawkers escorted an additional throng of dancing and banjo-playing contrabands through the streets. Later, they came "thicker and faster until they were coming by scores"; so many, in truth, that some people "almost regretted" the city's reputation.[12] And yet, when the ledger was tallied, many would have it no other way. Even though the financial burden on the town was great, even though the reality of the black was not always what most imagined, there were the rewards as well. But more than any one factor, just the former slaves' presence in Lawrence was itself a reward, for here was undeniable proof that the war was indeed being won. And in essence each bondsman who successfully reached Lawrence was a walking, talking, laughing nay vote to rebellion and another scoop of sod on the grave of the South. This to the old-time New England stock was comfort and reward enough.

Although certainly the most valuable, chattel was not the only Missouri property to make its way to the town. Since the start of war and the first jayhawking sweeps across the border, Lawrence had been one of the prime recipients of Missouri loot. Early in the war returning raiders brought back carriages, pianos, furniture, silverware, linens, and anything else that was portable. Homes were suddenly and lavishly furnished; ladies appeared on the streets in new silk finery; farms were outfitted; even churches were adorned with the booty. Later, however, most of the plunder came on the hoof—horses and mules, cattle and sheep—brought out by men like George Hoyt and his Red Legs, or arriving with fugitive slaves, or as was often the case, herded along by common thieves. To "save their bacon," most free-booters chose not to tarry in Lawrence but with a sly wink passed further west, beyond the law. Still, the city received more than its share of jayhawked contraband. Missouri owners had

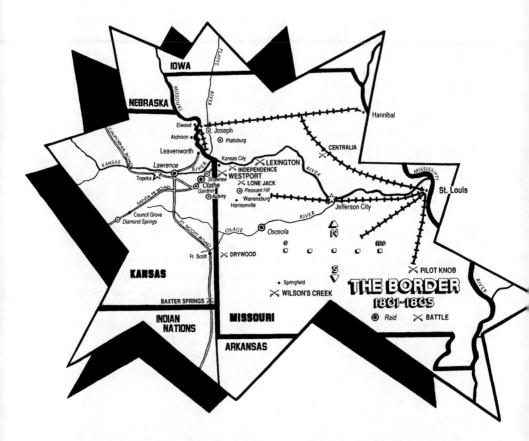

long ago ceased efforts to recover their livestock that had "strayed" the fifty miles to Lawrence—the few who did were run from town at gunpoint.

Certainly, some upright citizens recoiled at the thought of the thieving contagion spreading over their homes. But livestock nevertheless continued to find its way into local stables and barns, and for the great majority their sentiments were expressed thusly: "Horse hunters, from Missouri, must learn to talk less when they visit Lawrence; or the halter with which they hope to capture their stray horse, may be used to suspend an ass."[13]

Ever since the territorial days and the sack of 1856 there had been no question of the special hatred felt by Missourians for Lawrence. Life and progress would not permit the people to brood on the matter, yet the possibility of an attack never ventured far from their minds.

Unlike the harmless excitements of 1861, which stirred more thrill than alarm, the year 1862 gave rise to a host of terrifying rumors, threats, and panics. And the disheartening mire of Federal defeats in the East only compounded the gloom and made not only Kansas but all the Union seem agonizingly weak. Hardly had the new year begun when in March a band of men crossed the border and captured the village of Aubrey. Property was stolen and several men killed. In August Independence, Missouri, was taken by a small army of Rebels. Although the town was soon retaken and the secessionists scattered, Kansans increasingly began to regard the border with greater concern. And as fear grew so too did the demand for protection. But if speeches were long and promising, they were after all only speeches, and no military commander could seem to match his words with deeds. In September the heaviest blow to hit the state thus far came when a large party of guerrillas surrounded and sacked Olathe. Once again men were killed and a vast amount of property was stolen or destroyed; once again the raiders managed to escape unharmed. The sheer boldness of the attack—the capture of a small city ten miles inside the state line—spread panic up and down the border and started a frenzy of local defense measures.

"It is a very strange thing," grumbled John Speer of the *Lawrence Republican*, "that . . . a few companies cannot be stationed along the border, to defend the wives and children of our soldiers from such raids."[14]

"Place that force there and then we can retire to rest at night," echoed a correspondent from Olathe, a witness to the raid. "Men of Lawrence," he warned, "your turn may come next. . . . Join with us in getting a protection for our common border. Ask for that protection from the commander of the department."[15]

Then during the next month Shawnee, a dozen miles southwest of Kansas City, was looted and burned. As Kansans once more ran for cover, James Blunt, the man most accountable, was cudgeled as an incompetent, a fool, a "knave," an officer whose "dabbling in politics" had allowed the cities in his district to go up in flames while at the same time his troops were "rusting out with inaction."[16]

The pulse quickened at Lawrence, where the drills and watching of hundreds of militiamen had never really ceased.[17] Shops closed, meals were missed, sleep was lost, and although it was unnecessary for Speer to remind his readers yet again, he did anyway: "Unless we are *well prepared*, these fellows may make a desperate push some night, and pay us a visit of a most disastrous nature."[18]

Throughout the last weeks of October 1862 and into November each sundown in Lawrence kindled fear and fresh rumors of attack—some tales were as nebulous as the minds that inspired them, yet all were sufficient to keep the town in a habitual, weary state of alarm. It was in this climate, when every ominous report and every destroyed town seemed yet another signpost on the road to Lawrence, that an "extra stirring up" came and flung the city into the wildest panic ever.

At 10:00 P.M. on November 2, the mayor received information from a "most reliable source" stating that for some time now spies had been nosing about the town looking for weaknesses in the city's defense; supposedly upon finding them, they quickly relayed the word to Missouri bushwhackers. At that very moment, the informant added, the Rebels were on the move. A general alarm was sounded, and instantly the darkened town sprang to life. Within an hour thirteen militia companies replete with cannon, bayonets, and Sharp's carbines, plus every other excited man or boy who could wield a weapon, were in their places. For early warning three cordons of pickets were looped around the city, the farthest fifteen miles out. On into the night and following day the people waited anxiously for the first shot that would signal the attack—but it never came. And although later in the week George Hoyt and his boys rode into town and agreed that the report was true, it proved in the end, like all the others, just another false alarm.[19]

Finally, the harsh Western winter, as it had the year before, shut the door on the border war, easing tensions throughout the state. Although the holiday season carried on much as it always had and the war seemed at times far removed from Lawrence, the failure of Federal arms had an awful way of breaking through even the most tranquil surroundings. After Fredericksburg and Chancellorsville—national disasters both—a gloom blanketed the North, and hopes of peace and a restored Union appeared more elusive than ever. And Kansans looked upon the coming summer with a dread unequalled at any time in the past. For after the fury of 1862, an adage had been coined along the border: *As the grass commences growing the guerrillas will be raising.* It was a phrase truer than most would care to admit.

"There are mysterious movements all about us," whispered Hovey Lowman's *Journal* in early May 1863, as around the state spring burst to maturity. For several days residents along the route had noticed small knots of tough-looking, well-armed strangers drifting down the Santa Fe Road, less than a dozen miles south of Lawrence. Concern mounted and citizens stood nightly guard at the towns along the trail.

"Are they guerrillas?" asked the uneasy editor.[20] A few days later Lowman's answer was in the headlines:

GUERRILLAS!
THE BOLDEST RAID YET!![21]

As Dick Yager and his gang worked their destructive way back to Missouri from Diamond Springs, news spread outward like cracks from a fissure. And suddenly it was 1862 all over again. Once more Lawrence men sprang from homes and businesses to patrol the outskirts of town, to march and drill and target practice. An independent company of pursuit scouts was urged, two score daring horsemen to strike as lightning when the next Rebel force neared Lawrence.[22] But although attention might be riveted momentarily on immediate threats, no one really lost sight of the big picture, and through all the fear and rage the same old complaint surfaced again and again: Why was Kansas allowed to suffer from raids such as this when the remedy was simple? A border guard!

"A small force permanently located along the border . . . will be all sufficient to make inhabitants safe in their property and persons," pleaded the *Journal*. And once the military realized this and acted upon it, said Lowman, "no band of Missouri cut-throats . . . will risk their skins on the Kansas side of the line."[23]

Some hope was raised when Gov. Thomas Carney received permission to organize a body of militia to watch the state line. Although well intentioned, the inadequacies of the gesture quickly became evident: without state or federal aid the governor was forced to dig into his own pocket. How long one man could support the guard was questionable. Then, to the dismay of Kansans, the unit itself was grossly undermanned—not the regiment asked for but a mere one hundred and fifty men strung out to cover an area requiring a force ten times that number.[24]

In early June 1863, when word reached Lawrence that Shawnee had once more been sacked and four men killed, the alarm was again sounded. And with this grim news came the even grimmer understanding that only the people themselves could ensure their own safety, and to rely on the military would prove the greatest of follies. At this moment, not only did the summer of 1863 appear a reflection of the previous year, but all signs pointed to an even more disastrous time ahead as well. By June the wearied town had become so accustomed to rumors and alarms as to be "almost unaffected" by them.[25] The pickets simply kept the same monotonous watch on the same roads and horizons they had watched for the past two years, and the tired militia marched and drilled and performed their same old duty, a duty which seemed to have no end.

Then, just when the clouds were darkest and most forbidding, the skies began to clear and the first faint glimmers of light shone through. To the applause of all, the "amiable imbecile," James Blunt, was removed, and in his place came one of the brightest young stars of Kansas, Tom Ewing. Hope soared just as it always had when a change was made, but in this instance the feeling was naturally more pronounced. As he seemed able to do almost everywhere, Ewing hailed Lawrence on a positive note, for when appeals were made for troops to relieve the citizens of their nightly watch, a squad under Lt. T. J. Hadley was promptly sent over.[26] Into the last weeks of June anxious citizens watched intently while Ewing's rugged soldiers smoothly and swiftly went about their jobs. Old doubters began to take heart and smile once again.

"In justice to General Ewing," commented Lowman's *Journal*, "we must say that the bushwhackers are now unusually quiet on the border."[27]

It remained to be seen how his policies would affect the future of Kansas, but as they had with his predecessor, Lowman and all Lawrence men were quick to remind the general that even if Missouri Rebels were killed by the wagon load, Kansas would never be completely safe until Federal troops held the line. "It is by far the best way to protect our borders," argued the editor. "We must have troops continually there. . . . Kansas soldiers can be trusted there."[28]

Most Kansans, although optimistic, held a wait-and-see attitude. In the meanwhile, Lawrence militiamen continued to march, drill, and keep their powder dry.

Even in Kansas, however, no amount of local news could shade the fateful drama being acted out in Mississippi and Pennsylvania. Although the stranglehold applied by U. S. Grant was tightening, the Rebel defenders of Vicksburg yet bid defiance from their river fortress. Even more ominous, Robert E. Lee was taking the sting of war to the untouched North, driving for the heartland of Pennsylvania. Anxiously, the people awaited the results and prayed for the sounds of victory.

Those sounds came on July 4, 1863, when with a mighty roar the tide turned against the South. Lee, beaten and lame, retreated south from Gettysburg never to return. And when Vicksburg fell not only had Grant split the Confederacy in twain but he had once and for all secured the vital Mississippi Valley. Where token triumphs would have been most welcome and brought a shout to a troubled North, real, sweeping victories now came in a rush. After a grinding, futile two years of conflict, men were stunned that the course of war could change so swiftly and with such portentious results. From that day forward nevermore did thinking men doubt the outcome.

Throughout the North the summer war news brought one cheer after another. And news less earthshaking but fully as joyous, at least in Kansas, was confirmation that the border guard, so long desired, so long denied, had finally been established. With that, Kansans knew they at last had a man who saw the situation exactly as they did, the "live" man all had prayed for. As the days passed and no new calamity rippled the calm, it soon became obvious that all the earlier predictions were correct—the border guard was the answer and Ewing the general to put it through.

"The war is ending," cheered an elated Hovey Lowman.[29] Even the wheat and oat harvest had proven bounteous this summer. But best of all, since Thomas Ewing had taken charge, not one alarm had shattered the peace of Lawrence. Then, while the hurrahs continued and while Lawrence men were still congratulating one another on seeing the war through to the end, something happened.

During the last days of July, young Lieutenant Hadley met with Mayor George Collamore and spoke of an urgent message just received from Kansas City. Word had leaked out from the woods of western Missouri, warning that a desperate push against Lawrence was in the making, set to coincide, as the spies learned, when the moon was at its brightest, an advantage the raiders would use on their march through Kansas. The two men discussed the message, considered the source highly reliable, then debated a course of action. The plan proposed by Mayor Collamore was finally adopted.[30]

Thus, at midnight on July 31, when the moon was reaching its crest, the bell at the armory was sounded.[31] Startled, half stupid with sleep, militiamen came tumbling from their beds once more, throwing on clothes and hats and rushing for the door. Lamps began to dot the darkened town again as shouting, panting men raced through the streets to their stations. No one actually knew the cause of the excitement, but it spread the more for a want of it, from one to the next until the entire city was caught in the crush. The cannon was wheeled into place and shotted, and soon, with weapons leveled, several hundred militiamen were in their positions. Without knowing particulars, baffled citizens could only guess, but with

GEORGE WASHINGTON COLLAMORE
(courtesy of the Kansas State Historical Society).

the moon full and the land lit like a beacon the logic behind an attack was frightening. But the night slipped to morning and no one came to Lawrence.

The next day reinforcements from the country arrived, nearly one hundred extra men. A squad of soldiers and cannon crossed the river from Fort Leavenworth and joined the defenders. As the hours ticked slowly by, another night of nervous watch came. At dawn, however, when Hadley's scouts returned, their report was the same as the night before—no sign of the enemy. Try as they might, most still had no idea what the basis for the alarm was, and mysteriously, when questioned, Collamore and Hadley remained evasive.[32] On Sunday more help arrived and a company of soldiers passing down the valley stopped to aid the town. Tensions began to ease somewhat. Loafers and doubters, many of whom had little or no property to lose even if Lawrence were sacked, laughed at the clumsy spectacle of marching militia. While the light from the moon began to wane, suspense also started to fade; as another night passed with no unusual occurrences, townsmen, gaining in boldness, actually spoiled for a fight and loudly hoped the Rebels would indeed appear.

"Lawrence has ready for any emergency over *five hundred* fighting men," threatened the *Journal*, "every one of whom would like to see [them]."[33]

Finally, after three sleepless nights the alert was called off—the greatest of the war—and like all the rest, it too passed peacefully. Friends relaxed and joked among themselves once more and pointed in fun at their own fears and weaknesses. In retrospect, it all seemed so absurd. The likelihood that a hundred bushwhackers would dare risk the fifty-mile ride through an armed and aroused land only to take on a city the size of Lawrence suddenly struck many as not only remote but ridiculous. "It would be impossible," laughed one man.[34] And should any Rebel force be foolish enough to try, it could never slip past the blue wall protecting Kansas "without detection" and hence advance warning to the interior. If some people had responded to the alarm in a wild, irresponsible manner, the sum could be waved off as little more than a reflex from the days of uncertainty—the days before Gettysburg and Vicksburg and impending victory, and more especially, the awful, agonizing days before Thomas Ewing and the border guard.

While the Lawrence companies stacked weapons and wheeled the cannon back to its place, the country militia tramped home to thresh wheat, cut hay, and serve as the brunt of mirth and laughter by their neighbors. Hadley and Mayor Collamore, because of their secrecy, were themselves the target of sarcasm. "All the excitement," some laughed, "was engineered by the upstart of a young lieutenant, who wanted to make a noise in the world." And Collamore, still silent on the matter, henceforth wore the albatross of "our nervous mayor." Handsome George Hoyt, romantic in buckskins and his brace of ivory-handled revolvers, rode into town and snorted at the whole idea.[35] Kansas editors joined the sport, poking fun and offering Lawrence sage advice on how to avoid any future "scares." After all, they insisted, and as Hovey Lowman himself had admitted, "the war is ending."

"Thus the beginning of the end unmistakably appears," intoned the Reverend George Paddock from the pulpit of the Methodist Church. "Hope begins to smile again over the land."[36]

And townspeople longed to smile again and enjoy the pleasant side of life, free of worry, doubt, and fear. There were outdoor band concerts to attend, performed at dusk each week beneath the liberty pole. Excitement was growing over the Pacific Railroad and the telegraph that would soon link Lawrence to the world, and there was a lively interest in the coming visit of abolitionist and "Pathfinder" John Charles Frémont. Grand times were ahead, and there simply was no room for a flickering, faraway war.

Just after the full moon scare, the squad of artillerymen and their cannon returned to Fort Leavenworth. A week later, the company of troops continued their march down the valley. Even Lieutenant Hadley and his scouts were ordered elsewhere.[37] And not a soul raised a voice against it for as the last soldier left town that day there was a conscious, desperate effort among the people to begin the long journey back to peace and growth and business as usual. Then too, that night, for the first time in the war, Lawrence didn't bother to send out guards to the edge of town, nor the next night, nor the next.

As the melodies from the concert drifted sweetly over the city on a warm evening in August and folks sat drowsily on their porches sipping lemonade, reading the papers, and swatting gnats and flies, no one paid any mind to the strangers. There were always new faces passing through—immigrants, travelers, peddlers. But these strangers were different. They had been watching everything all along, with a veiled but sharper interest than most—the panic, the watch, the confidence, and finally, the laughter. When they had seen enough they quietly left, and no one noticed their going.

The days of August slipped slowly by and life along the border continued calm and unbroken. At Lawrence "the people never felt more secure" as the moon waxed and waned and the night sky grew darker.[38]

Although the column of horsemen was well behaved, more than a few residents of Gardner became suspicious after they had disappeared down the Santa Fe Road.

First, over a dozen hungry riders had dropped from the line and suddenly turned back to the village hotel. After bolting down a scratch supper the men then went to the stable and selected two fresh horses. In their place, a couple of jaded mounts were left with a promise that the others would be returned the following day. This in itself would have been no cause for concern, for such things commonly happened. What was strange, however, occurred when a few more stopped at a well. As the thirsty men drank they talked with a citizen and revealed that they were members of the Sixth Kansas Cavalry bound for Lexington, Missouri. The troopers had left without further ado, but their words hung perplexingly in the night air. To catch up with the column, the men rode west. Lexington was east![39]

5

THE FAIREST CITY

By 1:00 A.M. on Friday, August 21, Capts. Coleman and Pike had located the trail of the invaders and were tracking it west. Even without moonlight the path was plainly marked by trampled grass, twenty feet wide. When only three miles along, however, the trail came to a sudden and unexpected halt. Here, to stymie pursuit, the guerrillas had split and scattered over the prairie.

Crouching low to the ground, often striking matches, straining their eyes for flattened grass, hoofprints, and fresh droppings, Coleman's force moved west through the black, still night. Unlike the first few miles, however, the pace now was painfully slow, and as the ploy had intended, the already wide gap between the two columns grew even wider.[1]

"God might have made a more lovely country, but I am sure He has never done it."[2]

Thus spoke an inspired world traveler as he stood high atop Mount Oread surveying the beautiful scenes around him. Indeed, for those who made the steep climb up this day the panorama more than repaid their efforts. Looking west, the viewer beheld the historic California Road, gracefully winding its way to the horizon through a pleasant plateau of prairie and field. To the north, at the base of the hill, they saw the broad Kansas River suddenly but quietly slide into view as it rolls east, watering a wide, sandy valley of cottonwood and willow. Facing south, the dusty Fort Scott Road was spied descending through checkered farmland until it reaches the belt of timber along the Wakarusa River. There, at three miles, the road crosses the tiny, sheer-banked stream at Blanton's bridge; a few miles further it breaches the forested bluffs and disappears on the high prairie. Eastward, the California Road fades away through green meadows for several miles, then enters the village of Franklin. An-

46

other two miles and the road vanishes into the woods and fords the Wakarusa at Blue Jacket's crossing.

And down the eastern face, directly below the windswept summit, the viewer received his fit and final reward as he gazed on the "fairest city in Kansas"—Lawrence, August 20, 1863. From the heights the town lay open like a book. Because most lots had been stripped of trees and brush earlier, only saplings and shrubs betrayed a landscape almost bleak. Yet by frontier standards Lawrence was a well-plotted, trim, even pretty town of three thousand souls; its population in Kansas was second only to Leavenworth—a fact that troubled the residents not a whit. Second in numbers, as the adage went, first in integrity.

"Lawrence the commercial, literary and political center of the State," boasted one proud citizen. "More building going on here than in any other place west of the Mississippi!"[3] And so it was. New homes were "going up like magic." Already several hundred of the finest homes in Kansas graced the town. While building was stagnant elsewhere and other communities were failing because of the war, Lawrence had actually flourished. Nowhere was a house left unoccupied. Moreover, demand in lots was so intense that often two or three families shared a single home while awaiting completion of their own. And there seemed no end in sight.

Down the northern face of Mount Oread lay the limits of the city. Here, in West Lawrence, many of the town's prominent and wealthy citizens lived, and here too reposed most of the newer and more "tasteful" residences. To the east the older sections of the city began, and running three blocks from the river, East and West Lawrence were cleanly divided by a narrow but deep-sided ravine almost in the center of town. Several short bridges spanned the chasm and here, lining its banks, the city's only considerable growth of trees stood. Parallel with the ravine and a few blocks east was the business district. Beyond that, in the eastern river bottoms, the shantytown of nearly a thousand blacks had sprung up almost overnight.

From his home high on Mount Oread, George Bell, a former Union officer and current county clerk, could view the entire southern extent of Lawrence as well as the traffic coming up from the Wakarusa. He could also see the roads branching off to the city from the California road, one of which is the main thoroughfare, Massachusetts Street. Here in the south, the long business artery begins and reaches north through the heart of town to end at the banks of the Kaw over a mile away.

Up broad, dusty Massachusetts, seven blocks from the river, the South Park begins.

Nestled in the northwest corner of the park was the home of the Reverend Hugh Fisher, his wife Elizabeth, and their five small children. Although he wasn't exactly a legend in his own time, thirty-nine-year-old Hugh Fisher with his coy, wry smile could nevertheless claim title to a growing reputation, not only in Lawrence but along the border as well.

In 1861, when a brigade of jayhawkers made a sweep through western Missouri, Fisher tagged along as chaplain. The temptations on all sides were great, however, and shortly, like the men in his spiritual charge, the reverend joined the looting frenzy, even to the point of stripping "secesh" churches—just a few months before he had scolded children about "profane swearing . . . rum drinking and tobacco." The lord's work was carried a step further when the Kansan began coaxing slaves from Missouri masters. The spectacle of newly freed blacks—some joyous, some sobbing, all eternally grateful— was like scripture from the Book of Exodus; for Fisher it proved an appealing, satisfying side of the war. Later, the preacher became superintendent of contrabands, aiding displaced or runaway slaves by relocating them in Kansas. It was a rewarding but exacting job, and early that spring duties as superintendent even came within a whisker of proving fatal.

When guerrillas under George Todd stopped the steamer near Sibley, Missouri, one dark morning in March, they knew from informants downriver that escaped slaves were on the boat. But more importantly, Todd had high hopes of locking an iron grip around the throat of their escort, Fisher, who reportedly was also on board. When a search from stem to stern failed to flush out the quarry, the Rebels threatened three times to apply the torch if the jayhawker didn't come out. But the intended victim did not appear, and after murdering a number of the contrabands the bushwhackers finally left. Fortunately for the preacher, plans had suddenly been changed, and he chose to travel by rail rather than by the precarious Missouri River.

In mid-August Hugh Fisher returned to his home in Lawrence. Since the beginning of war he had seldom been around much, and even now it was not a visit but an ailment that brought him back. Quinsy, a debilitating throat infection, left the uncommon minister stretched on the sickbed.[4]

HUGH FISHER
(courtesy of the Kansas State Historical Society).

On New Hampshire Street, a block from the park, stood the just-completed brick home of the newlyweds Louis and Mary Carpenter. Judge Carpenter was a kindly, affable young man from New York who despite his age was one of the rising names in Kansas politics. Open and honest, Carpenter had recently served as probate judge to the county and in the past year had just missed in a bid to become the state's attorney general. Many a campaign was in store for this man of talent and drive, however, and the judge's future as a Kansan of the first order was as bright as it was certain.[5]

A block north of the park, in an open space on the west side of Massachusetts, a score of black recruits were encamped under the charge of the Reverend Samuel Snyder, captain, Second Kansas Colored Regiment.

On the opposite side of the street, a block down, twenty-two white recruits of the Fourteenth Kansas had also pitched their tents in a vacant lot. They were young local boys mostly—"babes," snickered adults—below the age for actual duty, yet eager and preparing for military life all the same. Although they wore their blue uniforms manfully and tried to play the role, when or if they would soon receive weapons was anyone's guess.[6]

From there for the next three blocks Massachusetts Street was framed by a series of solid, handsome structures that, said one admirer, "would be an ornament to any Eastern town." It was, in fact, the finest commercial street in Kansas with many two- and some three-story buildings. Much of the way was covered by shaded sidewalks with stores, shops, and offices occupying the ground floors and family apartments and more offices on the levels just above. Allen's Hardware, Fillmore's Dry Goods, Sargent & Smith's Meat Market, Marcy's Bowling Saloon, DaLee's Photography, Storm's Farm Machinery. Inside Storm's, a mockingbird showered the street with notes from "Old John Brown."[7]

A few doors down was Ridenour & Baker's. On the shelves of the two-story building known locally as "R & B's" was one of the most complete grocery selections in Kansas—everything from flour, sugar, and salt to cove oysters and canned figs.

The business began in the fifties when the two men, Peter Ridenour of Ohio and Harlow Baker of Maine, met, talked, became friends, and thereupon decided to form a partnership. It was an open-ended deal, however, for as both agreed, after three years the pact would be null and void and each could go his separate way.

Unlike other frontier merchants who sold dry goods, hardware, and such, as well as groceries under the roof of one general store, Ridenour and Baker chose instead to devote their entire attention to foodstuffs, not a novel idea but in a sparsely populated country certainly a daring one. "You can't make a living selling groceries alone," laughed a local competitor. "We sell that line at cost to bring trade for our other goods."

Undismayed, the men set to work, rising early, staying late, loading and unloading, buying, selling, cutting corners here, cutting costs there, dealing plainly yet fairly with their customers, learning each day and gaining while they did. In two years Ridenour and Baker bought out the merchant who laughed, and at the conclusion of three years the partnership had become so lucrative that ending it was out of the question. Soon a clerk was hired to handle retail while the owners began buying and selling wholesale. As the volume of trade increased the store itself was enlarged until it reached right up to the back alley. And as the hard work passed to others, the two owners assumed lighter tasks. By 1863 the once humble pair of grocers had become the strongest, most prosperous tandem in town.

On hand at R & B's was the largest inventory in the store's history. During a recent buying spree in New York, Ridenour had taken advantage of the fall in gold prices to sink every cent into fresh supplies. The times were so good, moreover, that he had also signed several thousand dollars' worth of vouchers.

Peter Ridenour also brought back a new employee. When a wealthy New York associate who wanted his son to learn business from the bottom—as well as distance him from bad sorts in the metropolis—asked his friend to take the boy west, the Kansan agreed, but not until after a good-natured protest. As Ridenour pointed out, the youth was a dandy, didn't know the meaning of labor, and would soon be writing home for ticket money east. But the boy had matured much since his discharge following the Battle of Gettysburg; he was big and athletic, had a pleasant disposition, and, insisted the father, he would work! In the end the New Yorker won out and the plan did go as hoped. By the time two weeks elapsed the son had smoothly made the shift; he found the hard work and clean air invigorating, the quaint, quiet village amusing in many respects yet comforting and somehow very reassuring. And not least, the crop of young females made the days and nights quite interesting. He and a fellow employee nearly the same age now shared an apartment above the store.[8]

Clark's Furniture, Eastern Bakery, Pollock's Cut-Rate Clothing, the Lawrence Bank, Arthur Spicer's Beer Hall, Danver's Ice Cream Saloon. Down Massachusetts Street, two blocks from the river, sitting on the corner solid, heavy, and proud was the keystone of Lawrence, the Eldridge House. Rebuilt defiantly on the foundation of the ruined Free-State Hotel, the four-story edifice was the most imposing structure in town.

Up the front steps of the Eldridge, under the arched passageways fancied with wrought iron trimming, through the dark wooden doors and onto the ground floor, an arcade of shops and offices was located. A wide flight of stairs led up from the street to the second-story landing. On this floor was the lobby, more offices, and a spacious dining hall. A noisy dinner gong nearby called the guests to meals. On the hotel's third and fourth floors were rooms and several elegant suites. Sixty patrons were currently lodged at the Eldridge, including a group of Eastern businessmen, a bishop and his circle of traveling priests, and in a room overlooking Massachusetts, the state provost marshal Alexander Banks.

A platoon of employees catered to the needs of the visitors, including the hotel seamstress, Sallie Young, a "bright and witty Irish girl." It was one of the largest, most luxurious inns beyond the Mississippi, and for the citizens of Lawrence the Eldridge always had been and always would be the seat of great pride and good memories. "Magnificent," praised a former guest, New York editor Horace Greeley.[9]

On Massachusetts just north of the Eldridge was the courthouse with a cannon parked nearby. A few doors down was the armory, and half a block further, by the riverside, sat the palatial home of Dr. Charles and Sara Robinson.

The first governor of the state, one of the wealthiest men in Kansas, just turned forty-five in good health; Charles Robinson should have been the happiest man in Lawrence. But he wasn't. Instead, the quiet, native New Englander was perhaps the most disconsolate and forlorn person in the state of Kansas.

To the best of his abilities he had tried. From the day he entered the territory in 1854 and staked his claim in Lawrence, it was Charles Robinson's hope that a sane, peaceful solution could be found for troubled Kansas. He more than any was responsible for holding back the storm by leading his free-state followers on a firm, yet moderate course.[10] "We must have courage," the bald-

THE ELDRIDGE HOUSE
(courtesy of the Kansas State Historical Society).

ing, bewhiskered doctor had insisted, "but with it we must have prudence!"[11]

And for almost two years his strategy had worked. His calm and wise decisions, his solid, steady leadership when radicals on both sides were pounding for war proved a blessing both for Kansas and the nation, and when all else seemed about to go under in an angry red sea of hatred and violence Robinson held forth like a rock for all to grasp. And to show their appreciation free-soil settlers had simply ignored the proslavery territorial government and voted Robinson their man for governor. But then came the sack of Lawrence in 1856, the burning of his home on Mount Oread, and the imprisonment of free-state leaders, including Robinson himself. And it was the cruelest of ironies that the doctor's internment as much as the plundering of Lawrence was the source of his waning popularity, for even from his prison tent near Lecompton one day he heard the free-state cannon shots that graphically thundered a change in philosophy. In his prolonged absence, the reaction caused by proslavery aggression gave the radicals of the Free-Soil party the unchallenged ascendency. Acts of violence in the next few years were the rule while Robinson and moderation were all but shoved aside.[12] Even so, the doctor's dedication to freedom was not forgotten, and when the issue had finally been settled and Kansas was admitted to the Union he was in fact awarded the laurel of governor. It was the crowning moment of his life.[13]

Charles Robinson was sworn in on February 9, 1861, as the first governor of Kansas. Within weeks he found that he had also become a war governor. Although privately he bristled at the sight of treason and revolt in neighboring Missouri, the new head of state stood by his old policy of moderation publicly, and hence the safety of Kansas became his chief concern, not the pillaging of western Missouri.[14]

"If we are careful," other moderates added, "it strikes us that Kansas will suffer proportionally less than any other State."[15] But the radicals, still riding high from the territorial days, would have none of it, and the governor's wishes were once more ignored as the jayhawkers swarmed across the border.

"It is true small parties of secessionists are to be found in Missouri," argued Robinson to military authorities, "but we have good reason to know that they do not intend to molest Kansas in force." If the jayhawkers could be forced from the line, he pleaded, peace might yet be restored and then, the governor confidently announced, "I will guarantee Kansas from invasion."[16] His entreaties were to no avail.

Later that year, incensed at what they termed his cowardice—yet in truth, Robinson was the last check to their designs on the border and political primacy in Kansas—a smear campaign was whipped up by the radicals and efforts were made to unseat him. Then, early in 1862, articles of impeachment were handed down against the state auditor, the secretary of state, and finally, against the governor himself. The charge was "high misdemeanors" regarding the sale of state bonds—stealing. Although the two cabinet members were found guilty as charged, Robinson was acquitted by a nearly unanimous vote. Nevertheless the odor of guilt by association lingered long after the judgment, and the governor found himself a ruined man.

At the end of his two-year term, Robinson retreated to his home by the riverside, a pariah in the land of his making. Lawrence and Kansas were more his creation than any other could claim, and

CHARLES ROBINSON
*(courtesy of the Kansas Collection, University of Kansas
Libraries).*

perhaps, deep within a troubled soul, they were the children he
was never allowed to sire. Now even the fatherhood of these was
denied him. Somewhere amid the broken hopes and shattered
dreams of his mind was the faith that healing time would erase the
memories of the scandal and enable his comeback. Then, once more,
Dr. Charles Robinson could assume the position in Kansas he so
rightfully deserved.

At the river's edge where Massachusetts Street ends, down from
the huge liberty pole with its gigantic U.S. flag, construction on
the new bridge was under way. One of the workers milling about was
Jim O'Neill of Lecompton. Originally from Ireland, he and his large

family were forced out during the famine of 1847, and all chose America as their ark. Much of the clan drifted south, and with war three brothers had entered the Rebel army. O'Neill was an antislavery man, however, and had been all along. He enjoyed his new home on free soil as did his wife and their six small children. Because of the distance, O'Neill chose to live in Lawrence during the work week and return to his family only on weekends.[17]

Across the wide river, brown and deep after heavy rains to the west, the sandy Leavenworth Road led up from the ferry and disappeared into a tall forest. A dozen soldiers were camped here performing guard duty on the Delaware Indian Reserve.

One block east of the liberty pole, on New Hampshire Street, stood the City Hotel. Nathan Stone ran the brown, two-story inn with help from his wife and son and attractive daughter, Lydia.

There were few businesses on New Hampshire, homes mostly, and much was the same with its partner across Massachusetts, Vermont Street. But in the second block of Vermont, on the west side, was the blacksmith and assembly shop of Ralph Dix. A little to the south was Dix's three-story home. The lower level of the house was used as a work place for the business, while the family—Dix, his wife, Getta, their children, and the three Dix brothers, all from Connecticut—lived on the upper floors. Adjoining the building on the south was a tiny barber shop, and one door further was the second-best hotel in Lawrence, the Johnson House.

Ben Johnson was one of the town's more strident abolitionists. He was also a man who split no hairs when it came to who he liked and who he allowed in his hotel. Last year, learning that a number of Missouri property hunters had signed his registry, the irate innkeeper collared the startled men and kicked them into the street, a sight that gave everyone a good round of laughs. If you're from Missouri, and you're looking for strayed property, "give the Johnson House a wide berth," chuckled editor John Speer.[18]

For quite some time now the white-plastered hotel had been a notorious Red Leg hangout where George Hoyt and his boys drank and "raised hell" between trips to the border. None were here today though, and only a dozen guests or so were in their rooms, riding out the torrid midday heat.

Directly across the street was the pretty, whitewashed Methodist Church.

Sundown comes earlier to Lawrence than to the rest of Kansas, one-half hour earlier. Mount Oread ensures this. In the evening the shadow from the hill crosses and cools the town, and the beauty of

JEROME AND ELLEN GRISWOLD
(courtesy of the Kansas Collection, University of Kansas Libraries).

sunset is captured each dusk in the cottonwoods across the river, glinting strawberry-gold.

Five blocks west of the Eldridge, through the Central Park and over a short bridge spanning the deep, wooded ravine, at the limits of the city sat the spacious home of Dr. Jerome Griswold.

Dr. Griswold, a curly haired, husky man, and his wife, Ellen, were just returning this evening from a long trip east. And the house they returned to was a house of friends as well as of guests. Three other families boarded with the Griswolds: Mr. and Mrs. Harlow Baker, newspaperman Josiah Trask and his wife, and State Senator and Mrs. Simeon Thorp.

A block south of Griswold's, close by a large cornfield, stood the finest home in Lawrence, the Lane mansion.

There had never been anyone quite like him before, and most Kansans supposed there would never be anyone quite like him after. He was "heroic," he was the "devil incarnate." He was the "liberator of Kansas," he was a "thorough bred demagogue." He was at once generous, loving, caring, even "saintly." He was at once a murderer, a liar, an adulterer, "as bad a man as they make 'em." He was anything, he was everything, but to his numerous friends, even to a few of his yet more numerous enemies, he was known simply and aptly as "one of our things." He was Senator James Henry Lane, the "humble servant of the people."[19]

Jim Lane blew into Kansas one fine day in 1855, and whatever small chance there had been for a peaceful solution to the territorial issue quickly went up in smoke. Although he announced shortly after arriving that he would "just as soon buy a nigger as a mule," Lane saw the shape of things to come and wasted no time in joining the free-soil cause.[20]

Vying with Charles Robinson from the first for control of the free-state forces, the sandy-haired scrambler could at once be all things to all men at all times. Part whoremaster, part camp evangelist, after taking the measure of an audience Lane had the uncanny ability to hold, mold, bend, and sweep it to such fantastic lengths that normally sane, sober-minded men rattled "like a field of reeds shaken in the wind." One wild moment he might blow thunder and hell fire at slavery and Missouri while he twisted and trembled with excitement, flinging down a coat, then a vest, then a tie, pausing just long enough to roll up his sleeves and, as if it were a white-hot poker, move a long, crooked finger slowly and threateningly over the torchlit crowd. A moment later, while listeners elbowed forward and strained to catch every word, "Jeems" might humor and toy with his audience and in a hissing, hoarse whisper carry on ribaldly about women or his "humble" Indiana childhood. Then, just as the crowd relaxed with this new theme, a chilling scream—"Great God!"—would shatter the night air and slam the audience back to earth.

"He talked like none of the others," said a spellbound listener. "None of the rest had his husky, rasping, blood-curdling whisper or that menacing forefinger, or could shriek 'Great God!' on the same day with him."[21]

Because he said the things Kansans wanted to hear in the raw and earthy way they wanted to hear it, Lane soon became a feature attraction. Quiet, pragmatic Robinson was never such a pleaser, and consequently the more excitable, impressionable—unfortunately, the vast majority in Kansas—flocked to the Grim Chieftain's camp. Eventually, a simmering dislike between the faction leaders bubbled into a boiling hatred—Robinson was for patience and peace; Lane for action and war.

And when that war he so feverishly worked for finally came in 1861, Lane lost no time in urging utter destruction on Missouri and slavery. Kansans needed but little prodding to assail the old foe, and advice from their newly elected senator and close friend of Abe Lincoln was merely icing on the cake. Some men, notably the moderates and Governor Robinson, pleaded with fellow Kansans to remain at their farms and shops and let well enough alone. But these were the sage minority, and amid the mad cheers for Lane their voices were all but drowned out as the border war he demanded began.[22]

The opportunity for the senator to exhibit his martial prowess, to "play hell with Missouri," as he styled it, came that autumn as Gen. Sterling Price marched through Missouri and briefly threatened Kansas. When the Rebels finally moved on, "General" Lane and his "smart little army" of fifteen hundred jayhawkers crept behind in their wake, supposedly to harry Price's rear and slow his movements. In truth, the army was little more than a mob of thieves and adventurers who immediately began treating themselves to the spoils of war.[23] At Osceola, a beautiful, bustling city along the Osage, the Kansans scattered a tiny band of Rebels, then broke ranks and got down to business. Stores were looted, safes emptied, homes, barns, and warehouses were torched, horses and mules rounded up, even the tobacco-chewing chaplain Hugh Fisher went to work on local churches. Reportedly, Lane's share of the booty, which included silk dresses, a piano, and $13,000 snatched from the hands of a widow, topped everyone's.[24] Later that day, with all that Osceola had to give loaded into wagons and carriages—including 300 jayhawkers too drunk to sit in the saddle—Lane and his men marched off to new fields of conquest.

"As the sun went down . . . Osceola was a heap of smouldering ruins," wrote a brigade correspondent. Later a visitor was shocked to find "not half a dozen houses" where before there were hundreds and less than a score of people where formerly there were thousands. Osceola, as a point on the map, had ceased to exist.[25]

That autumn, 1861, the senator and his jayhawkers thoroughly scourged the Missouri border, and the name "Jim Lane" inspired a terror fully equal to that of Jennison. "Destroy, devastate, desolate. This is war," cried the Kansan, his Mexican spurs jingling as he rode along. And like a prairie fire the brigade swept on, murdering, pillaging, and blackening a swath up and down western Missouri. As the flames shot up, Lane looked, to one New York correspondent, like "Nero fiddling and laughing over the burning of some Missouri Rome."[26]

Although the exploits of the senator from Kansas were widely applauded in the North and nationally his star was rising, no group of men could have been prouder or happier than those of his home state, most of whom savored the lesson being taught in "Secessia." And as John Speer of the Lawrence Republican smugly added, what his friend had done thus far was but a warm-up for what he would do in the future: a "miniature picture," warned Speer.[27]

Only Governor Robinson and a few others gave voice to dissent. Ever mindful of his adversary and well aware that Lane's stock always soared during periods of strife, Robinson reportedly spoke early in the war with Missouri governor Claiborne Jackson in hopes of snuffing the border war before it began. When this fell through the governor turned to the military, begging them to force the jayhawkers from the line before the Rubicon was crossed. Finally, when nothing came of this, Robinson rolled up his sleeves and continued the battle both orally and in print. The governor mocked the senator's claim in which he boasted that his brigade had routed "a greatly superior force" at Osceola. Lane's tenure on the border, wrote Robinson to the newspapers, was a history of theft, arson, and murder— of "pouncing upon little, unprotected towns and villages, and portraying their capture as splendid victories." The governor even insinuated that President Lincoln refused all reports from Kansas unless first endorsed by James Lane. He continued, "If our towns and settlements are laid waste by fire and sword . . . we will have Gen. Lane to thank for it."[28]

The senator easily brushed aside criticism from Robinson. Any man who made deals with traitors such as Claib Jackson, hissed Lane before a tumultuous crowd in Leavenworth, had no business talking about thievery and such. The gallows were the only high office the governor should hold, he concluded, "and I here arraign Charles Robinson as a Traitor to his country." To this the audience hotly agreed.[29]

JAMES HENRY LANE
(courtesy of the Library of Congress).

Shortly after the Leavenworth speech, and when the anti-Robinson ball had started to roll, the senator closed in for the kill. Sniffing feverishly among the sale of state bonds, Lane announced that profits were filling the pockets of individuals, not of the public. Then came the trial, thus beginning the end of a once-promising career. Battling gamely, Robinson refused to fold and continued the fight as did his dwindling cast of supporters. But soon the governor was forced to retire, beaten and disgraced.

With his long-time enemy now out of the way, and with western Missouri a blackened waste, Lane turned once more to Kansas and set about crushing what little political opposition remained. And with his popularity at an all-time high, and with a horde of more than willing henchmen to help out, it was a simple matter. By the summer of 1863 the "most radical of radicals" found himself in complete control of Kansas, both politically and militarily—a virtual king without a crown. Most men would have relaxed following such an achievement. After a seven-year climb to the top most men would have chosen to savor their triumph somewhat and bask in the warm glow of victory. But James Henry Lane was quite unlike most men. And whatever else the tireless senator was, stupid he was not. Well did he understand the volatile and precarious nature of Kansas politics, and when he saddled the radical tiger in 1855 he, above all others, knew that he could never dismount without being devoured. To keep his name dancing in the public's mind was and always would be his goal—never to let the people forget it, not for a month, not for a moment—for if the words "Jim Lane" were on everyone's lips there was no time to utter the name of another. And to keep his name there, as in the past, almost any excitement or pretext would do.

Now, a bit after midnight on August 21, Lane was back home following a railroad meeting at the Eldridge. Asleep were his grown daughter and teenage son. Also in bed, Mary Lane, a tired, troubled woman whose aging and careworn face spoke without words her tempestuous life with the senator. Throughout the mansion there were trophies and mementos: a shining sword, compliments of Winfield Scott for service in the war with Mexico; a beautiful black piano in the parlor, silk dresses hanging in the closet, and other appointments, courtesy of western Missouri.

General, senator, king; Jim Lane was riding the tiger in Kansas, and he had every intention of holding hard in the saddle.

Outside, others plodded home from the meeting. Save for this the town was still and the night black as a tomb.

A short distance from the Lanes lived the mayor of Lawrence, George Washington Collamore. A tiny, balding man with large, smiling eyes, George Collamore, like most of the leading citizens, was an early and active free-soil fighter. Mayor Collamore was also, like his old friend and law partner, Massachusetts governor John Andrew, an administrator who believed strongly in efficiency and the letter of the law in government. And like everyone else after 1862, the safety of Lawrence was the source of his greatest concern. Hence, upon entering city hall in the spring of that year Collamore had made some changes.

Although the old citizen guard had served a purpose, to the new mayor's way of thinking it had served it rather poorly. Unsophisticated, unreliable, though most had posted about the town cheerfully enough, other guardsmen had begged off or fallen asleep when they did show up for duty. It was a job best left to professionals. Thus from General Ewing the mayor sought and received soldiers for the task, much to the relief of everyone. Then, too, there was the town's weaponry. For much of the war the Lawrence militia used an odd array of arms with no uniformity whatsoever. When drill and target practice were through for the day each gun went to each man's home to suffer neglect and abuse in one form or another. Again the mayor petitioned and again the army delivered, this time with rifles and shot, enough to arm the militia. Unlike the past, however, Mayor Collamore insisted on storing these weapons in the Massachusetts Street armory where, after the town had rallied to any given alarm, a rapid and smooth distribution of arms could be effected.

It was in the midst of these preparations that the bottom had suddenly fallen out of the war—Vicksburg, Gettysburg, the appointment of Ewing—and two weeks ago, when Hadley and his guards left, even the mayor was convinced they were needed no longer. And after the full moon scare and all the ribbing he took, Collamore, the "nervous mayor," saw no reason to call back the citizen patrols, for even without a guard any emergency could be met by every man in town ready and waiting at the armory; this in fifteen minutes, thirty at the latest.[30]

Like Lane and Collamore, other prominent men were now home from the Eldridge, taking in something cool, a bite to eat, a quick glance at the newspaper before bed.

Kansas State Journal
Lawrence, Kans. Aug. 20, 1863

Why does a sculptor die a horrid death?

He makes faces and busts.

COURT REPORT
R. Wilson, drunkenness and fast riding, $5 and costs. Paid.
White Turkey [Indian], contempt of court, $2 and costs. Paid.
Calvin Ware [Colored], petty larceny. To be tried Aug. 24.

MILITARY
Army of the Potomac: Picket firing has ceased entirely . . . both armies seem to have settled down in a state of lethargy. . . . Parties recently arrived from Richmond represent the people there as sunk in deep gloom . . . sickness prevails to a fearful extent. . . .
Grant: Unimportant skirmishes occur daily.
Rosecrans: Very little news. . . . The rebel army has fallen back. . . .
Arkansas: There are very few Confederate troops in Arkansas. . . . Already our lines have been extended. . . .
Missouri: Gen. Ewing . . . to remove all suspected families . . . to end bushwhacking. . . . A three-story brick building in Kansas City, used as a guard house for she rebels, fell Thursday afternoon and killed four . . . badly bruised several others.

LOCAL
Ninety to one hundred degrees in the shade every day this week . . . . Fremont's visit postponed till October. . . . Bernstein & Cohn's burglarized last night . . . church affairs . . . politics . . . crops.

One by one the last lamps in Lawrence flickered out. Windows were thrown wide open to catch the absent breeze of a hot, sultry night, the kind of night when a person turned and tossed and shifted the pillow continually to the cool side, kicking sheets to the floor, rising tired and sweaty for a ladle of water. One o'clock, two o'clock, three—only the twinkling stars kept the vigil. All else slept. The war was over.

No one in the sleeping town would have guessed that, in fact, nearly two more years of smoke and death lay ahead. Even had the predictions been correct and had the Rebel army buckled on all fronts, few in Lawrence understood that for a good many Southerners, particularly in Missouri, the war was not over. Win or lose, the killing would never end now, at least not until the debt had been paid, not until someone paid and paid dearly for the destruction of their homes, for the loss of their loved ones, for the death of an age.

The signs were all there. Had any in the sleeping town bothered to study these signs they might have seen that the time for collecting this debt had come. But no one studied the signs and no one was awake. And no one would have guessed that at that moment, like a great heavy fog, dark and deadly, the collectors were flowing down through the bluffs into the quiet Kansas Valley, not a dozen miles away. Leading them was the only man who could, the man who by stealth and boldness had paralyzed the border for the past two years, and a man whose very name was the most feared word in Kansas. This man and those who followed were two hours from their destination—Lawrence.

By 3:00 A.M. Captains Coleman and Pike had discovered where the trail of the invaders rejoined—a trail now six hours cold. From Spring Hill the pursuers followed as rapidly as possible, northwest toward Gardner. A messenger sent back by Coleman to Aubrey ordered all arriving troops to push on without delay.

At the same time, fifteen miles to the southeast, Lt. Col. Charles Clark at Coldwater Grove received a message. It was a hastily written note from Coleman informing him that the guerrillas had crossed the border and that he, Pike, and 180 men were in pursuit. Throughout the night Clark had awaited more information from Pike. What were the Rebels doing on the Missouri side? Had they crossed the line? In what direction? Clark had called in scores of men from other posts and was prepared to march at once. But no further word arrived, and the troopers were sent back. Now came first news of invasion. With only a handful of horsemen, Clark quickly saddled up.[31]

6

VENGEANCE IN MY HEART

In the final hours before dawn on August 21, the last of the invaders entered the Kansas Valley. Now, to save time the scouts in advance often strayed from the winding California Road, cutting through pastures and fields, and leading the column over paths and lanes. But in the dark, among the woods, the work was slow. At length, a boy was taken from his home and forced to act as guide.

Several people along the route became uneasy. At Hesper, ten miles southeast of Lawrence, some heard the horsemen and quickly guessed the worst. A child was forbidden by his father to saddle and ride to the town. Because of his team's exhaustion, a farmer who might have gone didn't. One woman did send a servant rushing north to Eudora. But for most, their sleep was unbroken and others who were awakened suspected nothing.

Alarm might have spread had anyone discovered the list. The identity of the riders, their destination, and their purpose would have been clear then. Someone in the column dropped a scrap of paper while passing a farmyard. Had anyone found the note and struck a match they would have seen a long row of names—prominent Kansans mostly. Likewise, all the names were those of Lawrence men.

"Who we want," ran the heading.[1]

One year before, Olathe also slept. Although nothing separated the city of a thousand from "Dixie" except a ten-mile stretch of prairie, Olathe had earlier been lulled by numerous false alarms. The first came one night in August 1861, when a horde of Missourians were reportedly on the march to loot and burn the city. Even though the fear had been widespread and men, women, and children flew wildly about, dawn and scouts revealed not "a wolf, owl, or secessionist." It had been a terrible, yet groundless alarm. But as everyone later agreed, grounds for concern remained. And if it had done little more than redden faces, the embarrassing panic had at least hammered home one valuable lesson. Henceforth, an armed patrol would guard the town, just in case.

Later another false alarm rocked Olathe. But this time the city was ready. Still later, another scare hit the town and once more the people responded. And so on.[2]

Finally, in July 1862 the vigilance of Olathe was rewarded when three Missourians rode into town, robbed the deputy sheriff, then rode out again. The excited militia rapidly formed, and after a brief but furious chase the thieves were brought to bay. With that, townsmen buried their prey, congratulated one another on a job well done, and promptly returned to life and business as usual.

"Missouri had better send a few more of their bushwhackers through Olathe," laughed a proud resident.[3] And so, one dark night two months later, Missouri did. Except for the saloon, which was jammed with soldiers, Olathe was asleep and very unprepared as over one hundred shadowy horsemen drifted quietly through the streets. The first that anyone knew of their plight came with a simple midnight rap on the door. And suddenly, like some distorted dream, every man in town found himself standing in the square, huddled and helpless.

Then, from the crowd of Rebels a tall, graceful figure appeared. Instantly, most of the groggy townsmen were stunned. He seemed so different. Although dressed much like the rest, he was cleaner, neater, almost fastidious. His blond hair was trim and much shorter than the others', and quite unlike the fierce, mocking eyes all around, his were soft, easy, friendly. And when this strange man finally spoke his voice had a ring as clear and reassuring as his appearance. The man announced to the gathering in the square that his name was William Quantrill. If everyone kept their wits and remained calm no one would get hurt. They had come only for horses, guns, and ammunition, he went on, not to harm or destroy. Private property would even be respected, he added, *if* no resistance was made.

With that the raiders began the roundup of horses. One man protested, however. Drawing a butcher knife from his boot, the Kansan went for his mount. Just as he rose to swing in the saddle a shotgun blast ripped the top of his head off. While the horrified citizens watched on, the corpse flopped up and down on the street in wild death convulsions. Another man, an enraged soldier, grabbed a pistol and snapped the hammer at a Rebel three times. But each click was a dud, and before he could squeeze out a fourth his body was riddled with balls. And thus began the sack of Olathe. Guards watched the captives while shouting men broke away and kicked in the stores. Hotels and their guests were robbed. Another soldier was killed when he failed to leave his room as ordered. The offices of the two newspapers were demolished. The jail was thrown open and baffled inmates set free. Items were plucked from the citizens: jewelry, watches, miniature photographs of comely women. At dawn the guerrillas herded up the horses, loaded the plunder into wagons, and quietly marched from town.[4]

Olathe never recovered from the trauma of September 7. Businessmen whose stores were gutted chose not to reopen and risk another such loss. One editor was totally ruined and could not continue his paper. Many families moved away. Those who remained admitted they did so only because of the troops that now garrisoned the town. Even then most were apprehensive.[5] Indeed, so too were the residents of other border towns and farms, for the ease with which Olathe was taken left nothing secure. In one night one man erased for all Kansans any fine notions they might have had about the war, about wealth, about old age. In one night one man became to Kansas what Lane, Jennison, Montgomery, and Hoyt had been for months to Missouri—the blade of Western war.

Quantrill was no stranger to Kansas. A number of men in the crowd that night recognized their captor, and some actually spoke with him. Although he was remembered by many as not much more than a boy named Charley Hart, Quantrill had once been a friend during the territorial years and had even lived among them briefly. But all that was past. Things had changed. He was no longer Charley Hart, nor was he a boy. And Missouri was now his home, not Kansas. More important, when the war came it was the South with which he chose to side and not his native North.

Quantrill's war began innocently enough. Eagerly rushing off with the army of Sterling Price, he fought as a private in the opening battles for Missouri—Wilson's Creek, Drywood, Lexington. It was after the Rebel victory at Lexington, however, that a change was made.

Despite the best of Southern hopes, Lexington—a bitter, hard-won affair—came to nothing because Price soon retreated without a parting shot. And when he did, a veil of gloom and despair lowered over all Missouri secessionists. As the regular conflict receded south it left hundreds of Rebel soldiers in its wake. Some, maimed and crippled, would never fight again. Others, fed up with war and sensing that the cause was already lost, took the oath of loyalty and quietly returned to their homes. There were a few, however, who left the army only to pursue a more active, independent role. Quantrill was one of them.[6] Above the others he rose to command. Brave, intelligent, affable, from the start it was Quantrill's aim not simply to spar with the enemy in ravaged western Missouri but also to take the hard hand of war to untouched Kansas, and to do it as often as possible. So long as he led this would be his guiding star.

On a cold dawn in March 1862, a small, determined group of men took their first ride into Kansas. Quantrill, George Todd, and over thirty more ventured across the line to settle accounts with several jayhawkers living in Aubrey. As the guerrillas entered the village, they were fired upon from the hotel and were soon followed by three men who bolted from the building. They were swiftly chased down in a field of dry cornstalks and shot. In the melee others were wounded. The store was ransacked, horses taken, and although he was later released, a Union officer was led away as prisoner.[7]

The sack of Aubrey, although traumatic to those involved, was not a cause of major concern throughout the rest of Kansas. That a huddle of buildings a short jog across the border should be captured created no panic, although it did stir some interest. More important, to many who supposed that the war had retreated south with Price, it did come as a mild shock to find that it had not entirely. And although John Speer asked his Lawrence readers if they remembered Hart, it was the mysterious, foreign-sounding name "Quantrill" that swirled along the border from that day forward.[8]

A week later Quantrill reportedly swooped down and captured the Union garrison at Liberty, Missouri, a dozen miles northeast of Kansas City. After paroling the soldiers the guerrillas showed up next on the Missouri River, where they robbed a steamer after forcing it to land. A short time afterwards the bridge over the Blue River was burned, a soldier and tollkeeper killed, and suddenly Quantrill was everywhere.[9] Others took the cue and joined the war once more. Indeed, before the month of March was out, loyal Missourians and their brethren in Kansas began to hear the name *Quantrill* with disturbing regularity. But also before the month had passed, the cause for all the anxiety very nearly ended when the leader and over twenty of his men were surrounded one night while at a home on the state line. After a furious gun battle in which several were killed, the bushwhackers made a miraculous, fiery escape.[10]

But life got no easier from that point on. Within the next thirty days there were two other narrow escapes, a desperate encounter each, and each with loss of life.[11] As a result Quantrill disappeared altogether for the next few months, moving from place to place—the timber and bluffs above the Blackwater River; the hills and hollows along the Blue, a deep, dark wilderness east of Kansas City; or the even more tangled and vast Sni-a-bar country, a nightmare world of snakes, ticks, and flies accessible only by hog path or deer run. With his departure the guerrilla war in western Missouri perceptibly cooled.

April and May 1862 passed quietly. In June, however, there was activity, and then, in early July near Pleasant Hill Quantrill reappeared. Here the Rebels and a like number of Federals dueled for hours; first in a running firefight, then locking up for a savage hand-to-hand struggle in the underbrush. When the smoke had cleared nearly thirty men lay dead and many wounded, including Quantrill, shot through the leg.[12] More fighting broke out elsewhere. Adding a new dimension to the war, blue uniforms were stripped from the dead and donned by bushwhackers.

With reason, loyalists grew impatient. Because the military seemed unable to deal with the partisans there was talk of starting an Opposition Amateur Bushwhacking Company. Others began insisting that wives accompany them wherever they went because no man had yet been troubled by guerrillas while in the presence of a woman. And with both Union soldiers and bushwhackers now wearing blue, life in western Missouri became a double-edged game of survival with loyal and Rebel citizen alike never sure as to who they were facing.[13]

In light of the recent outbreak, drastic measures were deemed necessary if the exasperating war was ever to end. Thus from angry military commanders rolled a series of unfortunate acts that slammed the door on any sane solution to the border war. One such act issued from the quill of James Blunt. Characteristically exploding at the renewed fighting—because as district commander the millstone sat squarely on his back—that brash, headstrong individual responded by hoisting the black flag, transforming what had been until then a sputtering, reasonably humane fight into an all-out war of extermination:

> Whereas a system of warfare has been inaugurated, known as "bushwhacking" in which . . . rebel fiends lay in wait for their prey, to assassinate Union soldiers and citizens, it is therefore ordered . . . they shall not be treated as prisoners of war, but be summarily tried by Drum Head Court Martial, and if proved

guilty, be executed, (by hanging or shooting on the spot), as no punishment can be too prompt or severe for such unnatural enemies of the human race.[14]

Other generals had penned such statements, although in practice they usually fell by the board. Good to his word, however, Blunt followed through, and guerrilla captives either mounted the scaffold or faced the firing squad.

Bushwhackers pored over newspapers eagerly and were aware of events as they occurred. Some of the men with Quantrill were children when the territorial cry of "No quarter!" was raised in 1854. That threat, the threat of their fathers, never actually happened. Now, almost a decade later these sons read that in fact they were engaged in just such a contest; not the noble kind of romantic novels, but a brutal, vicious, primitive kind in which the defeated died and the victorious lived. A few would never respond in the manner Blunt's edict seemed to demand; instead, they quietly left the war. And for the time being Quantrill himself continued to parole captured Federals and seek exchanges whenever the occasion arose. There were a growing number, however, such as George Todd—tight-lipped, cold-eyed, deadly George Todd—there were a number like him who held no illusions about the border war, and the altered course of the struggle was for them one of the easiest paths in the world to take. In time most would think, and act, like George Todd.

By the second week of August 1862, anyone could see that western Missouri was ablaze with revolt. After the capture of two steamboats the Missouri virtually dried up from a Rebel blockade, and everywhere large bodies of men moved silently through forest and valley.[15]

When all was ready, Confederate recruiter Col. John Hughes appeared and took charge of this burgeoning army, then marched it to camp near Independence. There, on the tenth he was joined by Upton Hayes and his raw recruits, and that same day, still nursing his leg wound, in rode Quantrill and his seasoned guerrillas. In all, the assembled force approached four hundred men. Early the next morning the Rebels struck the garrison at Independence. The fighting raged for several hours, but after dozens lay dead on both sides, including Colonel Hughes, the white flag was lifted and the Southerners had control of the town.[16] Federal troops soon began converging, however, and after paroling his captives, Hayes—who now took command—led his army to the southeast. And while Hayes was gaining an even bloodier victory at Lone Jack several days later, Quantrill and his band were elsewhere, being officially sworn in as a Partisan Ranger Company. In suit, Quantrill was voted captain by his followers.[17]

The stir among loyal Missourians caused by Independence and Lone Jack was immediate. There was no lack of concern across the border either. If it was any consolation to Kansans, however, the Rebels showed small inclination to menace their state, and the whole affair had the appearance of an internal scrap between Union and Confederate Missourians. As the weeks passed, sketchy but welcome reports arrived, which stated that the Southern army, possibly five thousand men, demoralized and low on ammunition, was flying south in utter disarray. Quantrill was thought to be among them.[18]

"Heels up and coat tails streaming in the wind," clapped one Kansan. "They are running. That is the latest news."[19]

Within days, the sleeping town of Olathe discovered that not all of the Rebels were running.

> *Lawrence Republican*
> Lawrence, Kans. Sept. 11, 1862
>
> KANSAS INVADED!
> OLATHE SACKED!
> QUANTRELL AT WORK!
>
> The town of Olathe ... was visited and plundered, on last Saturday night, by the secessionists from Missouri, under the lead of Quantrell [*sic*]. Had there been a well organized and drilled company of fifty men in Olathe, with proper guard out, the town could never have been taken. . . . Let other towns take warning. The success of this raid will encourage similar ones on a bolder scale.

Five weeks later Quantrill returned to Kansas. On the night of October 17, 1862, the guerrillas surrounded and captured Shawnee. As at Olathe, stunned citizens were herded into the square to watch helplessly while the Missourians tore their town apart. The stores were quickly looted and torched, as was the large hotel. Townsmen such as William Laurie were dragooned to help load the plunder; Laurie, a photographer who had been run from Kansas City in 1861 for refusing to raise a Rebel flag, was stripped of his clothes and put to work. Seeing his opportunity, however, and clad only in underwear, Laurie quickly escaped to a nearby field.

A former resident of the place, a raider now with Quantrill, recognized a much-hated neighbor from the territorial days. He, George Todd, and several others approached the man. One of the gang baited the Kansan and asked him where he stood politically. Proud, defiant to the end, he boldly responded that he was a devout Unionist, same as always. In a twinkling Todd raised his gun, jerked the trigger, and shot him through the head. And as the man's wife and daughter screamed in horror, the old neighbor, feeling cheated, bent down, placed a pistol to the victim's mouth, and shot him once again. Another guerrilla, angry and wild, accused the wife of being an informer and argued to kill her too. At that Quantrill quickly stepped in and threatened to shoot the bushwhacker if he didn't calm down.

Finally, after setting a number of houses on fire and murdering another man, the raiders rounded up the horses and rode back into the night. When they thought it was safe to do so, many of the citizens raced in a mad attempt to save their property. A few were lucky. For most, however, the flames were too far advanced, and as they had been doing all evening long, they could only gaze on helplessly while their homes went up in smoke.

For his part, William Laurie was determined that he would never be driven from a town again. First Kansas City, now Shawnee. He would escape the war entirely and move to a haven beyond its reach. There, in faraway Lawrence, he would set up shop and live in peace.

After waylaying several more men, the guerrillas crossed the state line and finally disappeared into Missouri. With Kansas aglow to his back and a handful of dead in his wake, William Quantrill had carried the Civil War to still another Kansas town.[20]

In the weeks after the raid on Shawnee, as the days grew short and golden leaves sprinkled the valleys, Quantrill organized his men for a trip south. Unseen to a passerby in summer, junglelike lairs became entirely stripped of foliage in the winter. Also, mounts needed constant forage, and the frigid Missouri winter could chill even the most ardent fighting spirit. And so, around the first of November 1862, the captain led his company away from the Missouri River country and took up the southward march. They passed through ravaged western Missouri, moving swiftly over stretches of prairie and field, coursing when possible the timber along the Grand and Osage. Other bushwhacking bands, emboldened by Quantrill's presence, mushroomed on the countryside, engaged in a variety of acts, then vanished almost as quickly as he passed.

Kansas State Journal
Lawrence, Kans., Nov. 6, 1862

QUANTRELL
There have been fugitive reports circulated, for some weeks, that Quantrell [*sic*], the notorious predatory chieftain of the border

rebels, was making serious preparations to give Lawrence a call. . . .Were it not for . . . the probable loss of valuable lives, we should be inclined to favor Quantrell's purposes against Lawrence; for with any such force as he has yet been at the head of, we are quite well satisfied that to lead it to an assault on Lawrence would be the most fortunate thing that could happen for the future peace of the border. . . . Mr. Quantrell's reception would be warm, if he should venture up this way.

The guerrillas continued their march out of Missouri, through the Indian Nations and finally, before severe weather set in, crossed into Arkansas behind Confederate lines.[21]

Two months after the premature report, Quantrill had gone south and a great and abiding silence settled over the western border. Among Missouri Rebels, however, his aura lingered. He had been little more than a hope, a dream, a vision prior to Aubrey and Liberty and the skirmishes of spring. But over the long and bloody summer months, after Independence and a dozen other encounters, his reality had gained so, his image had grown so that finally, at Olathe and Shawnee, the Missouri ideal was fully realized. Whereas Price and other prominent Southerners had abandoned the state in its hour of need, this stranger, this answer to a thousand prayers, had remained to continue the fight. But more than any one thing, the war, in the shape and spirit of this man, was at long last and with a sweet, sweet vengeance being carried back to Kansas where it all began. Feeble old men, crusty veterans of 1812 and the Indian wars, saluted and hurrahed in their hearts again and secretly urged him on. Daydreaming girls, swept with emotion, dedicated poetry to their romantic, blue-eyed cavalier. One grateful woman, after giving birth to twins, paid the ultimate tribute and named one of her children Quantrill.[22] And in a hundred other quiet ways the people's love was thus expressed.

And even across the line, although many Kansas families slept in fields and quaked at the very sound of his name, there still was a curious respect building for the daring, phantom Rebel. Some boasted of their experiences in a Quantrill raid—"No counterfeit either," one man insisted, "but the real, genuine Quantrell"—while others told tall tales about narrow escapes from the hands of the captain himself.[23] But through all the yarns the respect held, couched at times, but there nonetheless; a grudging admission among a warlike race that this man, their enemy, was a bold and fearless fighter. And too, there was the tacit understanding that in a grim little war where

WILLIAM QUANTRILL
(courtesy of the Dover [Ohio] Historical Society).

restraints were rapidly slipping, Quantrill, despite "no quarter" edicts, managed to preserve a degree of humanity, even gallantry, as his parole of Union captives would suggest. A respect it was, but nothing more. All Kansans would concur that any repeat of the previous summer's onslaught would be the worst possible calamity to befall their state. There was hope that the year 1863 would be better. In the long intervening winter months there was the chance that their nemesis might be killed or that he might grow weary of a war that was looking more every day like a lost cause. Or perhaps he and his Missouri "whackers" considered the debt of 1861 paid and would trouble Kansas no longer.

But down in Arkansas William Quantrill had no intention of being killed. And if he agreed in his heart that the struggle for Missouri was over, his special war against Kansas was not. As he had said that night at Olathe, he would never be finished until the debt had been paid in full, until the border of Kansas was as stricken and desolate as was that of Missouri. Then all too quickly, and with this haunting thought still fresh in the air, the winter passed; soon from the spring woods of western Missouri a Federal spy was pushing on a secret message bearing the ominous words: "Quantrill is here."[24]

In May 1863, while troops were away on scout, a band of Rebels slipped into Plattsburg, Missouri, and set fire to the courthouse. Before the raiders left, the town's Unionist press was "knocked into pie."[25] For Missouri loyalists the omen was clear.

Even clearer to Kansans, however, was Dick Yager's march from Diamond Springs that same month. Thus the border braced for the summer of 1862 to repeat itself. Then, to the surprise of everyone, nothing happened. Thomas Ewing stepped onto the stage and the war for all appearances ended. Within a matter of weeks the "live" man generated a feeling of trust and confidence like no time in the past, and unlike his bombastic predecessor, the energetic young general allowed actions to speak for themselves. His troops took the field, attacked and scattered Rebel bands, and his spies mixed with the guerrillas so effectively that Ewing felt no major move could be made without his knowledge. Proof of his success, he felt, was Quantrill's inactivity. And finally, after two agonizing years of sudden descents from Missouri, a guard was placed on the open border in effect sealing off Kansas from the war, or more to the point, locking Missouri out. With this Kansans were given peace and a pledge: Quantrill will never invade the state again.[26]

No one bothered to inform Quantrill. As the best weeks for action passed—a time of good grass and water—the man who had wrought such havoc along the line in 1862 remained fast in the woodlands of west Missouri and did nothing; nothing, that is, except watch, wait, and plan.

Increasingly his mind locked on one place—his boldest stroke of the war: Lawrence. Returning after a three-year absence and taking a town he had left as a fugitive—no one could miss the irony. In view of the huge gamble, however—breaking clear of the border guard, the grueling fifty-mile ride through a hostile land, attacking a city the size of Lawrence, then returning with every Federal of the border between him and Missouri—convincing enough desperate men, enough needed to attempt such a ride, seemed at the time remote. But the wind was shifting. Already, although Kansas failed to see it as such, a fateful chain of events was rapidly unfolding.

In late spring, while Blunt was still in command, his troops captured a certain well-liked bushwhacker named Jim Vaughn. Clad in Union blue, Vaughn had prankishly come to Wyandotte one day to get a haircut and shave but was soon recognized and taken prisoner. In a bid to gain his release, Quantrill tried to bargain with Blunt, offering not one but three Federal captives, including a Yankee officer. The gesture failed, however, and Vaughn was given to the hangman. At the rope the condemned man spoke his last: "We can be killed but we cannot be conquered. Taking my life today will cost you one hundred lives, and this debt my friends will pay in a very short time."[27]

Then in July came what guerrillas feared most—the arrest of relatives and their exile from Missouri. Bill Anderson did make a mad dash to hide his family, and Younger and Yager lashed out as best they could. And George Todd did send a letter to Ewing threatening to burn Kansas City if the women and children were not released.[28] But the prisoners remained, the arrests continued, and in the end it was this frustration at preventing the banishment of their loved ones that loosened restraints to an attack on Lawrence. Quantrill worked out plans for the raid, scheduled to coincide when the full moon illuminated the Kansas prairie, around the first of August. He then did nothing. And, as expected, word of the impending march quickly reached Lawrence.

Then, on August 13, when the prison in Kansas City collapsed killing the five girls, something snapped and the border war was never the same. Murder! or so the guerrillas felt; the cool, calculated slaughter of women and children. No one seriously believed it was accidental. There were those like Anderson and Younger directly affected, and there were the many more who thought they got a glimpse of what lay ahead for their families. But all were acutely aware of their own inability to do one single thing to stop it.

"Vengeance is in my heart, death in my hand; blood and revenge are hammering in my head."[29] In this mood following the prison disaster, in the red rage and fury to strike at something, no suggestion had more instant appeal than that which Quantrill now proposed. Lawrence . . . a history all Missourians were well versed in: the New England colony, the Aid Society, abolitionists, jayhawkers, Red Legs, the proud, wealthy refuge of runaway slaves, a place of music and flowers, of pretty homes and united families—lying just beyond the cinder and ash like a sun-washed rose. Rebel spies reported that an atmosphere of calm, even apathy, had settled over the town following the full moon scare. It was agreed—Lawrence!

This time no Federal spies were around to pass the word when, on August 19, Quantrill led his column up from the Blackwater rendezvous and began the long march to Lawrence and his fourth raid into Kansas. And behind him, a good many who followed were determined that if this raid succeeded it would be unlike any raid of the past.

No one could miss the irony. It all began in 1857 when William Quantrill went west with several other Ohioans to file for homesteads in Kansas Territory. Sleepy little Dover, Ohio, might have been home forever had his father not died a few years before, throwing the young family on its own. The mother fended as well as she could and Will hunted and fished, but it was a shadow of their former prosperity. For a year the teenager, frail of health, tried a hand in Illinois and Indiana—odd jobs, teaching—but never sent back enough money to ease his mother's burden, a point that troubled him deeply and a concern that grew when the widow was forced to take in boarders. And thus the new start in Kansas.[30]

By late March the Ohioans had entered the territory and were soon staking claims near Stanton. Together the pioneers shared a cabin, clearing the land, plowing, planting corn by day, cooking, washing, and cleaning up by turns at night. A neighbor boy about his age paid visits, and although he was from a proslavery family whereas Quantrill was free-state, the difference was not enough to prevent the youths from becoming fast friends.[31] And unlike Ohio, Kansas offered a wholesome, invigorating life—the stiff outdoor work each day, the fine hunting and fishing along the river. It was a routine that young Quantrill enjoyed greatly. Writing to Ohio, the excited son asked his mother to sell out and come to their new home in the West. "We all will be square with the world," he explained, "& able to say our soul is our own."[32]

But it was not to be. The relationship among the Ohioans soured, Quantrill lost ownership of the land, and in the end his dreams of a farm in Kansas came to nought.

For almost a year following this, Quantrill shifted about the territory. But late in the summer of 1858 the youth struck off once more, and for the next two years he lived a restless, rootless life of roving and adventure, from the brawling army camps of Utah to killer blizzards in the Rockies, from back-breaking work in the Denver gold fields to Indian attacks on the high plains. It was a raw, rough-and-tumble, day-by-day life the Ohioan led, "pretty hard & scaly" in his words—a world of gambling, guns, and sudden death, but a world in which he was becoming more confident every day. Despite his age and gentle appearance, a rugged, resilient character was fashioned from the years in the wilderness, and although it was a life of rigor and uncertainty, it was a life Quantrill loved and thrived upon. Unmistakably, the West, where strength and wit prevailed, was his element.[33]

But still, there were the quiet frosty days of winter when the log schoolhouse near Stanton was emptied of its noisy children and the young teacher was left to his thoughts, to meditate and reminisce on his mother and Dover, on family and old friends and the placid, solid life surrounding them. Although he had seen and done much since leaving home—"enough incidents," he wrote to his mother, "to make a novel of adventures"—on reflection, this budding man viewed his life as empty and aimless. Exciting and free though the past had been, the other nature became increasingly preoccupied with the future and pondered the virtues of working for greater ends, absorbed with channeling his energies toward some lofty, though as yet undefined, goal. And at the same time Quantrill became utterly disillusioned with his home in the territory.

Shocked on his return from the West at the admiration shown by Kansans for John Brown and his attempt to foment slave revolt at Harpers Ferry, Quantrill's old notions gave ground. "Contemptible," he called them. His earlier stand had been naive, he felt; that in fact it was the free-staters, not the proslavery party, who caused the border troubles by raiding into Missouri for slaves and plunder. "The devil has got unlimited sway over this territory. . . . The only cry is, 'What is best for ourselves and our dear friends.' "[34]

Ohio, not Kansas, figured more and more into his future plans. After an absence of three years, the desire to return burned stronger than ever in Will Quantrill. He tried to maintain connections with Dover by copious letter writing, to learn of changes and old friends, but disappointingly, Caroline Quantrill was a poor writer and even the notes she did send were those of a mother fretting for the safety and happiness of her child. By the spring of 1860, the likelihood of Quantrill returning to eastern Ohio became more certain with each passing day. But then there was the school term to finish in Stanton and the scholars to educate, and the young man began spending much of his time in Lawrence.

Brief as it was, the stay in Lawrence was an experience unlike anything in the past. Quantrill worked with surveying crews for a time on the Delaware Reserve. But as the weeks and months passed he became deeply involved with several other men in the secret and mysterious trade of returning livestock and fugitive slaves to their Missouri masters—a legal, but delicate occupation anywhere in the North, magnified in Kansas, and doubly dangerous in Lawrence.[35] There were the lengthy clandestine trips to the border and back, and although he was known to some by his actual name, it was the assumed "Charley Hart" that Quantrill preferred for this work.

With difficulty the facade was kept up. Eventually, however, suspicion grew, questions were asked, and the game wound down. Late in 1860 an indictment was handed down by county attorney Sam Riggs charging Quantrill, alias Hart, with breaking into and stealing from R & B's powder house; with arson in the burning of a barn in which a runaway had been hiding; and finally, with returning that same slave to Missouri and bondage. To avoid arrest Quantrill hid in a number of places, including the hotel owned by Nathan Stone. The innkeeper had become especially fond of the young Ohioan, who was a frequent guest; in fact, his daughter Lydia had lately nursed him back from a long illness. Now through this friendship the hunted man was given asylum. In the end, however, Quantrill saw an opening and made good his escape.[36]

Shortly afterwards, the fugitive met with a small group of men about his own age—abolitionists from northern Kansas. And from this encounter a plan was conceived to carry out a daring raid upon one of the richer border plantations, to steal its slaves and despoil the master in the process. In December the men started for Missouri.

On a cool evening just after dark, Quantrill and three others entered the yard and strode to the house. While one of the raiders stood guard on the porch, the rest disappeared through the door. Inside, the owner was confronted. A candle was lit in a nearby room and Quantrill stepped to the side. Shotgun blasts roared out. One abolitionist fell dead. Another, although wounded, was helped away into the night by his friend. A few days later, the slave owner, Quantrill, and several others located the hiding place of the Kansans in a thicket. That same day the two men were buried.[37]

During the fateful winter of 1860–61, Southern states made the decision; one by one they began withdrawing from the Union. And that night at the plantation, Quantrill had seceded too in a sense— from Kansas, from Dover, and from much of himself as well.

At 4:00 A.M. on August 21, 1863, Quantrill was in Kansas again, crossing at Blue Jacket's ford, five miles from Lawrence. Behind him, splashing through the tiny Wakarusa were over four hundred tired, hungry Missourians. Many had been in the saddle for almost thirty-six hours. Some who had never suffered a night without sleep in their lives had now endured a second. More, the wiser, had snatched a few minutes of rest while they rode strapped to their saddles. None slept now, however. Already on nearby farms cocks were piping in the new day.[38]

When the servant sent from Hesper arrived in the darkened streets of Eudora, three townsmen immediately rose, saddled, and galloped west. In the excitement, one rider was pitched from his mount before he had cleared the city limits. Undaunted, the other two continued in their mad dash to Lawrence.

From Eudora, on fresh horses, Lawrence could easily be reached within half an hour. But just at daybreak and only a few miles from town one horse stumbled and fell, pinning the rider below. Unconscious, terribly crushed, the injured man was pulled to the roadside. And rather than continue, the friend raced to a neighboring home seeking help for his dying companion.[39]

With the first tint of dawn to their backs the raiders rode through the village of Franklin. A light fog covered the lowlands but several early risers could hear the clink and tinkle of brass and steel and a long, low rumble as hundreds of horsemen passed.

"Hurry up," came a voice from the mist, "we ought to have been in Lawrence an hour ago."[40]

Beyond Franklin the California Road was left, and a gradual ascent began up a small row of hills. After a mile the fog thinned and finally lifted. Ahead, dominating the western horizon was the black, spreading outline of Mount Oread, and suddenly there was no question of how much farther they had to go. A nervous excitement swept the column as the pace quickened. The rear, stretching for some distance, hurried to catch up. At last the guerrillas rode up the final rise. Slowly the rooftops on the outskirts appeared, then the tall Eldridge House emerged, and the business district, and more homes until the entire town lay at their feet. Here, at 4:55 A.M. Quantrill halted.

Nothing seemed suspicious about the town and there was no apparent movement, yet when the rest of the Rebels finally joined a tremor rippled through the ranks. Many were stunned at the size of the place. A city! A city more than double Olathe, Shawnee, and Aubrey combined. It was a certainty that somewhere to the rear hundreds, perhaps thousands, of Yankee cavalrymen and militia were closing by the minute. Now, before them was a place unlike any in the past. The calm was a ruse, some insisted; word must have spread and hundreds of men and cannon were now waiting to spring the trap. Caught in the jaws of two superior forces, the odds of reaching Missouri again on their bone-sore, spent mounts were nil.

The arguing continued and some refused to go further. At last Quantrill announced that any who wanted might return, but he was going in, and that those who cared to join should make themselves ready. With that the leader rode slowly ahead. Gradually the remainder of the men followed.

Finally, by 5:00 A.M. Quantrill was within a few hundred yards of the outskirts, and here he pulled up once more. Two men were called for and were sent to reconnoiter Massachusetts Street. As they passed through the town a few stirring citizens noticed them but paid them no mind. After several minutes the scouts rode back to the column. Once there, they said to Quantrill the only words in the world he wanted to hear: no one suspected, no one was waiting, the town was quiet and fast asleep.[41]

Kansas Territory, 1860

My Dear Mother,

It is a pleasant morning, this; the sun is just rising. . . . I stood in my schoolhouse door, and viewing this it made me feel a new life, and merry as the birds. But these feelings and thoughts are soon changed and forgotten, by the arrival of eight or ten of my scholars, who come laughing and tripping along as though their lives would always be like this beautiful morning, calm and serene. . . . And they, like all children, are enjoying more happiness now than they will at any other period of their lives. I sometimes wish that I was again a scholar in the old brick schoolhouse at Dover; and again with my companions on the playground. But scholars and companions are all far from me now, and I am left alone to contemplate. It all seems to me but a dream, a very little of which I ever realized; or, more like a sheet of paper on the first page of which there are a few signs, showing that something has been commenced, and all the rest left blank. . . . Thus my mind is ever recalling the past, and my conscience tells me that if something noble is not done in the future to fill up this blank, then it had better be destroyed, so that none may take it for an example. . . . I can now see more clearly than ever in my life before, that I have been striving and working really without any end in view. And now since I am satisfied that such a course must end in nothing, it must be changed, and that soon, or it will be too late. . . .

How I would like to be in Dover again and once again to see scenes and to call up recollections of the past. . . . And then to visit . . . most of all my own dear home and its occupants, then at least for a short time I would be happy as also those around me. . . . Give my love to all and a kiss for yourself. Good by[e.]

Your son,

W. C. Quantrill

P.S. I will here say that I will be home . . . as soon as the 1st of September & probably sooner by that time I will be done with Kansas.[42]

7

DEATH IN MY HAND

The day came clear and calm on Friday, August 21, 1863. Not a cloud in the pale morning sky, nor was there a trace of wind. Looking down from Mount Oread a few threads of white smoke were visible, curling straight up as early risers began preparing their breakfasts. Reaching to the heights came the faraway low of milk cows and the tiny, strained efforts of dueling roosters. Black, impassive, the Kaw turned the bend and silently slid east.

Although the land was yet dark, from the summit several figures could nevertheless be seen stirring in the twilight. There were the local hounds trotting their morning circuit, scouting leftovers from the evening past. But there was also Sallie Young, the Eldridge seamstress, taking her customary ride from town. Two beaux were with her, and at the moment the showoffs were racing their horses south down the Fort Scott Road.[1] Directly below, on Massachusetts Street, the boy recruits were just beginning to rise and dress. Charles Pease was close by, coming down the street from his slaughterhouse with a carcass of beef in the back of the wagon. His dog tripped along beside. Arthur Spicer had begun sweeping out the first of the day's dust from his beer hall, and in the streets George Sargent was making the rounds, tinkling his bell, delivering milk door to door.

At the Eldridge House all was silent save for the kitchen sounds of hired help beginning breakfast. Across the misty river, parked in the cottonwood grove, two teams loaded with salt for R & B's waited on the ferry to start service for the day. And winding his way up the face of Mount Oread was Charles Robinson. Leaving his wife at home by the riverside, the troubled former governor was taking advantage of the splendid new day. Above the slumbering town he approached the stone barn where his first house had stood. Here he would hitch a carriage and take a jaunt over the countryside while the air was yet

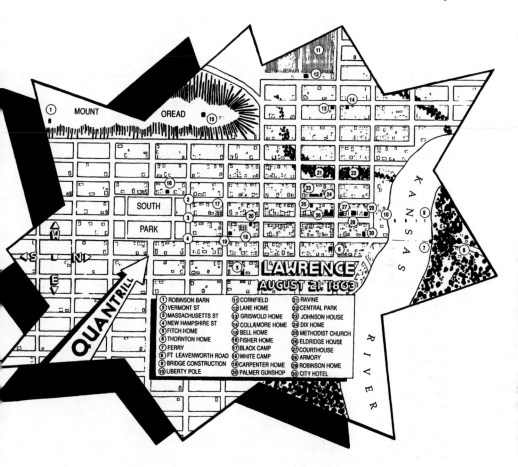

MOUNT OREAD

SOUTH PARK

LAWRENCE
AUGUST 21, 1863

QUANTRILL

KANSAS RIVER

① ROBINSON BARN
② VERMONT ST
③ MASSACHUSETTS ST
④ NEW HAMPSHIRE ST
⑤ FITCH HOME
⑥ THORNTON HOME
⑦ FERRY
⑧ FT. LEAVENWORTH ROAD
⑨ BRIDGE CONSTRUCTION
⑩ LIBERTY POLE
⑪ CORNFIELD
⑫ LANE HOME
⑬ GRISWOLD HOME
⑭ COLLAMORE HOME
⑮ BELL HOME
⑯ FISHER HOME
⑰ BLACK CAMP
⑱ WHITE CAMP
⑲ CARPENTER HOME
⑳ PALMER GUNSHOP
㉑ RAVINE
㉒ CENTRAL PARK
㉓ JOHNSON HOUSE
㉔ DIX HOME
㉕ METHODIST CHURCH
㉖ ELDRIDGE HOUSE
㉗ COURTHOUSE
㉘ ARMORY
㉙ ROBINSON HOME
㉚ CITY HOTEL

cool and fresh and where one could remain undisturbed and lost in thought. By his watch, it was five o'clock.

Songbirds began their morning ritual, and gradually, as it grew lighter, several more people emerged to stretch upon porches or visit a back building. In all, it was a tranquil scene—the dawn of a typical summer day in Lawrence.

The more he watched, however, the more George Bell realized there would be nothing typical about this day. He was the first to see them. From his home on Mount Oread the county clerk's attention had for some time been focused toward the Wakarusa where he spied a huge column of riders slowly materializing from the murky valley. He had naturally assumed they were Union troops. But then there had been the alarms and "great scare" of three weeks past, and the longer he watched and the more he thought, the greater his suspicion grew. As the horsemen neared, there were mysterious starts and stops and then, when they halted on the rise and two men rode into town and back and two more split off to Sam Snyder's farm, Bell became certain that this was not the Federal cavalry. They didn't even have a flag.

Grabbing his musket and cartridge box, the clerk ran for the door. His wife and children tried to stop him; if it were true, they begged, there was little one person could do, for the town was asleep. The man brushed their pleading aside. "If they take Lawrence," he announced, "they must do it over my dead body." Rushing down the slope, George Bell headed for the armory.[2]

Sallie Young was next. Someone with her said that the column to the east was a Kansas outfit. But no one had mentioned anything about their arrival yesterday. They watched for a bit, but their curiosity was up and soon they rode back toward town.[3] As it grew lighter, a few people in the south also saw them and turned to watch.

Finally, Quantrill paused for the last time. The young guide was passed to the rear. A number of men quickly jumped down, and loose saddle girths were hurriedly cinched. Blue jackets were stripped off, red sleeves rolled up. Revolvers were drawn, percussion caps checked. Some of the best stuck leather reins in their mouth and bit down hard, leaving both hands free. One final time Quantrill turned and reminded the Missourians why they had come. They knew. Then, at five past five, Quantrill's horse broke away at a gallop. Behind, a wild, explosive shout went up and the entire command lunged forward at a run. A few shots rang out but most held their fire.[4]

As the roar came nearer—an unearthly scream some thought, unlike anything ever heard in Lawrence—people in the south of town jumped startled from their beds and ran to windows, then to one another.

> Those men. . . . They have no flag!
> There's a regiment of them!
> The rebels have come!
> The bushwhackers are here!
> Quantrill's band as sure as you live!
> Quantrill is here!
> QUANTRILL!

At his barn Governor Robinson turned sharply to the east. He saw a number of tiny flashes followed by as many puffs of gray smoke and these in turn followed by the faint rattle of small arms fire. Unfamiliar as he was with actual warfare, Robinson nevertheless understood. As he inched his way back into the barn the governor saw below a long, dark mass moving rapidly through the south of town striking for the center.

In East Lawrence, blacks were already pouring from their huts and dashing for the river. "The secesh have come," they screamed. "The secesh have come."

Across the ravine in West Lawrence, those who were awakened by the gunfire thought first of Independence Day and firecrackers, then the marshal's dog killers, then the recruits acting up. But the Fourth of July was long past and most of the stray dogs had been killed. As for the recruits, they had no weapons. Jim Lane rose on an elbow and cocked an ear to the south window.

In the quiet surrounding his farm one mile west of Lawrence, Levi Gates also heard the strange sound. Without a second thought he reached for his long-range hunting rifle, and like George Bell and a good many others, Gates rushed straight for town.[5]

At the south edge of Lawrence, Sallie and her friends stopped by the yard of the Reverend Snyder. They could just make out the distant rumble in town, and here was Mrs. Snyder leaning over her husband Sam, sobbing uncontrollably. A milk pail was turned over, the cow was gone, and the front of the reverend's shirt was covered with blood. But the woman wouldn't say what had happened. The noise drew the riders further into town.[6]

Charging across open lots, the raiders soon began to separate. With waves and nods, scores of men, mostly farmers and the young recruits, split off to picket Mount Oread and the roads leading from town. A little further on, the main body itself broke into three columns, with Quantrill leading the larger to Massachusetts Street while two smaller groups turned down New Hampshire and Vermont. The shooting became more regular.

Ahead, as the roar approached, the boys in the recruit camp came falling from tents, struggling to get into their clothes. Across the street the black camp was already deserted.

When the main column spotted the tents and blue uniforms a moment later, it never slowed, but with shouts—*Osceola! Kansas City! Remember the girls!*—it rode right on through. As it did, there came a deafening explosion as hundreds of shots were fired up and down the ranks. In a few seconds, when they had passed, all that remained was settling dust, blood-spattered canvas, and a pile of twisted bodies, hands still clutching jackets and trousers. Seeing this, Charles Pease leaped from his meat wagon and flattened himself on the ground. Hard beside him, his dog shivered from paw to haunch.[7]

With the cry "On to the hotel," the main column stormed into the business district. Thundering down broad Massachusetts Street five and six abreast, shots were fired randomly at storefronts while on the adjoining streets others fired into the back doors.[8] At last, in a huge cloud of dust, the three columns converged and washed against the Eldridge House. Here they pulled up. A few shots rang out, but soon all became still, and as the shouts and swearing died away only the horses, rearing and plunging, were heard. With hundreds of guns moving from window to window the guerrillas watched and waited. A cannon was parked across the street at the courthouse, but no one was there to use it.

Inside the hotel, there was no panic. Most guests were still in bed, for it had been too sudden. After looking out, some men thought fast enough to slip their money to women. An employee quickly tossed his life savings of $100 in gold through a trap door onto the roof, and someone shouted that "half-wit" Jo, the hotel owner's brother, had been shot while scaling the courtyard fence. But most were simply too groggy to be frightened. Eastern guests were outraged at being roused at such an hour.[9]

One look and Alexander Banks knew it was hopeless. From his third-floor window the state provost marshal gazed down on a sea of upturned, fantastic faces—unshaven, deeply tanned, distorted faces, streaked with sweat, dust, and powder, burning with red-rimmed eyes, and framed in long, greasy hair. There were probably no more than a dozen weapons, including his own, in the entire hotel, so Banks made a quick decision. Yanking a sheet from his bed, he hung it out the window.

Below, there was a thunderous cheer at the symbol, and when all had quieted the provost marshal asked for the leader to come forward. As soon as Quantrill appeared, Banks wisely began bargaining for the safety of the occupants; the hotel would be surrendered without a fight, but first, he insisted, the well-being of the guests must be guaranteed. Quantrill was about to answer when a loud clanging echoed throughout the hotel. Startled, the mass of riders whirled and sprang back, ready to open fire. Quickly Banks yelled out, begging the Rebels not to shoot; it was a mistake—only the excited night clerk raising the guests with the dinner gong. For a moment, everything was "breathlessly still." Shortly, Quantrill again spoke with Banks and soon agreed to the terms, much relieved that the hotel had not become a fortress as feared.[10]

With wild shouts and cheers for Quantrill, many guerrillas then left for the stables and other parts of town while another group dismounted and, with brass spurs jingling, tramped into the plush hotel. Upstairs, fine ladies and gentlemen, scantily clad, had their rooms burst into by dirty, cursing men who with a splash of tobacco juice and wave of a gun ordered them out and down to the lobby. Trunks and carpet sacks were ripped open, and jewelry, currency, and ladies' apparel were crammed into pockets. The looting went from room to room as the stupified boarders, bishop and priests included, fled down the staircase. Banks and his assurance for their safety did little to calm nerves as the celebration above grew in fury. Downstairs, the trembling night clerk was forced to open the safe while other Rebels passed quietly about the crowded lobby, tapping men on the shoulder and asking, "Your money, if you please!"— much as a railroad conductor might pause for tickets, thought one. With some remaining humor another captive asked if he might keep just fifty cents for a drink or two. The bushwhacker stared at him for a deadly moment or two, gave a slow smile, and then handed back eighty.[11]

Down Massachusetts Street, store doors were kicked in and food and liquor were located. Miniature U.S. flags were also discovered, then with a laugh fastened to the rumps of horses. The offices of the *Republican* and *State Journal* were quickly put to the torch. Near the river, the rope on the liberty pole was cut and, amid loud cheers, the huge red, white, and blue banner came fluttering down.[12]

Among the twelve soldiers across the Kaw there was no longer any doubt. First came the mad flight of blacks furiously paddling boats and logs or simply swimming the swollen river. Then the flag fell. Then the cheers. Taking aim, the troops opened fire. On the opposite shore, several raiders trying to cut the ferry cable went spinning up the bank again. When a horseman was spotted, more slugs whizzed up Massachusetts Street and between homes near the river.[13]

Sallie Young and her two companions came into Lawrence quite some distance before they realized their mistake. Warning her friends to stay calm, the three quietly turned and rode slowly from town. When the outskirts were reached and a Rebel picket sighted them, the two boys set spurs and were off south. Sallie rode back into town.[14]

Soon, Quantrill entered the hotel. Stepping into the packed lobby he met a number of old faces, whereupon he shook hands and spoke briefly. He assured them of their safety. The guerrilla chief then climbed a flight of stairs and strode to the landing where he looked over the crowd and watched while his men went about their work. Everyone below seemed stunned. Terrified, most expected the leader to be the essence of his men; wild, vulgar, and snarling. On this score, however, they were gratefully surprised. Although he gripped a big pistol, with another in his belt, there was a pleasant, calm, even benign look spread over his boyish face and clear blue eyes. His gray hunting shirt was open at the chest and he wore a low-crowned Spanish hat with gold neck cord and little tassels dangling around the brim. A fine-looking man, mused a captive.

Some in the crowd attempted to humor and flatter, grinning sheepishly, reminding him of old times in the territory and congratulating him on his brilliant success in capturing Lawrence. Unmoved, Quantrill received the tribute with "marked complacency," simply adding that yes, it was by far his greatest exploit. Another ventured to ask why he hadn't come during the full moon as he had threatened.

"You were expecting me then," he smiled.

Then, after once more vouching for their safety, Quantrill asked if Governor Carney was in town. He was not, someone answered. Again he queried if anyone knew where Jim Lane lived. Arthur Spicer "volunteered." After ordering the captives across the street and assigning several men to guard them, Quantrill detailed a squad to follow Spicer to Lane's house: if he misled them, the saloonkeeper was to be shot on the spot; otherwise Spicer was to be returned alive as there was an old score yet to settle.

As they were being herded across the street, a number of bushwhackers cast crude remarks and curses at the captives. Already some raiders were glutted with liquor. One angry guerrilla, clamoring to murder the hostages, rode up, called a man a Red Leg, then aimed and fired. Although the shot missed, a guard threatened to kill the drunk should he fire again. This was seconded by Quantrill, who came out after hearing the disturbance. Quickly, he ordered the prisoners to the City Hotel near the river where they would remain safe.

At this, the terror-stricken men and women sprang headlong for the refuge, Quantrill escorting a short distance behind.

Reaching the hotel, the Rebel warmly greeted Nathan Stone and his beautiful daughter, Lydia, and shouted to the raiders nearby that the Stones were his friends and that neither they, the hostages, nor the building was to be touched. He then turned to leave. Before he left, however, Quantrill once more reminded the captives that Stone's hotel was their haven: "Stay in it. . . . Don't attempt to go into the streets."[15]

Although no Red Legs were there this morning, the Rebels didn't know it, and thus the three-story Johnson House was quickly surrounded by a large band. Unlike the Eldridge, however, the score of people inside refused to come out. Consequently, the bushwhackers began sniping at the windows, mixing the gunfire with calls to surrender. "All we want is for the men to give themselves up," they yelled, "and we will spare them and burn the house."[16]

Two doors down, in a home of screaming children, Getta Dix was doing everything in her power to get her husband to move. Earlier, while Ralph was still in bed, Getta had looked up the street and watched in disbelief while "half-wit" Jo was shot off the Eldridge fence; now with more shooting at the Johnson House the street was full of men. Again she pleaded—the raiders were too busy at the hotel—there was still a chance. But Ralph, his brother Steve, and several employees seemed frozen, uncertain, feebly reassuring one another that it was only a matter of time before help arrived.

Again the woman begged. But nothing. Putting her children in the arms of the men, she then ran down the flight of stairs to the side of the house and struggled to carry a heavy ladder up to a window. As she was coming back, however, Getta happened to look over toward the Johnson House, and there to her horror she saw several men leaping from windows only to be shot upon landing. Running back into the home, the woman barred the doors and told her husband what she had seen, warning the rest to stay inside. This and the fear of fire jolted the men. Together, despite his wife's pleas, Dix and the others decided that their only hope now rested behind the stone walls of the Johnson House. Thus after climbing out a window and crawling over the roof of the adjoining barber shop, every man did eventually reach the hotel.

After seeing Ralph safely on the other side, and after taking her children to a coal shed out back, Getta desperately searched for her black nurse. The woman was finally discovered locked in a closet, refusing to come out. Grabbing a meat cleaver from the kitchen, the frantic mother hacked open the door and ordered the frightened nurse toward the shed to mind the children while she herself went to the Johnson House.

No sooner had Getta left than she saw her brother-in-law tumble down the steps at the rear of the hotel. Running to his side, she settled his head into her lap and sought to comfort him. But Steve was dead, and when Getta tried to move, his brain fell into her hands.

Then, as the blood-smeared woman staggered to the front, she could see that the hotel had surrendered. And there, standing among the rest, Getta saw through a rush of pain and tears her husband.

"Oh my God, Ralph," she screamed. "Why did you do it? I know they will kill you."

Another prisoner nearby had just handed a pistol to his captor. As soon as the weapon was given up a gun exploded behind the man, blowing out his stomach. Horrified, Dix and the other seven captives screamed for mercy.

"I have killed seven 'red legs,' " laughed the head of the gang, "and I'll kill eight more."

Wildly pleading that it was a mistake, that they weren't Red Legs, the white-eyed, sobbing men knelt and crawled on the ground, reaching up to the guerrillas for life. Although she too was screaming and crying, Dix begged his wife to save him. At length, the prisoners were kicked and punched to their feet and driven by three guards across the street toward the Methodist Church, with Getta clinging to Ralph's arm, beseeching the men at every step not to harm him. Two of the Rebels bent, then broke, making her a promise. But the leader was firm.

"No, I won't let you take your husband away," he said. "I'm going to kill every damn one of them."

Hanging desperately on to Ralph, striking at the raider's horse as it tried to nudge her away, the woman walked sideways, never taking her eyes from the leader. Up from the church, in the alley, Getta stumbled over a pile of rocks, breaking her hold, and before she could rise again the guns went off. Somewhere in the swirling blue smoke she saw Ralph go down. As in a dream, she stood while all around her others fell away. Racing down the alley, another group of riders spotted the pile of bodies; without slowing they trampled them hard into the ground.

Getta wandered along Massachusetts Street for some time—to a store where looting guerrillas chased her away, to a figure that was still breathing. But nothing, it seemed, could hold her attention. She

RALPH DIX
(courtesy of the Kansas State Historical Society).

continued to drift aimlessly until at last she found herself again in the alley. Noticing a straw hat laying nearby, Getta picked it up, quietly placed it over her husband's face, then calmly walked back to her burning home.[17]

Although a number of raiders roamed Massachusetts Street, exploring one store after the other, most broke into squads and covered the town. Many, like George Todd and Bill Anderson, rode over the bridges spanning the ravine and paid a visit to affluent West Lawrence. From out of shirt pockets came the lists with the long row of names, and the firing that opened the morning so terrifically now settled into short, methodical bursts from every corner of town. The Missourians had finally gotten among those they hated most, and no power on earth could stop them now.

Panic gripped Mayor Collamore. Springing from window to window, he, his wife Julia, and their Irish servant saw on all sides only nightmarish guerrillas, angry and shouting. There was no way out. Suddenly the desperate man thought of his well and quickly ran for the rear. There, in a wing of the house the tiny mayor dove down the dark hole followed closely by his servant.

At the front door the gang entered, met by Julia and her frightened children. Cursing and yelling fiercely, they demanded her husband. Receiving no reply from the terror-stricken woman, the men crashed through the home, up and down, from one room to the next, madly hunting their prey. Failing in this, it was decided simply to smoke the victim out. Setting the house on fire, the raiders fell back into the street to watch and wait for the mayor's appearance.

Refusing to leave, Julia slipped to the well, and as the flames spread throughout the home, she spoke down to her husband.[18]

By the time George Bell reached the center of town, Lawrence was surrounded. There had been no resistance. Nowhere could Bell hear the distinct crack of a militia rifle, and as far as he could see he was the only citizen shouldering a weapon. His courage dissolved. Bell looked for a way to escape, returning to home and family his sole desire. At last he ducked into the ravine. There, to his surprise, he met many others, just as confused and frightened as he.

"Where shall we meet?" he whispered. Aghast at such a notion, those nearby warned that it was pointless to think about a stand any longer; fighting would only get them all killed. A friend urged Bell to throw down his musket and perhaps draw less malice should he be taken. The sounds of gunfire and pounding hooves were more than enough to convince Bell of the wisdom in this. Dropping the rifle and cartridge box, the county clerk inched his way up the ravine toward home.[19]

When Levi Gates reached West Lawrence from his farm he realized that it was too late. Across the ravine he could plainly see Rebels in the center of town and more to the south, and it was obvious there was little he could do. All of Gates's friends and neighbors who had come on the run had turned back home in dismay. He was about to do the same. But Levi Gates took pride in the fact that he was an excellent shot, and the once-in-a-lifetime chance to try his hand on a human target and bag a Rebel proved irresistible.

Dismounting, the farmer steadied his hunting rifle on a fence, sighted his mark, then squeezed the trigger. Although it was a long shot, a guerrilla in the distance jumped in his saddle. Tempted further, Gates once more loaded and fired, then raced for the wooded ravine. He failed to notice the man closing on his right, however, and after he was brought down and the Rebel had finished with him, Levi Gates lay sprawled in the dust, his head flat and mashed "to a jelly."[20]

The first Jim Lane knew of anything was when a "flying Negro" passed his home and yelled that the bushwhackers were in town. Instantly the mansion became a bedlam, and while the wife and children flashed about in their nightclothes trying to locate two guns stored somewhere, the senator peered out the window watching for the approach of the raiders. The guns could not be found. Grabbing his ceremonial sword as the only recourse, Lane quickly dropped it as the horsemen led by Arthur Spicer drew up at the front gate. Bolting through the house, the jayhawker flew out the back window and ran for a small gully, bobbing and weaving, pausing just long enough to look for Rebel pickets. In a few moments Lane emerged from the gully and went streaking west through his cornfield, nightshirt flapping in the breeze.

Meeting them at the door, Mary Lane politely informed the guerrillas that the senator was not at home. Foiled at not coming face to face with the most famous man in Kansas, the Rebels settled for next best and proceeded to dismantle his home. Pianos, furniture, china—much of it from Missouri—were broken up and strewn about, as were the senator's private papers. The rings worn by Mary and her daughter were snatched from their fingers. Having finally

THE LAWRENCE MASSACRE, BY LAURETTA LOUISE FOX FISK
(courtesy of the Kansas State Historical Society).

located one of the shotguns, James, Jr., was warned to give it up. He refused. When a blast smashed into the wall nearby he at last did as he was told. The home was then set ablaze. But the mother and children hurried and put it out. Again a fire was lit in a different spot and again the family rushed and extinguished it. Finally the flames caught and spread in a third area, and the frantic attempts to save the finest home in Lawrence at last ceased.

At that, the gang mounted and rode away. With them not only did they take Lane's "magnificent banner," presented to his Indiana regiment for duty in the Mexican War, but the "general's" fancy, shining sword as well.

By now Lane himself was almost a mile away, crossing over the California Road, still running.[21]

One block east of Lane's, another group surrounded the stately home of Jerome Griswold. The swoop completely stunned the four families inside. With loud, ugly shouts the men were ordered to come out. Looking down from the second-floor bedrooms at the terrifying array below, Dr. Griswold, Jo Trask, Harlow Baker, Simeon Thorp, along with their wives turned and spoke excitedly about what they should do. Again the men were demanded; again there was no response. A moment or two passed and then, anxiously, someone in the house called out and asked why the men were wanted.

"The damned sons of bitches must come out of there," yelled an impatient guerrilla. He was echoed by his companions. No one in the home moved at this awful demand.

Soon another raider, wiser than the first, urged the Kansans to come out, that he would guarantee their safety once they did. No one would be harmed, he insisted, adding that they came only to rob Lawrence, and "if the citizens quietly surrender . . . it might save the town." This last approach softened the four men in the home. And besides, there was nothing else they could do. "If it will help to save the town," Trask advised, "let us go."

The men—balding State Senator Thorp, handsome newspaperman Trask, and dark-bearded, husky Griswold—filed down the staircase and reluctantly walked out the door. While Baker was getting into his clothes, the bushwhackers quickly encircled the others. The captives were asked their names and occupations, then robbed, and when Baker at last came down, the raiders formed the four men into a line. As the wives watched, the husbands were ordered to march toward town, and with Baker in the lead and a guerrilla riding at the side of each, they walked off.

Just as they cleared the yard one of the Rebels cursed the men for going too slowly. This caused the prisoners to pick up the pace. Something exploded behind him, ripping through his neck, and before Baker hit the ground another shot shattered his wrist. The rest of the guns went off. Thorp fell down near Baker while Trask managed to run only a short distance before he too went down. Wounded several times, big Jerome Griswold stayed on his feet. He made it all the way back to the yard and was on the verge of escape, but just as he was scrambling over some cordwood a well-aimed ball tore the life from him once and for all.

As the women stood shrieking in horror the Missourians paused to scan their work. One man was dead outright, whereas the other three were still breathing. Screaming hysterically, the wives raced down the stairs and through the door toward the dying men. Before they could reach them, however, the raiders, cussing and shouting, drove them back again. Jo Trask, rolling and kicking in terrible pain, pleaded with a Rebel to let his wife come to him. The guerrilla listened for a moment, thought the matter over, then agreed. Cocking his pistol, he aimed down and sent a chunk of lead whizzing through Trask's heart.

"He's dead," shouted the killer to the wife. "You can come now."

It was decided to leave the two yet alive to lie and suffer as they were, and while the gang moved down the street a mounted guard was stationed a little beyond. After the others had left, the women again tried to reach their husbands but were once more frightened back when the Rebel rode down on them at a charge. There was nothing they could do. The mayor's house was burning and others were starting to smoke, and there were the men lying all alone.

In great agony from a stomach wound, Senator Thorp writhed in the blood and dust. His friend Baker lay a few paces off, bleeding from the neck and hand. Harlow Baker had come close to drowning once in a swirling black river of his native Maine, so he understood death a little better than most. Although they were painful, the grocer knew that his wounds were not mortal. He remained still nonetheless. Beyond, no sound or movement came from Griswold or Trask.[22]

Around the burning home of George Collamore all the guerrillas had gone. They left fully satisfied that Collamore had either escaped earlier or burned to death in the fire. But to them the most certain thing in the world was that the mayor of Lawrence could not be in the house and still alive. Even Julia, who had remained by the well talking down to her husband until the very last, was forced out by the murderous heat.

Standing back, she watched. The fire engulfed the house and spread to the wing, and then the orange flames crackled and licked over the mouth of the well.[23]

Old Joseph Savage wasn't in that great of a rush to leave town—at least not until he had hitched his buggy and safely loaded everything of value into the back, including his brand-new silver baritone, which he was eager to show off at the next band concert. But finally, he and his wife and a German friend did pull away from their home just south of Lawrence and drove up Cemetery Road. "Mine pipe, mine pipe," cried the German, who wanted to go back and get it. But Savage wasn't turning around just for a pipe, and the German and his smoke would simply have to wait.

After a short ride they came to the home of Otis Longley; here they stopped. To their surprise they saw Otis suddenly bolt out his back door and run to the front, "making a frightened noise, unlike any other sound I ever heard," thought Savage. Close behind came two men cursing him to halt. He kept going, however, and just as he was about to reach the fence along the road, a shot rang out. Otis went down. As the stunned people watched on, the moaning man struggled to climb the fence. But another explosion sounded behind him and another bullet blew open his jaw, knocking him back to the ground. When the two Rebels walked up—one greedily chomping slices of cantaloupe—Otis was on his hands and knees, coughing streams of blood. Again he tried to rise. A loud blast at close range dropped him for good. The men then crossed the fence.

Joseph Savage, "some times crawling, and some times running and rolling," had already made a break for cover. But trembling and pale, the German sat beside Mrs. Savage stiff with fear. The woman's pleading and the sight of the horrified German was just too much, however, and the wagon was allowed to pass.

The two guerrillas strolled back to the house, the one still eating melon and the other merrily tooting his new silver horn.[24]

"Now is your time to make your escape," whispered one of the raiders behind Lemuel Fillmore. Earlier, Fillmore had taken his valuable horse to the ravine for safekeeping. Instead of staying there, however, he returned to his house for a pistol. That was when they caught and disarmed him, and that was why he was now being marched toward Massachusetts Street.

"Now is your time to run," the captor whispered as they neared the ravine. At this, Fillmore decided to make his move. He got only a few paces, however, before he was shot in the back and killed.[25]

In West Lawrence an old man stood by a fence, idly spectating. A Rebel rode up. Water was demanded. The old man ambled off and soon returned. Taking the cup with his left hand, the bushwhacker shot the man dead with his right.

Like these victims, most common people were at first impervious to the peril around them. Many were still under the impression that as with Olathe, Shawnee, and the others, this raid was for plunder alone, where only "marked" men would suffer. Otis Longley had seen Rebels on Mount Oread earlier, but he went right on with his chores. When finished, he drew buckets of water and sat patiently waiting, just in case his home was set on fire. The attorney Sam Riggs, despite the warnings of his wife, Kate, continued to help neighbors along his street by removing furniture and dousing flames.[26] Many others reacted similarly.

Looking down from his stone barn, however, Charles Robinson harbored no such illusions about this raid. Below, he watched the drama unfold. He saw the home of Mayor Collamore ablaze, as well as that of Ralph Dix. He saw Lane's house burning. As the sun rose, Robinson also saw through the smoke the machine movements of the guerrillas, their door-to-door calls, the citizens breaking from their homes at a run, the pursuit by men on horseback. The governor also heard the muted pistol fire, the shrieks of wives, the shouts and laughter of killers.

Charles Robinson had founded Lawrence barely nine years before, and a kind fate had allowed him to be absent during the first sack in 1856. Now, to his utter misery and grief, he had a front-row seat to the second, but this, unlike the other, was a much more thorough, much more tragic affair.

Larkin Skaggs was accustomed to having things just his way. He had already laid claim to one of the finest horses taken in the Lawrence stables, a magnificent white, and few were the men to contest it. He was big and burly and strong, and his long hair and beard were grizzled because he was quite a bit older than the rest. But Larkin Skaggs was also exceedingly cruel. When drunk, the bushwhacker was even crueler than usual, and thus when Lydia Stone's sparkling diamond ring caught his eye, it was wrenched from her finger in the same brutal way Skaggs took whatever else he wanted in life.

LYDIA STONE
(courtesy of the Kansas Collection, University of Kansas Libraries).

When Quantrill entered the hotel the attractive young woman made a tearful appeal. Still in the building, Skaggs was located terrorizing the Eldridge captives; after a few words from the leader, he was "obliged" to return the ring. On his way out, Skaggs paused just long enough to glare down at Lydia Stone. "Miss," he said, "I'll make you rue this."[27]

Not long after she arrived back in town, Sallie Young was taken prisoner and robbed of her pony. But shortly afterward she was put back in the saddle and ordered to go with a squad of Rebels to identify men and point out which homes were which. But Sallie wasn't very helpful. Every other house it seemed was that of a brother, a cousin, or an uncle, and with tears rolling down her cheeks she begged the raiders to spare the home and occupants. They did so repeatedly, but after this the girl was allowed to leave whenever she chose. Although she might have left at any time, Sallie tagged along instead and followed the squad wherever it went. Some of the people who caught a glimpse of her were confused: how odd she looked in her natty riding habit, they thought, alongside the rough and ugly men.

Arthur Spicer was also with a group of Rebels. Unlike Sallie, however, the saloonkeeper was religiously pointing out men, homes, and businesses. And unlike the girl, Spicer couldn't just pick up and leave anytime he wanted; to have had so many relatives would have been his end. It was coming soon enough, he thought, when he was handed back to Quantrill.[28]

The man with the salty little grin wasn't grinning today; he was praying. As he lay on his back in the dark cellar, squeezed up between a dirt ledge and the kitchen floor, he knew it was only a matter of time before they came.

Like his old boss Jim Lane, Hugh Fisher entertained no rosy notions about tomorrow should he fall into Rebel hands today. That morning at Sibley had proven how important he was to Todd and the Missouri bushwhackers. Nor was he as ill as previously thought. At the initial shout, the jayhawker jumped from his sickbed and bounded out the door. First, he turned his horses loose from the barn, and then with his two young sons, Willie and Charlie, he ran for Mount Oread. The illness had sapped the preacher, however, and the sight of Rebel pickets on the crest made him think twice. Sending the boys on alone, Fisher fled back to his South Park home. Elizabeth, with a baby in her arms and a tot by her side, thought her husband was insane to return and said as much, but as he slipped into the tiny cellar the woman made up her mind to do everything she could to save her man.

His wait was not long and Fisher soon heard the sounds—horses to the gate, spurs on the porch, knocks at the door, boots on the kitchen floor.

"Is your husband about the house?"

He is not, lied Elizabeth.

"I know a damned sight better," snapped the guerrilla. "He's in the cellar; where is it?"

Startled, yet composed, taking the four men to the door, the woman pointed with a straight face: "The cellar is open; if you think he is there, go look for yourselves."

Staring down into the black, a light was demanded. While the mother went upstairs to fetch a lamp, still keeping a grip on herself, the baby was placed in a bushwhacker's arms. Waiting, the man made faces and cooed to keep the infant from crying.

Below, Fisher could hear everything. When he heard his wife returning with the lamp and the cocking of revolvers, his left foot began to tremble uncontrollably. He placed his right foot over it to keep it still. Then as the light entered the cellar and boots came slowly down the steps, Hugh Fisher's heart and lungs slowed, then stopped, and his whole life flashed across his mind in an instant. And Elizabeth, holding her baby tight to one ear and pressing her hand hard to the other, went quickly into the front room.

As the Rebels reached the bottom, they were forced to stoop under the low ceiling. The man holding the lamp came to where the reverend was lying and stopped. In the glow of the lamp Fisher squinted upon the guerrilla's face, less than two feet from his own. Because of the low ceiling the lamp too was held low; thus the preacher's face remained in the shadow cast by the ledge he lay on. The men looked a bit longer but soon walked back up the stairs.

"The woman told the truth. The rascal has escaped."

There was no time to listen to the echo in her ears. Elizabeth Fisher reached deep down, drew up every ounce of self-control she possessed, and let the words roll.

"You will believe me now, I hope. I told you my husband had gone."

The Rebels lingered awhile, robbed the house, torched it, then left one of their men behind to see that the fire spread. But it wasn't in him to stop the woman as she raced from the well to the blaze and back again, and so the reluctant guard just left. When the last of the flames were doused, Elizabeth came to the cellar door and spoke softly to her husband.

"Pa," she said, "Pray and trust in the Lord, and I'll do all I can."[29]

After leaving their father, the two Fisher boys became separated somewhere in the hazel and sumac up the hill, and twelve-year-old Willie fell in with Robert Martin, a lad a little older and bigger than himself. Young Martin wore a blue shirt made from his father's old uniform, and he also carried a musket with a cartridge box slung from his shoulder. So when a picket spotted them, he gave chase.

The two boys raced over the hill, side by side, as in a game where home base and blue sky are always just ahead and everything somehow ends as it should. But a blast sounded behind them, and as Robert tripped, Willie felt something wet and warm spray his face. Robert didn't get up to finish the race because half his head was gone. And when Willie wiped his face he found his hand dripping blood, bone, and bits of brain.

Little Charlie Fisher also joined with another boy and together they hid in the cemetery. But a child's superstition forced them to a nearby cotton patch instead.[30]

As he crept along the ravine toward home, George Bell soon came to realize the futility of it all. He was cut off. Peering between the weeds and limbs, he could see no hope of reaching his family on the hill. In the streets, in the alleys, around burning homes and barns, only guerrillas were about. To climb the barren slopes of Mount Oread would be suicide. But his nerves cracked. Bell panicked.

Convinced it was just a matter of time before the raiders swarmed in and murdered them all, the county clerk and another man ran into the street. Once in the open and alone, the two abruptly returned to reality. But then, as fortune would have it, they spied a familiar sight—a partially completed brick home. The men dashed in, climbed to the second story, and crawled up among the joists. They could only keep quiet, count the seconds, and pray they hadn't been seen.

But they had.[31]

When a gang came to the home on South New Hampshire Street looking for Louis Carpenter, they didn't have far to look. He was right there.

Absorbed with the more important things in life, the good judge had never given much thought to fear; and so, being unfamiliar with

GEORGE BELL
(courtesy of the Kansas State Historical Society).

it, he could not fully express it. Thus when hate and the big black guns stood around him he didn't react as most men might. He certainly didn't run because running never entered his head. His hands didn't tremble. His bodily functions didn't betray him. His voice didn't waver, and when lethal questions were posed the New Yorker replied straightly and honestly in a clear upstate accent. There was also a strange, kindly quality about him. Some Rebels could not resist the temptation and stole a few items from the house, but no one was in a mood any longer to burn it. And certainly no one could bring himself to harm the judge. When the guerrillas left the yard, Carpenter was still standing there while behind him, his bride, Mary, and her sister, Abigail, began to breathe once more.

It was no act—the judge was always like that. A little later, another mob came and, seeing the pretty home, decided to burn it. But once again and as calm as ever, Carpenter met the raiders and sent them away disarmed. The pressure on the women, however, was almost unbearable.[32]

It was a miracle! The bushwhacker just started shooting at the men clinging to the beams when George Bell yelled out. The firing stopped, and everything became still.

It was true. The Rebel was actually Bell's old friend. In happier times the two had often broken bread together at the Kansan's table, and each had greatly enjoyed one another's company. Bell and his companion were told to come down, for from that moment on both men were home free. The old friend would talk to the Missourians and straighten things out. The county clerk jumped down followed by the other man, and together the three walked outside. That's where the miracle ended. The crowd of guerrillas standing around them, wild and bitter, didn't care a dime about old acquaintances.

"Shoot him! Shoot him!" was their cry, and not a word was uttered by the old friend. A religious man, Bell asked for a moment to pray. Granted. Finished, the clerk said *amen*, and in a burst of fire his companion fell down and George Bell dropped dead.

From there the gang scaled Mount Oread to complete the job. At home Mrs. Bell met the raiders and recognized the former guest. "We have killed your husband," he blandly informed her, "and we have come to burn his house."[33]

When a group of bushwhackers broke into the home of Edward Fitch and shouted for him to come from hiding, he did. While Sarah and the three terrified children watched, the Massachusetts native walked down the stairs and into the circle of waiting men. As soon as Fitch hit the foot of the stairs he was dead. But just to make certain, the Rebel who shot him grabbed another revolver and continued to pump slugs into the corpse until that gun too was emptied. The guerrillas then moved on to rob and torch the home.

As the smoke began to drift about, Sarah pleaded and tried three separate times to remove her husband's body. But three separate times the murderer forbade it. She then ran to retrieve a small painting of Edward, but once more was denied. Finally the woman ceased all efforts and just wandered from room to room watching as her home was destroyed. At last, when the place was engulfed in flames, and with sparks and debris showering about her, a guerrilla forced her to leave.

Sarah walked with her screaming children across the road, sat on the grass, and watched while the home and everything she owned crackled and roared over the body of her husband. Above, on an adjoining shed, a small Union flag hung limp. The children, playing soldier a day or two before, had planted it high so that everyone in town could see they were loyal and proud to be Yankees.[34]

Escape was the thing, escape by any means. Politicians, doctors, and merchants bellied toward safety side by side with local layabouts and town drunks, crawling in underclothes through flowerbeds and cabbage rows, along weedy lots and ditches until they finally reached what to them seemed a God-sent sanctuary—a cottonwood chicken coop or a tiny, stinking outhouse. Others simply hurled headlong into wells or shimmied beneath wooden walkways. An outdoor cellar in the center of town with a hidden entrance was a haven where many fled.[35] But more found refuge in the ravine, along the tangled banks of the river, or in Jim Lane's vast cornfield. Often chasing a victim right to the edge of these places, guerrillas always slammed to a halt and galloped away as if expecting a volley of shots to ring out. In the cornfield, scores of thirsty citizens were hidden. Several times the raiders rode along the perimeter; some were for going in. Uncertainty, however, always held them back. A woman living on the hem of the field who had carried water to the fugitives was asked by a group of Rebels, who themselves stopped for water, what was in the corn.

"Go in and see," she replied, in a tone that left no doubts.

Had they gone in they wouldn't have found Jim Lane. Nor would they find him anywhere near the field. Instead he was among the bluffs far to the southwest of Lawrence, "on his belly under some bushes."[36]

Escape was the thing; there were other ways. After somehow avoiding the slaughter, the lieutenant of the recruits eluded his pursuers and ran naked into an abandoned shanty. There he found clothes and quickly dressed. In a moment or two he left the hut and walked into the street unnoticed, wearing a dress and bonnet.

Another man burst into a home occupied by three women and begged for help. Soon a noisy gang stomped through the door. Searching the rooms without success, the guerrillas loudly entered the parlor. At this the indignant ladies scolded the Rebels to please be quiet and more considerate, since "poor Aunt Betsie" was neither well nor accustomed to such excitement. Sitting in an invalid's chair, "Aunt Betsie" was eyed suspiciously—an old woman's cap, a shawl across her lap, medicine bottles and cups nearby, a "niece" fanning her. Finally, the raiders left and the grateful "Aunt Betsie" and three resourceful women breathed easily once again.[37]

Some men without recourse simply put on the dirtiest, most ragged set of clothes they had and mixed with the Missourians. One dentist went even further. Besides finding money for the guerrillas and guiding them to the best stock of liquor in town, he also joined in and set several homes on fire.[38]

When raiders knocked on their doors, women too employed almost any device in an attempt to save their homes—and very often the men hiding just above or just below.

> Where in hell is Fred Read?
>   Gone east for goods.
> Peter Ridenour?
>   Gone east to buy goods.
> What are your politics?
>   Sound on the goose.
> Has your old man ever stolen any niggers in Missouri?
>   Never been in Missouri.

But as often as not, no amount of pleading or lying would suffice, and a home was put to the torch anyhow. And as soon as the bushwhackers had done their work and moved on, behind them women and children rushed with quilts and slopping buckets of water in an attempt to smother the flames. But as was commonly the case, after gamely battling and subduing a blaze, the soot-smeared ladies looked up only to find another squad approaching with the same intent.

"Put that out if you can!" said an exasperated guerrilla to a woman who had just stopped one fire. When he had gone, she did just that.[39]

Those at the home of John Thornton were more persistent. When the straw bed they ignited was put out, the Rebels returned and started it again, but this time Nancy Thornton was forced to leave. In a short while, when the husband too appeared and raced out the back, the guerrillas were ready and waiting. A chunk of hot lead burned into Thornton's hip. He didn't go down, however, but turned and fled back into the house. Again the heat became unbearable, and when he reappeared another shot was fired, this time blowing his knee apart. Once more, and followed by his horrified wife, Thornton limped back into his blazing home.

Blinded by smoke, the wounded man soon came out again, leaning on Nancy for support. One of the raiders rode up, took aim, but just before he could jerk the trigger the Kansan lunged for his leg. Thornton was unable to reach the weapon, however, and a slug at point-blank smashed into his eye and exploded out the cheek. Another gun went off and a ball entered his back, ripped down the spine, and tore into a buttock. But still Thornton clung to his attacker. Frustrated and out of ammunition, the bushwhacker tried again.

"I can kill you," he growled as he used the heavy revolver like a hammer to bash the head of the struggling man. At last John Thornton lost his grip and released the leg. But he wasn't dead.

"Stand back and let me try," yelled an impatient guerrilla nearby. "He is the hardest man to kill I ever saw." With that, the enraged attacker let fly every ball in his weapon, striking the target three times. Thornton stumbled a few steps, then collapsed in a heap. Still doubtful, one of the Rebels reared his horse back to stomp the body, then leveled his pistol to fire again.

"For God's sake," shrieked the hysterical wife as she grabbed the horse's bridle, "let him alone, he's killed now." Satisfied, though amazed at the time and energy needed to do it, the bushwhackers finally moved on.

To preserve it for burial, Nancy managed to drag the body away from the fire to an open space across the street. There, she saw that her husband had a wound for almost any given place and was literally soaked in blood from head to toe. Looking closer, however, the woman saw something else—John Thornton was still alive![40]

"Fred, one of them damned nigger-thieving abolitionists ain't dead yet; go and kill him." Neither Harlow Baker nor Simeon

Thorp could be sure which of them had moved, but it was certain that one would soon find out.

Since being shot, the two had lain in the street feigning death as the guerrillas rode nearby. When it was clear, they had whispered back and forth to one another describing where they were hit. Baker still had the strength to get up, but dared not. Senator Thorp, hurt much the worse, could not.

The horse stopped beside them and they heard the Rebel dismount. When he was kicked over onto his face, Baker knew he was the one. He heard the explosion, felt a sharp sting, and in a rush all the air left his right lung. He grew dizzy and almost fainted, but through the pain Baker was still around to hear Fred congratulate himself as he rode back to his pal.[41]

This time George Todd came in person. Only a twist of fate had kept him from meeting the preacher that morning near Sibley, and Todd today wanted no stone left unturned.

Despite this, Elizabeth Fisher, as unflappable as ever, insisted that her husband was not at home; that he had gone over the hill long ago and was by now probably well on his way to Topeka. And again the woman boldly invited the doubting Rebels to search the house. To his great relief though, Hugh Fisher did not hear the cellar door open, nor did he hear the thud of boots down the steps. He did hear, however, the breaking of chairs and shutters for kindling and a guerrilla swearing to kill his wife if she tried to extinguish the fire.

Ignoring the threat, Elizabeth slammed the door in the raider's face and raced to the well to fill buckets, pans, and tubs. This took time, however, and meanwhile more fires were being set. By the time she returned with the water, her two-story home was hopelessly ablaze. Running back to the front of the house, the desperate woman turned her energies toward saving the one-story kitchen and trying to keep her husband from being broiled alive. Climbing on the cookstove she doused the ceiling first. Then lugging two tables outside—setting one atop the other—Elizabeth scrambled up to the roof and threw more water on. But just as these flames were quenched much of the burning roof on the house crashed across the kitchen. Dipping up more water the woman drenched her clothing, then once again waded into the flames. But it was hopeless. At length, as the Rebels stood around the home watching her futile efforts, Elizabeth ran for more water and began flooding the kitchen floor under which her husband lay. A neighbor woman, as mystified

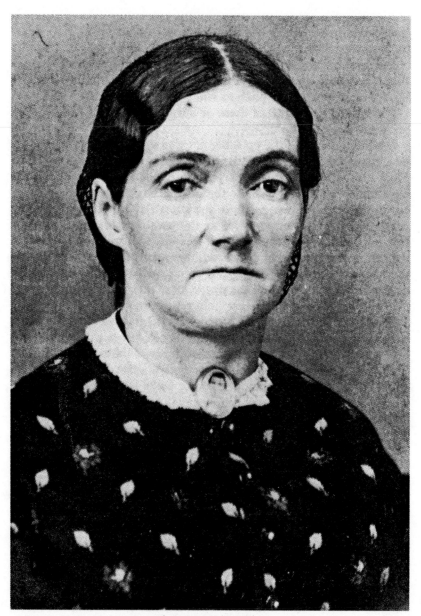

ELIZABETH FISHER
(courtesy of the Kansas State Historical Society).

as the bushwhackers, asked her why she was trying to save a piece of floor when her entire world was burning. "A memento," she yelled back above the roar.

But as the fire and debris fell into the kitchen even Elizabeth saw that it was only a matter of time. Slipping into the smoke-filled cellar, the frantic woman spoke to where her husband lay.

"You must come out of there or burn alive; I can't keep the fire back any longer."

"Almost roasted," the preacher decided it was his last chance. As he crept out the cellar door Elizabeth quickly threw a dress over him. Then as she lifted a heavy carpet the husband ducked under, and crawling as low and as close to the woman as possible, the two went out of the burning home. While the guerrillas watched on, the carpet was laboriously dragged across the yard until the weary wife at last dropped it down beside a small weeping willow. Running back to the house she grabbed chairs, bedding, and other items and stacked them over the rug. And finally, like candles on a cake, the mother sat her two children on top of the heap. After this, she could only wait and watch and pray the Rebels didn't suspect.

With guns in their grip the bushwhackers glanced from the house to the pile and back again. They always looked from a distance, however, and much to the woman's relief, none of them approached.

Sitting quietly by the baby, Elizabeth's little boy was startled when he heard from far below a hoarse voice whisper for water. "Pa is here somewhere; I heard him speak," he said, looking up to his exhausted mother. The child was quickly hushed and the father ordered from here on out to *keep still.*[42]

Not every raider had the stomach for it. Caught up in the pathetic efforts of a crying woman struggling to remove a divan, desk, or piano from her burning home, some could not hold back and soon found themselves wrestling over a piece of furniture just as frantically as the woman. And after setting a fire, not a few who imagined their hearts stone beyond hope caved in to tearful appeals and joined to save what they had intended to destroy.

After fleeing her home one woman returned to find it ablaze, yet curiously, neatly laid under a tree was a box containing her family photographs. Other Missourians stared like children at the beautiful parlors they entered, and many simply could not bring themselves to destroy the pretty cups, saucers, and heirlooms. Had it been left to them, some would have spared even "marked" homes. But harder sorts were always just around the corner. "No, God damn the abolitionists," shouted an angry guerrilla. "Why should this house be saved?"

And most were not cold killers. Rummaging through homes, searching for plunder, many obvious hiding places were avoided, and often a raider either winked or turned his back while a man escaped. But others were quick to remind that these same Kansans were the ones who had been in Missouri "killing our people." Most were not cold killers—but enough were.

> You have killed my husband; let me keep his ring!
> No matter.[43]

The Germans fared the worst. Their antislavery views were well known and, unlike other men, they couldn't escape by lying; their tongues were judge and jury.

"Nicht versteh," said one when the Rebels popped him a question.

"God damn you, we will make you versteh!" they shouted as they shot him dead.

For some time the town's German blacksmith had remained hidden with his little child amid a patch of corn in the Central Park. Later the baby grew restless in the heat and began to cry, prompting several passing guerrillas to venture in. When they left the father was dead with the child still crying in his once-powerful arms.

At a German home, the people were ordered out while the Missourians sacked the contents and torched the place. Among the occupants, a man on his sickbed had to be carried from the house and placed upon a mattress in the yard. When the gang finished indoors they walked over to the invalid and pulled out their guns. With pistols staring down, the German strained on weakened arms to rise but was instantly blasted back upon his cot.[44]

Again a squad came to the home of Judge Carpenter bent on burning and killing. But just as the others did before, the men left quieter than they came.

When they had finished with him, Arthur Spicer was brought back to Quantrill at the City Hotel. Despite his earlier threat, however, the guerrilla leader now seemed totally unconcerned at Spicer's return, and after entering the building the saloonkeeper passed discreetly to the rear.[45]

Activity picked up on Massachusetts Street as many of the raiders drifted back. Stores gone over lightly before were now cleaned out. Some merchants and clerks were compelled to wait on bushwhackers as if they were regular customers while liquor and food was being served and boots, shirts, and hats were being tried on.[46] In the apartments above terrified families were forced out, but not until they had filed past the Rebels and been robbed.

I'll take that watch!
Give me those earrings.
Fork over them greenbacks.
Shell out, God damn it . . . and be quick about it!

As fewer Rebels moved through the lesser streets some people came out and made their escape. With his wife, little daughter, and a friend, the Reverend Richard Cordley left his home and splendid library and quietly threaded through the streets. After some "exciting moments" the four entered the brush and walked to the riverbank. There, in a marvelous stroke of luck, an alert friend on the opposite shore recognized the Cordleys and, risking his own life, rowed a boat across and ferried the group to safety.[47] One man and his wife stuffed a change of clothes in a pillow slip, sat their children in a play wagon, and simply walked away.[48]

If one could muster the courage, getting through the streets and beyond the first line of pickets was to escape, for those patrolling further out—farmers and boys mostly—showed little inclination to stop or harm the refugees. Most citizens, though, remained fast in the same places they had throughout the morning—whether indoors or out.

One man holding an umbrella sat in the open undisturbed, shading his wife and child. Another, after being chased and shot at, fell and was immediately covered by his wife. Long after the assailants had left the woman continued to wail and shriek. Afraid she would draw even more attention his way, the husband at last whispered, "For God's sake, wife, don't take on so. I don't know if I'm even hit."

After helping the bushwhackers load packhorses, the two young clerks at R & B's, still barefoot and half-clad, eased off to the bushes and raced to the river. The frightened New Yorker saw no point in stopping there, however, and after swimming the Kaw he sprinted up the Leavenworth Road.[49]

At last, the Eldridge House, thus far spared though picked clean from "cellar to garret," was put to the torch. As some raiders were busy spreading the fire on the ground floor, a woman ran up screaming that a black baby, left by its mother and forgotten in the excitement, still remained inside. After listening for a moment, the men went on with their work.

"Burn the God damn little brat," was the grim reply.[50]

The fires caught, then climbed rapidly to the fourth floor. In a very short time "the finest building in Kansas"—plush carpets, chandeliers, music, dancing, laughter, and all—was enveloped in flames.

On the adjacent corner the courthouse went up. Across the street from that, Danver's Ice Cream Saloon burned, and so on down the street until both sides were completely ablaze. And while the fires were set the Rebels celebrated; walking or riding through the street in fancy clothes and shiny new boots, wearing rings on their fingers and gold chains and crosses from their necks; gulping down lobster, oysters, figs, and ice cream; smoking black cigars; guzzling beer, brandy, and French champagne; waving top hats in the air as the huge liberty flag was dragged past them in the dust. From time to time there were small explosions as stocks of powder and sealed canisters heated, and the acrid smell of tar and oil mingled with the sweet scent of burning tea and molasses.

At the end of the business district, a large gang of drunks spotted Dan Palmer and a friend standing in the door of Palmer's gun shop. Before they could duck back in both were shot and wounded.

While some of the bushwhackers set the building on fire, others stood the two men up and bound them together with rope. Then, when the flames caught and began to roar, the startled captives were pitched inside. Wild with fright, Palmer and his friend regained their footing and struggled out the door, pleading with the Rebels for mercy. But amid hellish laughter and waving pistols the men were again hurled into the furnace. At last the rope broke, but there was nowhere to run. By this time only Palmer was able to rise. Standing in the flames, arms reaching for heaven, he screamed above the roar, "O God save us!" This brought a new round of applause and laughter. Soon, the cries inside ceased and the drunken gang moved on.[51]

Except for a number of pickets, by nine o'clock most of the raiders had drifted back to the South Park and much of the residential area was left deserted. That's when Mary, Abigail, and Louis Carpenter "began to breathe again." But then there was another violent pound on the door. As they had done all morning, the family kept its composure, and while Mary went to the door the judge came down the stairs to deal with these Rebels as he had the rest.

The door was opened. Stepping partway in, a stone-faced guerrilla stared at the judge, then asked him where he was from.

"New York," came the even reply.

"It is you New York fellows that are doing the mischief in Missouri," was the cold comment. The Rebel raised his pistol and fired.

Breaking from the door, the wounded man bounded up the stairs and into a bedroom. Pushing Mary aside, the guerrilla gave chase. As his pursuer was searching the rooms above, however, Carpenter slipped by and ran to the basement. But a Rebel below saw this, and when his friend came down, the two found windows leading into the basement and opened fire. The judge was hit immediately. And because the room was unfinished there was nowhere to hide. Helplessly, Carpenter could only flatten himself against the walls and try to dodge the bullets. As the Rebels paused to reload, the blood gathered in pools at the victim's feet. Finally, with no other hope, Carpenter broke for the stairs leading outside. Once in the yard, however, he stumbled and fell and was unable to rise.

As the guerrillas approached, Mary ran screaming to her husband's side and covered his head with her arms. Walking around them several paces, a bushwhacker at last bent down, jerked up one of Mary's arms, jammed in his pistol, then fired. Within inches of her own, the judge's head shuddered for an instant, then splashed apart.[52]

A lone Rebel walked to where Harlow Baker was lying and stopped. Partially turned on its side, he looked down at the dusty body for a moment, at the blood—black and caked on the hand, neck, and back. "Poor devil," he muttered.

Pulling out a sharp knife the bushwhacker knelt down and ripped open a pocket. Finding nothing he rolled the body over and slashed the other. Again nothing. Spotting Baker's hat, the man mumbled that at least here was something, something good at that. Taking his prize, the Rebel walked back into town.[53]

At last the pickets rode in and the entire force of guerrillas converged on the South Park and began forming. Packhorses high with plunder were brought up, as was an ambulance. A large, fat ox was selected, killed, skinned, quartered, then quickly stored for travel. Amid the movement and general excitement, Quantrill found the young guide, and handing him a new suit of clothes and the reins to a fresh pony, the lad was pointed toward home. The Rebel leader then said goodbye to his friend Nathan Stone, his wife and son and daughter Lydia, and hoped that someday, some place they might meet during happier times.

"The ladies of Lawrence were brave and plucky," he confided to someone before he left, "but the men . . . were a pack of cowards."[54]

Quantrill then joined his command. And at a little past nine, with the smoke from Massachusetts Street rolling up like the walls of some towering black canyon, the raiders moved south and the long, uncertain retreat to Missouri began.

Several minutes passed. Only the sounds of the inferno were heard in the deserted streets. Across the river, the squad of soldiers watched intently. Finally, with a few citizens they boarded the ferry and inched toward the town.

But one man was not quite finished. Although he had bragged about the streets that eleven Kansans had been sent to hell by his gun, for Larkin Skaggs this was still not enough. Skulking around until Quantrill left, Skaggs galloped back and pulled up beside the City Hotel.

"All you God damned sons of bitches come in front!" he shouted. "Come right out here!"

Foolishly, many did step out the door. But others, including Lydia Stone, either remained inside or, like her brother, dove out the back. As they filed down the steps, men and women were ordered into separate lines, and while waiting for the rest to appear, Skaggs, terribly drunk and teetering in his saddle, asked one of the captives where he was from. "Central Ohio," answered the man. He was instantly shot. "That is worse than Kansas," growled the bushwhacker.

Another round was fired into the hotel itself, which brought an immediate plea from the owner, Nathan Stone. Without a word Skaggs turned and fired again, striking the innkeeper flush in the abdomen. While the screaming people fled the front of the hotel, more jumped out the back. Spying a boat, two men quickly pushed off from shore. In their haste, however, they failed to attach one oar properly and the two furiously paddled around and around in circles as the current carried them down the river.

Hearing the gunfire and seeing the renewed exodus, the men crossing on the ferry quickly returned to the north shore.[55]

Growing impatient, Skaggs finally wheeled and rode back through town. After killing a man along the way and chasing another, the burly bushwhacker trotted leisurely from Lawrence down the California Road, confident that Quantrill had left the way he had come. He soon realized the mistake, however, when he saw farmers coming in his direction. Spurring cross-country toward Eudora, the drunken man weaved and wobbled in the saddle as the big white horse raced through fields leaping fences and ditches. But more men were riding from that way, and cornered, Skaggs was finally captured and taken toward Lawrence.

When the party reached the outskirts and learned what had taken place, the prisoner without further ado was slain on the spot.[56]

Slowly, slowly the people began to come out—peering cautiously from the brushy ravine, parting carefully the stalks in the cornfield. The ferry started inching over again. Governor Robinson stepped out of his stone barn. The county sheriff crept up from under his floor. A man who had feigned death even though he lay near a building on fire rose with the clothes burned from his back.[57] And Harlow Baker, too, on painfully weak legs pulled himself up and staggered to the house. Others emerged from the hidden cellar in the center of town, popped up from tomato patches, or, dripping wet, gazed over the mouth of a well. What they saw when they came out was overwhelming.

Everywhere one turned, the enormity of the raid attacked the senses. Those cut off, who thought their experience an isolated case, were numbed to learn that similar acts had been going on all around the city. Like a twister it had come so swiftly, so tremendously, so utterly—yet like a twister it too had gone so quietly and completely that many were confused and still had no conception of time. And the bodies . . . no one had expected this. "One saw the dead everywhere," said the Reverend Cordley as he moved through the town, "on the sidewalks, in the streets, among the weeds in the gardens."[58]

And the day was actually darker than it had begun. Burning homes and barns sent spires of smoke upward until they converged to form a huge pall over the city, blotting out the sun and sky. Massachusetts Street was a raging wall of flame and churning black clouds. Crunching timber and toppling bricks fed the roar, and the heat was so intense that none dared enter the street. Even the sidewalks were burning. And everywhere was the suffocating dark fog. Women, some carrying babies in their arms, ran through the streets shielding their faces from the fire, crying and screaming for husbands and sons. Some, like Charles and Sara Robinson, found one another.

Then, down a side street, flaying the hide of a plowhorse and shouting at the top of his lungs came Jim Lane trailed by several farmers. "Follow them boys," cried the senator as he passed, "let us follow them." Some did respond, and together they galloped south. But even had more felt the inclination, there simply were no horses left in town.[59]

By noon a goodly number of citizens had straggled back to town as had curiosity-seekers from the countryside. And by this time even Hugh Fisher, sweltering all morning under the rug and furniture, felt safe enough to crawl from his torrid hiding place to get a drink of water.

Later, as the fires subsided, several men began the grisly task of trying to retrieve the dead and wounded. One of those thus engaged was George Deitzler. At first glance the victims nearest the fires were thought to be blacks. Coming closer, however, the old general was shocked to discover that the corpses were not Negroes, but white men "completely roasted. The bodies . . . crisped and nearly black." Reluctantly, Deitzler bent down to pull a man up, but to his horror as he yanked he merely came away with two chunks of steaming dark flesh. Reeling backward, the general retched and had to leave. Most others, try as they may, could fare no better and turned away "crying like children."

One corpse lay on a sidewalk near a fire. The body was normal in every respect except that the skin of the head had been burned away, leaving only a grinning skull. Another man was half body, half skeleton. Others had rendered down into a "shapeless mass." And without a trace of wind the stench of cooked flesh weighed like a blanket in the hot fog. Relegated to stronger sorts, recovery did go on.[60]

After the pews were moved out, many of the dead and wounded were taken to the Methodist Church. While two physicians probed an ugly hole in a man's face, searching for a lodged ball, another, lacking both medicine and instruments, performed delicate surgery using only a sharp penknife. Lying in a corner, "half-wit" Jo Eldridge, also shot in the face, raved deliriously. Crying women, themselves on the verge of collapse, tried to help those waiting by bringing water, cleaning wounds, and fighting off the swarms of blowflies. The mangled bodies of Ralph and Steve Dix were brought in and laid out; Ben Johnson, some Germans, and others not recognizable were also carried up the steps. In his rush to get the wounded

AFTER THE RAID

(courtesy of the State Historical Society of Missouri, Columbia).

indoors, one minister keeled over from exhaustion. Elsewhere it was much the same as people waited for the few available doctors.[61]

A young woman, just as confused and frightened as she had been all morning long, ran into the Griswold home for comfort. In the back parlor she first saw Mrs. Baker fanning her husband who lay on the bed, his clothes bathed in blood. Fleeing into the dining room, the girl suddenly froze at the sight of Doctor Griswold and Josiah Trask stiff, white, and stretched side by side on the dinner table. In the front parlor she glanced in to see Senator Thorp, twisted and rolling in terrible agony, his clothes black with blood and dust. He was struggling to speak to his wife but couldn't. Bearing no more, the sickened young woman left the house entirely.[62]

Just up the street, surrounded by the smouldering ruins of her home, Julia Collamore could get no response from either her husband or the servant as she shouted into the well. When a close friend arrived, he volunteered to go down. Tying a cord around himself, and with the aid of two men to lower him, the friend entered the hole. About halfway down those above felt a sharp yank and frantically began to pull the man up. The strain was too great, however, and the cord snapped. But to the surprise of everyone above, there was no cry for help from below.[63]

Despite everything, some paused a moment to behold the phenomenon. Flocks of killdeer, attracted for some reason, flew about carefree from yard to yard, calling their sprightly refrain.[64]

Throughout the afternoon and into the evening the people continued to trickle back. Some returned wearing the same nightshirt they had awakened in, while not a few husbands came back in the dresses that had enabled their escape. Strong men, finding a dear friend whom they had presumed dead, fell into one another's arms and wept. The devout knelt in circles and prayed.

Those who had fled Shantytown that morning also began appearing, coming across the river or out of the woods. One black, atop a white horse, rode bareback down Massachusetts Street singing with all his might "John Brown's Body." Behind, with a rope around its neck, he dragged the naked corpse of Larkin Skaggs. With other former slaves, the rider hauled the body to the Central Park and tried to burn it.[65]

As the fires cooled and gardens and weedy lots were combed, more dead were discovered. The floor of the Methodist Church filled until there was no room. Forty identification tags had already been provided, but for others only a number distinguished each from the next disfigured form. Robert Martin, killed by the side of young Willie Fisher, was found and carried down from Mount Oread in the arms of his crying father. Charlie and Willie Fisher also returned, and the grateful parents sped to heaven their thanks and bowed to pray. But both Elizabeth and Hugh couldn't help noticing that there was something different about Willie; he was not the same Willie who had left that morning.

It wasn't so easy for editor John Speer. Of his three sons, the youngest was alive and with his mother. Another son, Junior, was dead. Someone said he was murdered while running along a street, shot by a mounted Rebel dragging the Union flag. But the other son, seventeen-year-old Robbie, was still missing. Speer refused to believe that Robbie too was gone. And so, covered with soot and ash, the father kept up his search, calling out as the night descended. "I want you to help me find my boy. They have killed one, and the other I cannot find."[66]

"The fires were still glowing in the cellars," noted the Reverend Cordley as he moved through the darkened streets. "The brick and stone walls were . . . standing bare and blackened. The cellars between looked like great caverns with furnaces glowing in the depths. . . . Here and there among the embers could be seen the bones of those who had perished."[67]

John Speer and others seeking a son, a brother, a husband were praying that the bones they saw down among the cinder and fire were not those of the loved ones they sought.

That night the dogs howled without ceasing, and for miles around a vast angry glow was seen shrouding the skies above Lawrence.[68]

8

THE HEATHEN ARE COME

Saturday, August 22, 1863. Hardly had glint of dawn reached Lawrence when the weary people, straining to gain a few minutes of sleep, were jolted by a long, piercing scream heard throughout the town. Followed to its source, a woman was discovered in a gutted building sitting among the rubble. Her husband, she feared, had been shot and burned there the day before, and after searching the wife had found his remains at last—a blackened skull that she hugged to her breast.[1]

This chilling scene "added much to the . . . sadness and horror which filled every heart," said a viewer, and stamped an accent on what was already becoming known as "Black Friday."[2] There was no awakening from the nightmare. Massachusetts Street, normally a hive of activity on Saturday, was black and idle now, only a jagged gash through piles of ash and debris. Red coals still glowed in the basements. At the south end of the street, two stores remained standing; to the north, by the river, several more stood, including the armory with weapons intact. In between, all else was ruin. Vermont and New Hampshire streets were much the same—a barn, the ice house, the City Hotel, a home in which George Todd had taken breakfast and left his voucher of safety.

In the residential area the condition was somewhat better. Although close to one hundred homes were destroyed, many of these the beautiful structures of West Lawrence, anyone could see how much worse it might have been. Dozens of houses were torched and torched again only to be saved by the women. And for those not doused, the absence of wind prevented the flames from leaping to a neighboring home. Most brick and stone dwellings stood untouched, and because of the soldiers, all the houses along the river, including the Robinson mansion, went unscathed. Except for a Negro church, every other still stood. The county land records were somehow preserved.[3] But all this in itself, as the citizens viewed things, was small cause for thanksgiving. The bushwhackers had been meticulous. The town was devastated. "Lawrence," wrote one, "is as much destroyed as though an earth quake had buried it in ruins."[4]

And even had there been anything left to buy, there simply was nothing left to buy it with, for very little money remained. Of the three banks in town, two were robbed of every cent and the third spared only because a stubborn vault could not be blown. Practically all the cash and merchandise in the stores and offices was stolen or burned, and among the citizenry as a whole, the gold, silver, jewels, notes, and watches that were not outrightly stolen were generally lost or destroyed in the confusion. Much of the furniture, clothing, shoes, and linen was also gone. Most people, young and old, wore the same grimy apparel in which they had come away twenty-four hours before. In addition, there was virtually no food in the town.

Although the suffering and privation were extreme, the material loss paled beside that of the human. At first glance even the most sanguinary estimate placed the toll of dead at no more than sixty, a staggering number considering that nearly all were unarmed civilians. But even this grim figure was soon surpassed as more victims were discovered hourly.

When workers finally entered the Collamore well they brought up three dripping bodies—the mayor, his servant, and the would-be rescuer, all dead. After filling the Griswold home with hideous screams and groans, Simeon Thorp, in terrible agony, at last succumbed. As for the photographer, William Laurie, his flight was ended. Kansas City . . . Shawnee . . . the war had overtaken him once and for all in faraway Lawrence. The charred bones of other victims were raked in from the embers or found sprawled among the weeds and gardens. The dead seemed to crowd the living as the toll grew to one hundred and climbed.[5]

The human loss was as unfathomable as the material loss was seemingly irreparable. There was little talk of rebuilding. Fear of a similar occurrence ran so high that it seemed foolish to do so, and some raiders had even warned that Lawrence must be entirely abandoned or they would return. The herculean task of trying to reconstruct their world also caused many to despair. But perhaps most disappointing and unbearable of all was the lack of anything tangible to strike at; the inability to reach out and smash the authors of so much misery and woe. For some, at least, this simple, savage act could not but help ease the pain and frustration.

Throughout the morning, travelers, emigrants, teamsters, and curiosity-seekers, jammed on the main roads for twenty-four hours, began to stream into town. One unsuspecting arrival quickly found himself surrounded by an angry mob. Identified as a proslavery man and active during the territorial struggle, he was led away to the barn by the river. There, despite pleas to the contrary, he was accused of being a spy for Quantrill, and being thus charged he was promptly convicted. A noose was thrown around his neck, and in a few moments the stunned man was drawn up and left kicking in the air. There was no hard evidence, as most admitted, but the victim was a Missourian, and that was close enough.

The body was then cut down and given to a black on horseback, who galloped through the streets followed by a snarling crowd. As the corpse was dragged along, the clothes tore away and the mob pelted it with rocks, sticks, and anything else available, each person dealing their share to the lonely trophy. Four other men blundered into town and were collared under the same pretext. Fortunately for them—and for consciences later on—they were only held, not hanged.[6]

Sallie Young was next. Hooted and jeered viciously wherever she went, the girl was arrested, accused of collaborating with the raiders, then confined to await transfer to Fort Leavenworth.[7] The fury temporarily vented, Lawrence turned to more pressing matters.

As the morning wore on and the temperature rose, the stench from the corpses became insufferable. Already, many bodies had swollen so great that the clothing had burst, revealing grotesque wounds "full of flies & worms."[8] Frantically, the work began to identify the victims and get them under earth as rapidly as possible. There was little wood left and certainly no coffins. Many of the carpenters were either dead or wounded and nearly all the tools of the trade destroyed. Nevertheless, the citizens began. Oak and walnut logs were sawn and fashioned into rough boards. Most nails had melted in the kegs, but enough good ones were found and the planks were soon joined to form crude boxes. The dead were quickly deposited and the covers hammered down. For many, "it sounded rather harsh . . . to have the lid *nailed* over the bodies of their loved ones." But there simply was no time for anything more elaborate, especially since the threat of epidemic increased with every hour.[9]

When the Methodist Church was full, bodies were taken to other churches. Not all victims remained in town. After identification, three corpses, including that of the Irishman Jim O'Neill, were loaded onto a wagon and returned to Lecompton for burial.[10] Coming

SALLIE YOUNG
(courtesy of the Kansas State Historical Society).

from the opposite direction, farmers brought fruit and vegetables and gave freely. And from Leavenworth the first real relief came when several wagons loaded with food, clothing, medical supplies, and caskets arrived.

Throughout the day and into the night the tempo increased and the sounds of the terrible work continued. At the cemetery atop Mount Oread, a ghostlike gathering moved in an arc of lamplight, and some of the boxes were at last lowered down. Slowly the recovery began.

When he wasn't helping out around town, Peter Ridenour was at the bedside of his friend. "Well, Mr. Ridenour, I am gone up," Harlow Baker had whispered when his partner rushed into the room on Friday. But though he wasn't given much hope by others and could barely breathe, Baker surprised everyone, including himself, by continuing to hang on.

And so the old friend stayed by his side, waiting for the end—fetching ice, tending the wounds, chatting. Jokingly, Ridenour admitted that the only reason he was sitting around this moment was because of a few potato plants and a garden bed he'd hugged so dearly that a leaf might have covered him. His home was gone, he added, even though he had naively taken the precaution of locking the door. But the two young clerks had made it. After running so long and hard that his feet bled, the athletic New Yorker hadn't stopped until he had reached Leavenworth. There, he went straight to a family friend, Governor Tom Carney, and borrowed money enough for clothes and a one-way ticket east. But after some rest and reflection he was hesitant. The boy had come back today on the Leavenworth stage. Although admittedly he had never been so scared in his life, not even at Gettysburg, the youth discovered that indeed he had survived the battlefield and now, although his feet were very tired and sore, he had survived Black Friday as well.

Ridenour didn't mention to his partner that the business was wiped out. Five years of savings had vanished in a blink when the banks were looted. The store's huge inventory was also gone and although their insurance covered most everything, including fire, a clause excluded "invading enemies." There were also many outstanding debts and no way to meet them. Although he didn't burden his friend with business matters, Peter Ridenour had already taken the first faint look down the long road back. He was yet young and strong and energetic and his name was respected by all. And if he lived long enough, every creditor would get his due. The store's safe with the books and a modest sum of cash had somehow weathered the storm, and if one put stock in such things, there was a benign omen of sorts—the salt wagons from Leavenworth had arrived and were now parked outside the gutted store.

But while he sat and waited and watched his old friend suffer, the thought uppermost on Mr. Ridenour's mind was not salt or creditors or even the store, but whether the partnership, the friendship would continue as always or if the B would yet be stricken from R & B.[11]

Early Sunday morning at the usual time, work was set aside while a few citizens gathered to worship. They were women and children mostly at the Reverend Cordley's church, dirty and disheveled and dressed in men's work clothes. No one said much. For some, the press of the past two days had been a sore test of faith, and a moment's respite to collect their thoughts and drift in meditation was a welcome balm. There were whispers and silent prayers and then a passage from Psalms, verse 79: "O God, the heathen are come into thine inheritance. They have laid Jerusalem in heaps. The dead bodies of thy servants have they given to be meat unto the fowls of the heaven and the flesh of thy saints unto the beasts of earth. Their blood have shed they like water round about Jerusalem, and there was none to bury them."[12] After a moment more of silence, work was resumed.

Again as the heat of the day approached, workers were made aware of their dilemma. The coffin building was not keeping pace with the decay of the bodies. The caskets that came from Leavenworth helped, but there simply weren't enough coffins there, nor in all Kansas to meet the needs. And more victims were being found. At last, in desperation, it was decided to dispense with formalities altogether and inter the more advanced cases with as much speed as possible. Into a long, deep trench gouged from the cemetery ground, forty-seven black and bloating bodies were finally lowered down. Similar burials, like that of Judge Carpenter and Edward Fitch, took place in backyards.[13] With this, some of the terrible trauma and urgency began mercifully to wear off.

More help came from the countryside and another large wagon train of food, clothing, and supplies arrived from Leavenworth. Visitors continued to enter the city, some to aid and some simply to gawk and assess the destruction. Early estimates placed the damage in the millions of dollars, with over $250,000 stolen in currency alone. Almost every businessman and merchant was totally cleaned out. Still, there were increasing murmurs of rebuilding and renewed investments. Flagging spirits began to revive somewhat as a few took heart. Included among the strangers in town were a number of correspondents and illustrators from large Eastern newspapers who began sketching scenes and taking down eyewitness accounts. A few unabashed individuals came forward with their stories. One black related that when the raiders had entered Lawrence on Friday morning, he had dashed over the meadows south of town and hid in a tree above the Wakarusa, outlegging his imagined pursuers and establishing some kind of record for the three-mile course. When asked about the feat, his simple reply: "The prairie just came to me."[14] Another man, a dentist, described his escape and return to Lawrence and his utter amazement to find that, though everything else was gone, the Rebels had entirely overlooked his inventory of gold and silver plate.[15]

Others had similar tales to tell, though not always so jocose. They told of a morning replete with hairbreadth escapes and terror, of miracles, irony, and death. But as the journalists scribbled away, always from each new tale there surfaced the same consistent theme—the steely defiance and grit of the women. Almost all their acts, although carried out under fantastic duress, were marked by an uncanny degree of calmness and courage. Instances of their heroism, their "sand," ran on. There was Lydia Stone: When the Eldridge prisoners became frightened of retaliation, the young woman, risking her own life, raced down the riverbank in the teeth of the soldiers' bullets waving a hanky for them to stop. There was Kate Riggs: By grabbing the horse's bridle and hanging on until she had been dragged around the house and over a woodpile, the tenacious woman succeeded in saving her husband Sam from the monster Skaggs.[16] There were Elizabeth Fisher, Eliza Turner, and a score of other equally doughty heroines. And never had female ingenuity been better displayed, from the "nieces" of "Aunt Betsie" to the woman who saved not only a featherbed to sleep on but a neighbor man as well, whom she rolled up inside and carried to safety.[17] Another woman fooled the Rebels by burning oily rags in kettles, thereby making it appear that her home was engulfed in flames.

And even after their bravery and resourcefulness saved many a man and home, the women's work had but begun. When the initial shock had passed, many, like the "ministering angel" Lydia Stone, carried on, moving with quiet grace among the crowds of victims, "attending to their wants and speaking words of comfort and cheer."[18]

As Sunday wore on, the women, arms scorched, hair singed, continued their labors with an air of increasing confidence. Some optimistically saw in their great trial a hidden treasure. Although they left little else in Lawrence, the guerrillas overlooked something very precious nonetheless, something that could not be burned with a torch or strapped on a packhorse: courage, the only thing in life that really mattered. When all else was taken, this at least remained and gleamed more brilliantly than ever before. Then others took note and drew inspiration from a familiar sight at the river's edge. Amid the ruin and devastation the old liberty pole stood straight and tall, defiantly holding its ground. Even the tortuous hot spell was at an end. Late in the day a refreshing north wind kicked up, clearing and cooling the air. If the truth be known, for many of these women, as well as the surviving men, there was within them the dawning of that warm and golden glow that shines only in the hearts of those who have faced off with the worst in life and come away victorious. For Lawrence, the worst had come. The trial had passed. There was nothing more from life to fear.

As the work progressed into the evening, a lookout on Mount Oread, watching the activity below, happened to glance south toward the Wakarusa. There to his horror he saw rising from the valley floor an all-too-familiar sight—smoke and flame. Without a second thought the rider flew down the hill and galloped into town, screaming with all the power in his lungs, "They are coming again, they are coming again; run for your lives, run for your lives."

With these startling words reserves cracked, then crumbled, and suddenly there was nothing left. In a moment, as if from one mind, panic seized all, and like a cannon shot the race from Lawrence instantly became a mad stampede. Someone rang the armory bell but no one was fool enough to rally. Men who had naively held to their homes at the onset of the first raid and who thus experienced the most terrifying hours of their lives didn't wait around for the second, but broke from town at a run, hair streaming in the wind. Women, whose courage hadn't wavered during the Friday attack and whose poise had been a comfort to all, now caved in completely and became "utterly unstrung." Men, women, children—all raced blindly, filling the streets with a bedlam of sobs, shrieks, and shouts, expecting the slaughter to overtake them with every bound. *Run for your life . . . Quantrill is coming back and will kill all of us. . . . Run to the country, Quantrill is coming. . . . Take your children and run . . . Quantrill is coming!*

After a few short minutes the dust had settled. The town was deserted. Except for a few wounded, not a soul, black or white, resident or visitor, was left in Lawrence. As time passed, men on the opposite shore anxiously watched for the attack to begin. But mysteriously, there was only silence. Shortly, one hundred citizens recovered sufficiently to cross back and pass out weapons from the armory. Their plans for a stand went for naught, however, for they soon learned the cause of the lookout's alarm—imprudently, a farmer had chosen this moment to burn off a field of straw.

Knowledge of the error came too late to reach the majority of people, however. Some were far away and still running while others were even further along and had no intention of ever stopping, like the clerk at R & B's, who this time would not pull up until he reached New York and absolute safety. But for the rest, many carrying footsore children, there was no run left, and they simply alit in fields and thickets fringing the town.

That night proved to be one of the coldest, cruelest summer nights in border memory. The temperature plunged, the rain and hail came in sheets, the lightning cracked, the thunder roared, and the wind blew with all the fury of a cyclone. But still—soaked, frozen, and huddled as they were—few ventured back, for the wind and cold and rain were far preferable to Lawrence, where they firmly believed Quantrill was adding the final touches to the bloody work begun on Friday.[19]

One of these miserable refugees, seeking an answer to it all, later questioned his aged father. "Why have we been so terribly punished? Why so infinitely worse than any other place in all the history of this war? Why beyond comparison and precedent?" After brief reflection on the territorial days of the fifties, the war on the border and the sagging fortunes of the South in the sixties, of the bloody days of rampage when Lane, Jennison, and their jayhawkers had turned western Missouri inside out, the son found the answer to his own question. "It has come," he finally admitted, "and they have had their revenge."

But another, angrier than the first, and speaking for a great many more than the first, considered the scales once more uneven.

"Oh! God!" he implored heaven, "Who shall avenge?"[20]

Who shall avenge? Surely they had not been forsaken. Surely, no matter the past sins, surely they had not been so entirely and utterly abandoned. Surely a just and righteous God, even while his children were being returned to dust, must have parted the clouds and sent fiery bolts, red with uncommon wrath, thundering down to smite the devil's host. Surely somewhere between heaven and hell the fiends had been brought to bay and slaughtered as they stood. Surely they had. Where then had it happened? When had it occurred? Who then, oh God, had indeed avenged?

9

THE CHASE

At dawn on Friday, August 21, Charles Coleman, Joshua Pike, and almost two hundred cavalrymen rode into Gardner. As the troopers paused to water their mounts, residents revealed that the trail they were following was now six hours old, that the raiders had passed through before midnight riding west on the Santa Fe. Once more Coleman sent runners to alert the region, and as the sun rose to his back the captain led his command west. After but a short distance, however, it quickly became obvious that scanning the ground for hoofprints as he had done the past ten hours would no longer be necessary. From then on he need look only to the sky above Lawrence, twenty miles away, to know precisely where the path would lead. Coleman pushed his horse harder.[1]

Seven miles to the northeast, Maj. Preston Plumb and forty troopers were just entering Olathe. They found the town wild with excitement, a condition that had existed throughout the night. As he was making inquiries among the people Plumb's gaze was attracted to the west. There an immense black thunderhead appeared to be building in the otherwise cloudless sky. After a stunned, silent moment the major turned to his command. "Quantrill is in Lawrence," he shouted.

Gathering the men available in Olathe, including Lt. Cyrus Leland, Jr., Plumb quickly led his force cross-country toward the smoke. Along the way messengers were sent north to warn the Kaw Valley, and as they passed fields, gaping farmers were told to get their guns.

Several miles behind Plumb, nearly one hundred Federals hastily gathered at Kansas City were pushing ahead.[2] To the rear others gained their bearings as the sun lit the landscape. Near Paola, Lt. Col. Charles Clark and thirty men were angling north toward

Gardner. At the same time, two hundred regulars and a piece of ar-
tillery were moving up from Spring Hill. Another fifty followed.

At Westport, as news arrived, Maj. Linn Thacher hurriedly outfitted men drained from Missouri. As the morning wore on an additional eighty troopers were sped west while Thacher remained to
organize more streaming from the countryside.[3]

Indeed, by mid-morning and under an already-blazing sun, all of
eastern Kansas was marshaling to arms. Military couriers traced
and retraced the area, spreading the word while civilian volunteers
did the same. And as the messengers arrived, farmers dropped their
axes and scythes, grabbed muskets, and ran to join their militias.
For the first time in the war, most of settled Kansas sprang to a common alarm. But for those living in the six counties surrounding
Lawrence, no messenger was needed to interpret the dark sign in
the sky.

By 10:30 A.M., Captain Coleman and his men were less than an
hour from Lawrence. At Blue Jacket's crossing they reined for a short
rest before the final jog into the burning town. In a few moments, to
his surprise, Coleman was joined by Major Plumb. With Plumb assuming command the Federals forded the Wakarusa and rode onto
the flats of the Kansas Valley. After clearing the timber, however, it
soon became obvious nothing could be done to save Lawrence.
Plumb's duty now was to head off a similar disaster on the Rebels'
line of retreat. To the west he saw a row of smoke columns extending
south along the Fort Scott Road, as well as a large cloud of dust. The
guerrillas were moving south! After a word or two Plumb wheeled
his men back across the river, striking south for Baldwin City and
the Santa Fe Road.[4]

A few minutes later, thirty miles northeast, amid the cool splen-
dor of towering cottonwood and elm, a messenger rode into Fort
Leavenworth and delivered a handful of telegrams to the commanding general. The telegraph office had opened on schedule at eight but
only now did Thomas Ewing read the unbelievable words that came
screaming from the notes: Invasion! The border guard had been broken. Somewhere in Kansas bushwhackers were loose. Another message: The guerrillas, 800 strong, had passed through Gardner,
heading west. Holding for no more, Ewing ran to gather the troops at
the fort. Slashing protocol he commandeered several hundred men
outfitting for service on the plains, five companies of the Eleventh
Ohio. But alas, many of the Ohioans were without horse or weapon,
and for the next two hours the shaken general would race in a des-

perate bid to get them equipped while time ticked off and events un-
folded miles away, beyond his control.[5]

Down the Fort Scott Road they came. Some were riding fresh
mounts and leading their old, while most made do with the same
poor beast that had brought them there. Many were drunk and reeling. All were very tired. And all had some form of plunder either
hanging from saddle horns or strapped on packhorses—boots, shoes
and coats, fancy lace shawls, bolts of cloth, silverware, tea services,
picture frames, clocks, gadgets of all kinds, even ladies' sidesaddles.
Most wore new hats, shirts, and trousers. Many had pockets stuffed
with paper, jewelry, and gold. All had a share according to his taste.

The column continued down the road four abreast, raising an immense cloud of dust. Along with the horsemen creaked the ambulance with several injured raiders inside; driving it was a Lawrence
captive. At the Wakarusa, when everyone was over, attempts were
made to burn Blanton's bridge. Once across the river, squads fanned
out on both sides of the road. Farm homes, most of their occupants
having long since fled, were looted and put to the torch, as were
barns and outbuildings. Tinder dry crops in the field and recently
stored grain were also set alight. After two miles or so, the squads
rejoined to make the steep climb out of the valley.[6]

Upon gaining the high, open prairie, the guerrillas advanced a
few miles until they reached the deserted hamlet of Brooklyn at
the crossing of the Santa Fe Road. Since it seemed impossible to
attempt a retreat via the shortest route, the California, or back the
way they had come, Quantrill announced his aim to march toward
Osawatomie where, by using the cover of the Marais des Cygnes
timber, they would try to escape far to the south. But before that, he
yelled, they would lay waste everything in their path—a charred
swath one mile wide and fifty long. His men loudly agreed. At
Brooklyn this plan went into effect.

Shortly, with the sun directly above and with the village and surrounding countryside engulfed in flames, a cloud of dust was sighted
back in the smoke-filled valley. Unsure just who or how many there
were, the raiders ran for their horses and were soon headed up the
Santa Fe, two miles from Baldwin City.[7]

A few minutes passed. From the north, the cloud of dust approached Brooklyn and soon the first of the riders slowed and cautiously entered the burning town. More came on. In fact, strung
down the road came the rest of the pursuers—a fantastic mix of
farmers, merchants, and boys, some clad in nightclothes, some in

their underwear—armed with everything from shotguns to corn knives. A few had good mounts but most rode mules or mares with colts tagging behind. And bouncing atop his plowhorse with blinders, and clad in a filthy nightshirt tucked into ridiculously large trousers, in rode the senator from Kansas, James H. Lane.

Already, as the guerrillas passed, men were emerging from their hiding places and "swarming on the trail." Around Brooklyn alone, over one hundred came crawling from the brush and cornfields. After a brief halt Lane and the van of this growing force tumbled east on the Santa Fe, where the dust of the Rebels was only minutes away.[8]

Unseen several miles up the trail, Major Plumb was advancing west. By 1:00 P.M. he and his men had finally covered the eight miles from the Wakarusa and cleared the forest above the valley. Without dismounting, famished troopers snatched bread and water from generous farm wives. The forced march also took its toll on the young mounts. Some could go no further; ascending the final slope they simply dropped dead, quivering in their tracks. Near Baldwin City Plumb learned that the raiders were still thought to be moving south on the Fort Scott Road. Indeed, he could already see smoke over Brooklyn several miles west, and spurring ahead the major led his men down the Santa Fe hoping to block the retreat somewhere beyond. Another company of regulars followed close behind, as did local militias.[9]

Between Lane and Plumb, on a road framed by fence-lined cornfields, Quantrill advanced. The rear of his column was already crowding toward the front as the menacing cloud of dust near Brooklyn gained steadily. At last the guerrilla leader reached the crest of a small hill. He abruptly halted. Ahead, for the first time in three days, he saw the inevitable blue line of approaching cavalry—a large force at that. The route east was closed. Behind, an unknown; maybe as many, maybe more than faced his front. To stand meant disaster. Through the cornfield a narrow lane ran south. There the captain pointed his men, who even now were shaking off plunder to lighten the load. After a short distance the Missourians stopped at a small crossroads where Quantrill spoke hastily with Todd and other lieutenants. Should they attempt the Santa Fe around Baldwin or try the Fort Scott below Brooklyn? All agreed—the Fort Scott! With that, Todd and sixty of the best-mounted, best-disciplined men fell behind and formed a rear guard while Quantrill led the rest toward the Fort Scott Road.[10]

A few minutes later the militia and citizens under Lane joined with Plumb on the trail down which Quantrill escaped. No sooner had the two forces met and revealed what had happened in Lawrence than Senator Lane demanded complete control of the operation. Startled yet firm, Major Plumb absolutely refused. Wildly, "General" Lane again demanded control. Once more the major refused and "high words" passed while above the corn the fleeing raiders could plainly be seen. Ignoring Lane, Plumb and his men hurried down the road followed closely by the militia and citizens. Upon reaching the tiny crossroads Charles Coleman was ordered up for a charge on the Rebel rear just in the distance. Only two hundred horses were found still able to move above a walk. Nevertheless, the bold captain led his two hundred down the lane, followed by farmers and three companies of militia. With the rest of the regulars Plumb rushed south in an attempt to bar the ford at Ottawa Creek, less than a mile away. Along with him went the remaining militiamen and at his elbow, Jim Lane, who continued to badger and curse the major for total control.

Moving rapidly, Coleman's force gained on the raiders and soon came up with them. There, spread across the road were George Todd and thirty guerrillas. Behind a short distance were another thirty. Instantly the Rebels opened fire. Bullets whistled up the lane, sending most of the militia diving for cover. More rounds were exchanged as the troopers opened with carbines. Todd and his thirty then wheeled and fled west behind the remainder of the rear guard, who waited across the road. When the cavalry crept close, another volley was fired, and so on, until Quantrill had finally put his command back on the Fort Scott Road and started south. Seeing this the Federals ripped down a fence and went racing through the cornfield in an attempt to strike the flank of the retreating guerrillas.

Hearing the rattle of gunfire to the west and aware that he could not possibly keep pace with the fresh mounts of the militia, Major Plumb turned and rode back toward the fight. Lane, by his side, managed to gallop ahead.

Through the field raced the soldiers and militia, rustling and trampling the corn stalks, shouting, hats flying, sweating and cussing they came on. Suddenly they reached the fence at the field's end; there the headlong rush slammed to a halt. As if from nowhere, facing them on the prairie to the south stood George Todd and his rear guard. Surprised and exhausted, the Kansans watched the Missourians while the Missourians watched the Kansans. Minutes went by, the two sides staring at one another, neither group moving. Finally, the calm was broken when crashing through the field came Jim Lane. Raging at the halt when Quantrill was in plain sight less than a mile away, the senator demanded that the fence be thrown down and the charge started anew. No one moved. Leaping from his horse, Lane tore into the fence himself, shouting "with all his command of language" for everyone to begin the attack. At last Coleman yelled to his men, "Dismount and give them a round or two."

Quickly the troopers jumped down, and using the fence as a rest, a loud volley was fired up and down the line. The blast startled the horses. Rearing and bucking, many bolted through the field and a number of men broke from the line to give chase. At that moment Todd made his move. With a wild war whoop the guerrillas sprang forward at a run. And at this terrifying sight, and at this even more terrifying sound, a complete panic seized the Kansans. Forgetting discipline or valor, it was simply every man for himself. Hundreds of soldiers, civilians, and riderless horses stampeded back through the corn, bumping and trampling one another as bullets whizzed and screaming bushwhackers pounded closer. Only then, when everyone else had fled did Lane—who was still struggling with the fence— look around and realize his predicament. And when the lead Rebel, with both pistols blazing, was almost upon him, Lane too dashed back through the corn, dodging this way and that.

Finally, the breathless Union men reached the fence from which they entered. No one had been killed in the rout, although a few had scratches and bruises, but the fear had been perfect. Gathering up their more manageable mounts the Federals began to regroup as Lane came in. Looking back over the demolished field the Kansans were forced to watch miserably as the Missourians laughed and hooted, waving their hats mockingly in the air. At length, when all were remounted, the pursuers crossed the field once more and there, uncontested, they saw the last of the raiders fording Ottawa Creek.[11]

By now, after all the running back and forth, the horses, especially those of the military—which were closing on their hundredth mile with little feed or rest—were utterly useless; most could barely walk. A survey was taken and eighty animals were found still able to hold a trot. An equal number of regulars and militiamen led by Lieutenant Leland were assigned to take these mounts and push the Rebel rear. They were to fight if possible, but above all they were to hang on Quantrill's heels and prevent further looting and burning.

After a mile or so the scouts did overtake the raiders on their equally worn mounts; once again the chase resumed. But as before,

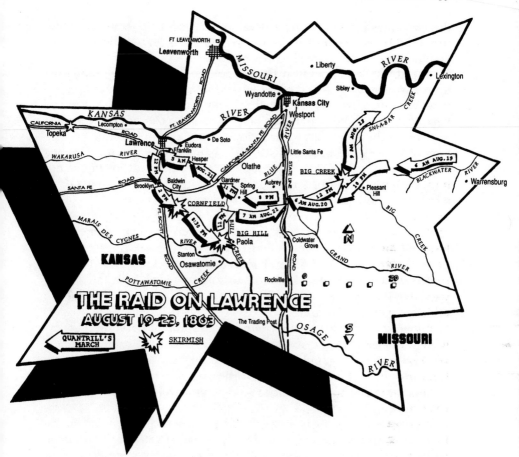

the guerrilla rear guard formed a line when the pursuers drew near, fired a volley, then retreated behind the second line, which in turn fired and retreated and on and on, alternating mile after mile as Quantrill and the main column marched unmolested.

Throughout the afternoon the chase continued in this manner: over the parched and waterless prairie, under the merciless sun, with the bushwhackers in front, the skirmishers in the middle, and Plumb and his burgeoning army always at least one mile in the rear. Four raiders, possibly drunk, whose brains had been boiled to paste in the murderous heat, straggled and were slain without ceremony. Plumb's mount gave out and collapsed beneath him. Another was taken from a nearby farm and again the major rejoined the pursuit, over a trail littered with dead and dying horses, "strewn with . . . all descriptions of plunder." And always near Plumb or ahead, watchful lest something occur that demanded his participation or deft leadership, Lane too remained in the saddle.

Ahead, the Rebel column slanted southeast, "generally following no roads or paths," still on line with Osawatomie. A scout sent beyond led the way, watching ravines and brush for ambush and the vast horizon for dust clouds. When hills broke contact between the two forces the guerrillas spurred to a "lope" and nothing more. The plan of wasting all in their path was abandoned now with Kansans close behind, but it was evident that they could not or would not attack again. Mercifully, with each agonizing mile the raiders drew a bit closer to the Missouri woodlands, to sleep and rest.[12]

By 1:00 P.M. Thomas Ewing had mounted and armed the three hundred men of the Eleventh Ohio and started south. Upon reaching Leavenworth City the general learned for the first time that the raiders had finally struck. Another source added that the Rebels were driving for the capital, Topeka. Without pause Ewing and the Ohioans galloped south.[13]

As word of the raid on Lawrence raced through Leavenworth, everyone rushed into the streets. Stunned citizens gathered in groups and spoke quietly, genuinely concerned for the well-being of fellow Kansans. Some fretfully discussed the fate of friends and relatives. Others were not so altruistic, however, and were quick to grab the advantage.

Thieves and black-marketeers, idled by martial law, leapt to the fore, screaming aloud that someone was responsible for the disaster. The angered people agreed. And the most likely candidate, they pointed, was the man who had just left—the man who had been bullying their town and arresting good, solid Union men while miles away the cities of Kansas went up in flames. None seized the initiative quicker than did Mayor Dan Anthony. No sooner had Ewing left than the younger brother of Susan B. Anthony issued a blistering proclamation nullifying martial law and ordering the city to arms. Nailed to walls and rushed to press: "The know-nothing, do-nothing policy of the General commanding this District, who has shown his utter incapacity, with five thousand soldiers under his command, in allowing a few hundred guerrillas to get fifty miles into the interior of our State . . . is ample proof that we must depend upon ourselves for the defense of our city and State."[14] Such was the storm cloud rising as Ewing rode south.

On into the blazing afternoon the general pushed his column, driving man and beast to their limit. Horses buckled and dropped dead from exhaustion. Four soldiers toppled over from sunstroke. Halts were few and fast, and after a minute or so the order to move was given. For Thomas Ewing, the day that opened so cool, calm, and promising proved in the end a flaming nightmare—one long, mad, furious race to reach the scene of action and patch the damage done to Kansas. Behind, trailing in the thick, blinding dust, his fellow Ohioans kept up as best they could.[15]

If Leavenworth, a city of nearly twenty thousand, was "excited" following the news of Lawrence, the smaller towns south of the Kaw were absolutely alive. At Olathe, where citizens had watched the smoke all day, and whose populace had good reason to remember and fear Quantrill, "men ran in all directions" when he was rumored to be retreating their way.[16] And at countless other towns and villages the situation was the same. While menfolk flew to their local militias and joined the pursuit, frantic, confused women were left on desolate farms with only crying children to help remove household goods. Some took time to bury valuables, but most simply fled to fields hugging a photograph or keepsake.

When word reached Paola that Quantrill might be coming, the place sprang to life. Maj. B. F. Simpson, at home recruiting, speedily sought to organize a defense. Only a dozen regulars under Capt. Nicholas Benter were in Paola, but as the day wore on more men and weapons arrived until the town soon resembled an armed camp.[17]

By five o'clock Lieutenant Colonel Clark and his company also rode in. After turning north that morning when nearly to Paola, Clark had hit the guerrillas' trail at Spring Hill and followed it to within a few miles of Gardner. There, to his chagrin, he learned that he was nothing short of a half day behind. Knowing there was a large force in pursuit and assuming Quantrill could not escape Kansas over the same route he entered it by, Clark pivoted and drove south once more—the proximity of the Marais des Cygnes woodlands made Paola a natural line of retreat. Upon reaching the town and finding it already well organized, the colonel sent scouts fanning south and west. As evening approached, more defenders rode in until eventually over five hundred guns faced the setting sun.[18]

Shortly before dusk the dreaded news arrived. A scout had spotted the raiders five miles out, advancing south for Paola. Clark immediately ordered Major Simpson to take his men to the west edge of town. There at Bull Creek ford, the main crossing to the Marais des Cygnes and a point Quantrill most likely would pass, Simpson, Benter, and their militia pulled up. The ford itself was dry, as was nearly all the creek. Just above the crossing, however, was a long run of deep water with sloping land on the west side but high-banked and brushy to the east. Well aware of the arid stretch of prairie between Lawrence and Paola, Simpson rightly guessed the condition of any horse crossing it. Upon reaching the creek and smelling water, the thirst-maddened creature would prove uncontrollable and bolt headlong into the pool. That's when the order to fire would come—when the guerrillas were trapped in deep water on animals that refused to budge. Positioning his men in the woods atop the eastern bank as well as along the ford, the major then sent a squad up the road to give advance warning. With orders to hold their fire until a signal was given, the ambushers settled in to await the Rebel approach.[19]

At dusk Quantrill and the main body of raiders passed over the summit of Big Hill, two miles northwest of Paola. Here atop the high ridge the column overtook the scout and halted momentarily. Taking the lead himself, Quantrill then steered down the slope. After only a short distance, however, he ordered another halt, and soon Todd and the rear guard appeared.

Pressing ahead, Lieutenant Leland and forty militiamen advanced up Big Hill, over which the Rebels had disappeared. Far to the rear came Plumb and the rest of the Union pursuers. When partway up the rise, Leland and his men drew rein. On the opposite side of the hill an eerie sound was heard. As the men stood and listened the noise grew louder and louder until, suddenly, over the top burst Quantrill and two hundred screaming bushwhackers. Instantly, the dark crest of Big Hill flashed with gunfire.

Reeling back, Leland's little band fled for their lives as the Rebels charged downward. After a mile the militia paused just long enough to turn, then let fly a wild volley into the night. Again, a little further on another round was fired until at length they reached Plumb and the main column. Behind them, all had suddenly become quiet; there was not a guerrilla in sight. Together the Federals rode back cautiously toward Big Hill. Once atop the ridge, however, no Rebels were discovered, and it soon became obvious that Quantrill had used the charge and time created to slip away into the now totally darkened landscape. Thus the only option open to Plumb, as he saw it, was to continue in the same direction the pursuit had followed throughout the day—south to the Marais des Cygnes. Despite the many failures, his force might yet overtake and press the raiders until some other unit could block their retreat.[20]

In the quiet along Bull Creek, Simpson and his nervous militia waited. The scouts had been gone an hour and still no word. But then, just when the major began to despair, a scout galloped in reporting that indeed the bushwhackers were on their way and would be at the ford in less than a minute. Quickly, the men took their positions. Soon, unseen in the dark, hundreds of hooves were heard approaching. In a moment, the walk of the horses up the road became a trot, then a run, then a wild stampede, and as riders tried in vain to control their thirsty mounts, shouting and cursing filled the air. At last, when the uproar reached its peak, the unmanageable beasts crashed madly through the brush and plunged headlong into the creek. Simpson readied to give the signal, but just then he yelled for everyone to hold their fire. Above the tumult he heard a voice.

"Is that you, Plumb?" shouted Simpson over the din.

"Yes," came the astonished reply. And with that a bloody calamity was narrowly averted. After watering their horses, the two groups agreed that returning to Paola and handing over control of the pursuit to Lieutenant Colonel Clark was the wisest decision. Thankful a grievous mistake had been avoided, yet disheartened at their inability to box Quantrill, Plumb, Simpson, Lane, and the rest rode away from the ford.[21]

Immediately after the fight on Big Hill, under cover of darkness, Quantrill moved east until he came to the banks of Bull Creek. At this point the plan of marching to the Marais des Cygnes and hence crossing Bull Creek somewhere to the south was abandoned. Instead, the raiders broke sharply to the north seeking a ford further up. And after a ride of several miles, the column finally crossed a branch of the stream; here, at eleven o'clock, a camp was made. Pickets were sent out, horses allowed to graze, and in a few minutes most of the men were down and fast asleep.[22]

At midnight, Maj. Linn Thacher reached Olathe. There he learned that Quantrill's march during the day had been on a direct line for Paola. With over one hundred men Thacher rode out, driving due south.[23] A few miles away two hundred additional Federals were also pushing for Paola. Near Osawatomie, another company of regulars was pounding north. On the border, Lt. Col. W. King and the Fourth Missouri Militia were marching directly southwest for Paola.[24]

Meanwhile, well over a thousand soldiers and militiamen were in Paola, cooking meals on open fires and sleeping in the courthouse square.[25] Although it was clear that Quantrill had not gone south over the ford, nor with the many scouts watching had he passed east near the town, and with Plumb to his rear he certainly hadn't slipped deeper into Kansas, it seemed fairly obvious that he must have escaped north. But from sundown on into the night, the Union force at Paola remained camped and idle.

Sometime around 1:00 A.M. news arrived that the guerrillas had been located. A squad of militia scouting the forks of Bull Creek had stumbled upon their bivouac. Unfortunately, although there was no exchange of gunfire, the Rebels had grown wary and resumed the retreat.[26] At this revelation a stir began anew in the slumbering town. Men, especially the comparatively rested and avid militia, packed food and prepared to saddle. When all was ready Major Simpson and Captain Benter checked in with Clark for further instructions. Instead of being told to mount and strike the trail, however, the stunned officers were ordered to remain in Paola. Major Simpson protested, exclaiming that Quantrill would escape. Clark rebuffed this bit of impudence, stating that the pursuit would begin when he said it would and that the more rational approach was to start first thing in the morning when both man and beast were reasonably fresh.

Again the two implored Clark. Tough Captain Benter, "the very man to fight Quantrill," even offered to take his company out alone if necessary. But the colonel was adamant and to the overture again said no! Even as forty fresh regulars arrived from the Trading Post the militiamen were ordered to unsaddle, stack arms, and return to bed. Clark was firm in his decision that neither he nor anyone else would move until dawn. And thus the golden opportunity to throw the weight of the Union army between the guerrillas and the state line was fiddled away and "a great occasion was lost."[27]

The only man who could have rescinded Clark's order and launched an immediate full-scale pursuit was not there—nor was he anywhere near. Supposing that the commander of the district, after hearing of the raid on Lawrence, would return at once from Leavenworth to his headquarters, Major Plumb had throughout the day sent a host of couriers to Kansas City. In these notes Plumb advised General Ewing to place every available man along the line as the raiders were most certainly coming that way. When the messengers arrived and found the offices at the Pacific House vacant, the news was relayed by telegraph to Leavenworth, the general's last known whereabouts. But alas, Ewing was at neither place. Instead, he was pacing the banks of the Kaw, thirty miles north of Paola, enduring an "unavoidable delay" of hours, waiting for the DeSoto ferry. Collapsed around him, the Ohio troops slept in the dust.[28]

After abandoning their camp the guerrillas struck due east. Quantrill had no intention of halting again until the border was crossed and the woodlands were gained, perhaps by sunup. There was little way of knowing how near the Yankees were, but the Rebel chief responded as if they were just behind—or just ahead.

A few hours before dawn, vedettes of the Fourth Missouri Militia galloped back to the main column and informed Lieutenant Colonel King that they had just seen the shadows of a large body of eastbound riders. King quickly deployed his skirmishers, then ordered the regiment forward. The militiamen advanced cautiously, feeling in the dark inch by inch, waiting for the flash of gunfire that would signal the fray. But again, a fight was not to be. Sliding smoothly, silently around King's flank, "aided by the darkness and broken character of the prairie," Quantrill was far to the rear and on his way to Missouri before the Yankees realized no one was now to their front.[29]

At glimmer of dawn on August 22, the bugles were sounded and the command was given in Paola to mount and move. First to leave was the young officer who had ridden further during the thirty-two-hour chase than any other Federal, Charles Coleman. At the head of seventy Kansas regulars and an equal number of militiamen, the sturdy captain rode north until he caught the trail, then raced east. Shortly afterwards, Clark led the remainder from town and struck the trail. Others who had been converging throughout the night were not far behind. Indeed, no sooner had the last of Clark's men passed east than an additional two hundred troops followed in their tracks. Directly behind this came Linn Thacher's company, and not far back King's Missourians fell into line.[30]

From this point on the pursuit became a much more lively affair. The rest and feeding of the horses enabled the Federals to move rapidly and appreciably narrow the margin between themselves and the raiders, and in time they would have overtaken them. But time had ceased to be of the essence—distance was. The eight-hour delay in Paola, necessary though it seemed, opened a gap simply too wide to be closed. And as Charles Clark was leading his refreshed command forward at sunrise, William Quantrill was leading his weary column across the line, leaving Kansas at the least likely point—by the very trail over which he had entered it.[31]

By break of day Thomas Ewing was already entering his third consecutive hour in the saddle. For most of the night he had stalked the DeSoto landing trying desperately to get his troops over, and even then, impatient, he had struck south leaving a third on the opposite shore. And now, if such was possible, the mad pace he set was even more terrific than that of the day before, as if he were trying in minutes to recover hours lost at the ferry. Horses stumbled and fell, throwing their riders; men slipped from the saddles and were dragged in the stirrups. And always, even in early morning, there was the heat and suffocating dust cutting visibility in the rear to only a few feet.

"Riding like maniacs," thought one private.

Somewhere along the way it was learned that Quantrill was not advancing west for Topeka but was, on the contrary, retreating east to Missouri. Frustrated by the delays, on the brink of mental and physical exhaustion, Ewing made a quick decision. There was only one way whereby he might yet reach the field in time to take control of the pursuit. Spurring his horse ahead, with only a few men able to keep up, the general rode south alone. The rest were ordered to follow as fast as possible. And as if the race had taken on a mind of its own, the Ohioans did come on. But later the limit was reached and they too finally collapsed by the wayside, many unconscious or unable to move. One young lieutenant dismounted and, far from home or glory, simply pitched over and died from sunstroke.[32]

Upon gaining the woods along Grand River, the raiders stopped, dismounted, and began to celebrate. "Home," they said, and all the troops in Kansas couldn't get them now. Food was fetched from nearby farms while the business of dividing the loot got under way.

It was not long, however, before pickets disrupted the party, announcing that thousands of Federals were at hand. Once more the Rebels ran to their horses. At this time one hundred men, mostly farmers, chose to split and follow the river to their homes. Also at this time the Lawrence ambulance driver inched into the brush, unnoticed. Many abandoned their lame mounts and took to the paths on foot. Oblivious to danger, a few simply sought a deserted cabin or barn, a hidden cave or rotting log and promptly fell asleep. Leading the balance of his shrinking command out of the valley, Quantrill pushed northeast toward Pleasant Hill, passing over the same trail he had traveled three days earlier, steadily aiming for the Sni Hills and safety.[33]

Several hours later the advance of Lt. Col. Bazel Lazear's Missouri militia was just clearing the timber along Big Creek. Oddly enough, by holding slow and hard to the same track made by the guerrillas on Wednesday, Lazear found himself on Saturday in a position not attained by any Federal officer during the entire chase. Unbeknownst to the colonel, he was the last obstacle to Quantrill's escape. And with almost three hundred fresh men and mounts, he was certainly the most formidable.

After moving a short distance from the creek the militia halted. Half a mile to the west a large number of blue-clad horsemen was seen approaching on the prairie. Suspicious, Lazear rode forward. As he neared, the mysterious column reached the top of a ridge and began forming a line of battle parallel with a fence. All doubts now removed, Lazear turned and quickly prepared for a fight. Dismounting a company and passing their horses to the rear, the colonel ordered the men forward to act as skirmishers. As these time-consuming procedures were taking place, Quantrill quietly faced south and rode down the fence, leaving Lazear with some of his force in the saddle and some not. By the time the militia was entirely remounted the guerrillas were half a mile in the distance.

Galloping south, Lazear soon gained on the raiders and came up just as they disappeared behind a rise. Without pause the Yankees thundered over the hill. There on the other side they found the Rebels faced and waiting. Shots rang out as the guerrillas opened with revolvers. Momentarily checked, the militia replied with muskets. Several bushwhackers were hit and dropped from the saddle while a number of horses, struck by stray bullets, reared in the smoke and crashed to the ground. After a few more rounds the raiders broke for the timber. On their tired mounts, however, they were easy targets. Some had animals shot from under them, and as they gained their footing they were in turn cut down. Others ran for their lives or leaped on a friend's horse. By the time the shooting stopped and the last of the Rebels had reached the woods, five of their number lay dead and several more, unable to move from wounds or sheer exhaustion, were executed on the spot.

Racing over the littered ground Lazear and his men entered the brush in hot pursuit. Finding the trail had divided, the Federals in turn split, and shortly another band was run down and five more killed. After this, the militia reformed on the original field once more, buoyant and proud of their victory. While his troops raked over the plunder, discovering everything "from a horse to a finger ring," Lazear set up camp and announced that a well-earned rest was in order. And well-earned the rest was. Had the colonel but pushed the initiative, however, he might have earned something far beyond his wildest dreams.[34]

Behind, just breaking camp on the Grand after his latest halt, Charles Clark with nearly two thousand men was also dividing his command, sending Plumb and Thacher north following the main trail while the colonel himself chose to scout the brush to the east. Little was accomplished this day by either group. Clark did succeed in killing a number of stragglers, and just at dusk Thacher attacked a party of men he thought were guerrillas. But other than this, Saturday the twenty-second was spent in fruitless search.[35]

That evening after dark, as though the lead role in a poorly acted, poorly directed tragedy had suddenly stepped onto the lighted stage, Thomas Ewing, tired, sore, and very, very alone, rode into the bivouac on the Grand. Around the campfires he found Colonel Clark, George Hoyt and his scouts, and what probably seemed like half the population of Kansas. He also found the most powerful man in the state, Jim Lane, still clad in his grimy nightshirt and baggy trousers. The tirade levied on Plumb that opened the chase—and afterwards at any other officer who didn't measure up—now had a final and fitting outlet. And for the first time, Ewing heard the lurid details of what had transpired in Lawrence.

With the chase for all practical purposes over, the two men retired and held a lengthy "interview," shouting and arguing into the night about the next course of action.[36] As to that, Ewing had already reached a verdict. He had pondered the thought earlier and was about to propose it to General Schofield when in truth the calm prior to the raid did not seem to warrant it. Now, with the sudden swirl of events, everything had changed; the day for hesitation and half measures had passed. Ewing's former plan, the exile of Rebel families, severe though it seemed at the time, was scrapped, and in its stead a much more drastic, sweeping course was adopted. And though the distraught general didn't need the senator's curses and threats to convince him about the wisdom of his own plan, he received it nonetheless.

"You are a dead dog if you fail to issue that order," warned Lane.[37]

With both men in agreement as to what would be done, the meeting ended. But even while Lane was threatening, his crafty mind was spinning.

The hunt in western Missouri continued for the next few days with diminishing results. Clark, Lazear, and their small armies combed the Grand and Blue River country, the hills and valleys, the forests and fields, in the vain hope that they now could accomplish in the guerrillas' backyard what they had failed to gain on the open prairie. And thus the pursuit ended. The race was lost. Only a score of actual raiders had, as Clark put it, "gone the way of all the world." The bulk had escaped cleanly and scattered to their stronghold along the Sni. None of the leaders was killed: Todd, Anderson, Younger, Yager—all escaped.

But the greatest disappointment was that the man who planned and led the raid lived to savor his triumph and bask in glory. And glory it was. For his role that morning in Lawrence he gained the eternal respect and admiration of thousands who had long since given up; thousands who felt that though it had come ever so slowly, justice had after all come ever so surely. There was a deep, quiet sense of satisfaction for some; there was a lifting, hardly contained elation for others upon learning that their old foe had been paid back for Osceola, Kansas City, Order No. 10, and a slate of other wounds, paid back, to borrow the old Kansas term, "with interest." And although it was the most terrific, punishing ride of their lives, he had also won the undying love and devotion of his men. Indeed, the march over and retreat back had few equals in the war, and it was a feat many in the North might have secretly envied had circumstances been different. Five grueling days in the saddle—over two hundred miles—across much of occupied western Missouri, through four counties of the most warlike state in the nation where he had "dodged," "bewildered," and "baffled his pursuers," all with the loss of only a handful of men. But even as he settled in along the Sni to rest and reflect upon the success, even then his name was flashing across the wires of the Union and being rushed to press in newspapers everywhere. And as it was read and pronounced on the lips of an incredulous, horrified public, the name became an abrupt and bitter curse. What normally might have been lauded as the most astonishing and dazzling light cavalry raid of the war was instead being transformed into one of the blackest pages in American history. The man and the deed, together, inseparable:

Quantrill—the infamous monster
Quantrill—the border butcher
Quantrill—a crime . . . terrific, inhuman and bloody
Quantrill—the Lawrence Massacre!

IO

THIS SAVAGE WAR

"Disaster has again fallen on our State," wrote Governor Thomas Carney to John Schofield on August 24, 1863. "Lawrence is in ashes. Millions of property have been destroyed, and, worse yet," he continued, "nearly 200 lives of our best citizens have been sacrificed. No fiends in human shape could have acted with more savage barbarity than did Quantrill and his band in their last successful raid."[1]

Thus, word of what came to be known as the Lawrence Massacre spread to the outside world. The reaction was swift . . . and mighty.

New York Times
Quantrell's massacre . . . is almost enough to curdle the blood with horror. In the history of the war thus far . . . there has been no such diabolical work as this indiscriminate slaughter of peaceful villagers. . . . It is a calamity of the most heartrending kind—an atrocity of unspeakable character.

Chicago Tribune
What pen can depict the horrors . . . fiends incarnate . . . shooting down unarmed citizens . . . butchering them with wives and mothers clinging to them and begging for mercy.

Leavenworth Conservative
Shot down like dogs. . . . No fighting, no resistance—cold blooded murder.

Boston Post
The atrocious murders . . . exceed almost anything recorded in history. . . . The brutality, the cold-blooded ferocity. . . . Citizens butchered at their hearthstones, penned in like cattle.

And elsewhere throughout the North people were shocked, stunned, sickened. Terrible though the war had been, nothing even approached this Lawrence butchery, either in numbers or grim, barefaced brutality. And it came like a slap in the night to find that this region, which outwardly seemed so quiet, so uneventful—especially when contrasted with the titanic struggle in the East—should now explode in flames of fury and hate and provide the war's worst incident. But perhaps even more sobering was the realization that the "cruel war" had become by tenfold even crueler.

Amid the swirl and storm following the slaughter there was a rush of angry and frightened men, each trying to explain how a thing of this magnitude could happen. The easiest way, of course, was to point. At first those handiest—the military guarding the border and those participating in the hapless chase—were the most likely candidates. There was Capt. Joshua Pike at Aubrey, whose tragic "error of judgment" opened wide to Quantrill the gates of Kansas. Although first to detect the invasion, Pike sat idly in camp, sending a few messages up and down the line but not a word west, while he frittered away hours waiting for help. Maj. Preston Plumb, whose seemingly cautious pursuit over the scorched prairie to Paola had the look to some of an honor guard escorting the raiders safely to Missouri, was branded a coward and a traitor for his role. When overall command fell to Lt. Col. Charles Clark at Paola, the last real chance to halt the Rebel retreat was squandered when the zealous subordinates were denied permission to leave town and move to the attack. With the chase resumed on Saturday, Clark's creaking gyrations, especially after crossing the state line, were charitably described as "slow." And the farmers and villagers along Quantrill's route, those who either through fear, ignorance, or "criminal apathy" failed to warn Lawrence, did not escape the headhunting. The men of Franklin, where a stand of one hundred arms remained stacked in the arsenal all Friday morning, did not fire a shot. Those who scattered in quailish terror on the guerrillas' line of retreat. And so on.[2]

Naturally, the pointing quickly worked to the top, but in the end no one was certain just who or what merited the greatest share of guilt. The one thing Kansans were certain of, however, was where the source of trouble lay.

"I must hold Missouri responsible for this fearful, fiendish raid," continued Governor Carney. "No body of men large as that commanded by Quantrill could have been gathered together without the people residing in western Missouri knowing everything about it."[3]

On this score there was no debate. Kansas, not three years old, would remain a state in name only unless something was done—and soon. And at the time no means of guaranteeing its safety seemed too severe. The people of western Missouri were guilty, either as "aiders & abettors," as Carney put it, or as pathetic pawns skillfully played in the hands of the bushwhackers. But these were fine points. Kansans held all western Missouri "responsible" and therefore all western Missouri would pay.

Soon after the chase Thomas Ewing returned to the Pacific House in Kansas City. The District of the Border, a model of confidence and ability the week before, was now a shambles; along with it Ewing's own heretofore spotless career had been blackened, perhaps beyond cleansing, by the smoke and soot at Lawrence. Ewing realized this only too well. Already an avalanche of criticism was thundering down: charges made by certain "political Quantrills," as the general styled them; his untimely absence from headquarters on the night of August 20; Leavenworth, where no precautions had been taken to link the commanding general to the telegraph office and the office itself, opening and closing shop as if the border were at peace rather than home to a lightning guerrilla war; Ewing's decision to march overland, an arduous ride in the best of conditions, absolutely murderous in sun-wracked August, with only the flimsiest of information as to the raiders' whereabouts; the DeSoto ferry, a history of slow crossings and "poor accommodations."[4] The list went on.

A cooler man, cried critics, would have boarded a boat at Leavenworth, steamed downriver to Kansas City, disembarked fresh men and mounts, read the latest dispatches, then, after a comparatively short ride of twenty or thirty miles, thrown himself across the state line barring Quantrill's path.[5] That no soldiers were stationed at Lawrence when in truth they were at every other town less despised by the Rebels was charged to the general. "No man, woman, or child ever suggested the idea of stationing troops permanently at Lawrence," he burst out in a letter to his superior, John Schofield.[6]

Although most accusations would not bear up and all were laced with character slurs and patent lies, each had its audience in the wake of the Lawrence disaster. "My political enemies are fanning the flames and wish me for a burnt-offering," he continued to Schofield. "It is all mere mob clamor."[7] A court of inquiry was demanded, the light of which would reveal the truth, Ewing felt, and clear his name of any incompetence or wrongdoing. But still the clouds of failure hung black and heavy over the Pacific House, and when the hail of criticism didn't trouble the general's mind, the "horrors of the massacre" did.[8]

To his credit, however, Ewing was not one to stew in self-pity or waste his time fending off every assault. Instead, he got down to business. So long as "half or more of the people are disloyal of all shades, as in western Missouri," he explained to Schofield, the border would remain in turmoil. To this both men agreed. Thus Ewing did that which he felt he must; he issued General Orders, No. 11, calling for the dismantling and destruction of the Missouri border. Since virtually nothing seemed to work at wresting the bushwhackers from western Missouri, then western Missouri would be wrested from the bushwhackers.

Effective on August 25, Order No. 11 decreed that within fifteen days all persons residing in the border counties situated between the Missouri and Osage rivers would remove themselves from the land. Rebels, "either openly or secretly disloyal," living in the towns occupied by troops were also expelled. Those individuals fortunate enough to live within a mile of these stations, and who were able to prove their loyalty to the federal government, might remain. The few Unionists who yet lived on the countryside could move to the military posts or any part of Kansas beyond the border. But all else were banished. Where and how they went was their problem. But they must go, and quickly!

"To obtain the full military advantages of this," all grain and hay, either stored or growing in the fields, was to be burned. Nothing useful to the partisans was to remain in the region—no food, shelter, livestock, or forage, but most importantly, no people. Those lingering in the void after September 9 would be considered Rebels and hence guilty until proven innocent, if they were given the chance.[9] As he inked his signature to the bottom line, Ewing understood as well as any the hardships that must result from such an edict. But in his mind, at least, to save Kansas the border cancer had to be removed, once and for all.

"Though this measure may seem too severe," he told Schofield, "I believe it will prove not inhuman, but merciful."[10]

His word a law, the officers and men versed on their assignments, Ewing set the clock in motion and the fifteen-day countdown began.

Soon after Order No. 11 became known, famed artist and statesman George Caleb Bingham stepped onto a boat at the capital, Jefferson City, and steamed upriver. Stomping through the doors of the Pacific House, Bingham found the commanding general at his desk and got right to the point: the proclamation must be rescinded! Momentarily taken aback, Ewing replied that it was out of the question; the order would stand. Thereupon a heated argument ensued.

Of Southern background, although a staunch Unionist currently serving a term as state treasurer, the popular, toupeed little man confronting Ewing did not represent the sentiment of George C. Bingham alone but uttered words that a good many loyal Missourians and moderate men everywhere felt: namely, that Order No. 11 was an odious crime, an intemperate, vengeful, unprecedented act against a vastly innocent society that had nothing whatsoever to do with Lawrence, Quantrill, or even the rebellion. The edict must be cancelled.

"This is war, Mister Bingham," said the general. "I do not propose to alter my course of action regarding it. And may I remind you that I am commander of this district."

"And may I remind you," fired the artist, "that your whole course is stupid and outrageous. . . . Your mind is closed . . . as is your heart."

"To meddlers," Ewing shot back.

"Is it possible that unless you do something drastic to appease Kansas for the Lawrence raid that your own political star is quenched?" stabbed Bingham, alluding to the next senate election.

Furious, the big general approached and glared down on the little man.

"Mister Bingham, you can get out of here."

"Then you absolutely refuse to rescind the order?"

Ewing was firm.

"If you persist in executing this order," the artist threatened, "I shall make you infamous with my pen and brush." When the general said nothing the Missourian flew out the door.[11] But as Bingham left, others—politicians, editors, clergymen—with the same demands were waiting to enter.

And even over the state line, some Kansans who agreed in principle had little faith that the order would work in practice and feared the consequences if it did not. This measure, they felt, in the hands of the same "dull and incompetent" man who could not prevent the destruction of a town deep within a loyal state was certain to be mismanaged, and then not only would Quantrill continue to scourge the land at will, but suddenly his ranks would swell with a whole new legion of wrathful, bloodthirsty killers freshly kicked from their homes. If this came to pass there were many black, smoky days ahead for Kansas and much new sod to be dug.

Even if the order were carried out to the letter, however, there were many who didn't feel this was enough. In the eyes of most Kansans, the farmers and planters of Missouri were just as guilty as the guerrillas. Whether by actual complicity, whether by simple silence, either way they had made the nightmare at Lawrence a reality and just as certainly killed the men in that town as if they'd been there to squeeze the trigger themselves. Now Order No. 11 was granting these murderers ample time to collect their stolen goods and escape the border altogether, no doubt to carry on a sneaking, silent war elsewhere. Ewing's order, as these excited men saw it, was a pardon to Rebels, not a punishment; and if there was one ounce of justice yet left in the world, punished they must be, and severely.

"Hanging, disemboweling and quartering are not half severe enough to satisfy the righteous vengeance of the people," wrote one observer.[12] And many were determined that this was exactly what would happen, regardless of Ewing or his law.

Caught in the ideological crossfire of radical and moderate Unionists, too soft for the one, too harsh for the other; commanding a token army of 4,000 men in a land swarming with bushwhackers and jayhawkers; criticized mercilessly as a "pimp and an idiot," a man "without heart or brains"; his finely crafted world crashing down all around him, the embattled thirty-four-year-old brigadier resumed his post and got on with the job at hand.

The Sunday storm had extinguished the last embers in Lawrence, and by midweek, those who were coming back following the panic had done so. For most, the work began where it left off.

Over one hundred and fifty bodies had at last been buried; mercifully that grim business was nearly at an end. In the rush to inter the dead over the weekend, only the briefest of words were spoken, but with matters less strained, something more fitting seemed called for now. "It was a week of almost uninterrupted funeral services," noted a weary Reverend Cordley, who, while waiting for rites to begin at various homes, would fall fast asleep outside the doors.[13]

Some of the terribly wounded died, but others such as Harlow Baker and John Thornton, although both in critical condition, continued to improve. Produce arriving from the country had not stopped and, happily, supplies from Leavenworth still poured in. And money was being raised. Already "with less talk than would ordinarily be required to raise $100," Leavenworth had subscribed $15,000. Governor Carney opened his pockets and personally chipped in another $1,000, and to the widow of the Eudoran killed in the heroic attempt to warn the town, Carney gave $500. Four men, including Sen. Samuel Pomeroy, pledged $100,000 each to help resurrect the Eldridge House. Throughout the state and nation others were coming to the aid of the stricken town, and in a short while money and supplies would be on hand to rebuild Lawrence anew.[14]

But all this, though encouraging, still seemed oceans away and did little to check the deep despondency. The want was dire, the memories vivid. Some felt the moral damage caused by the Sunday panic greater than that of the raid itself. Passions ran high, higher perhaps than at any time since Black Friday. There was hope that some of the wealth stripped from the town might be recovered. Many people, especially ruined merchants, were more than interested in the reports sifting back that said that a good share of the loot and currency and nearly all the fifty horses stolen had been retaken. Rumors also had it that Lane, in a pursuit bungled by stupidity and downright cowardice, was the lone bright spot.

Hopes of recovered property were soon burst, however, for when Jim Lane and his bedraggled men rode into town the dismayed citizens saw no extra horses and no cash and goods worth mentioning. The wealth of Lawrence was gone. That part of the report had been untrue; the part about his own glorious role in the chase was not, however, or so said Jim Lane. Alighting from the saddle tired and sore, just completing a circuit that would have laid men half his age low, Lane was never so entirely fatigued that he could not summon the energy needed to advance his own name. He announced to the gathered citizens that he and his squad had killed over two score of Quantrill's men and undoubtedly wounded more. Some others in the chase, others whose imaginations were just as fantastic, said they counted between eighty and one hundred guerrillas "lying or hanging dead," and had the yarn spinning gone on much longer, or had anyone been willing to listen, few if any of the raiders would have made it to the border alive. But the people were not amused or impressed by these tales; they had heard them for years. They were instead more concerned about who would answer for the mounds of fresh brown sod on the hill. Moreover, they angrily asked, how and when was Missouri to be punished?

After making arrangements to have his home rebuilt, Lane called for a meeting of townsmen. There he revealed the plan to depopulate western Missouri, assuring the men present that he had personally cornered Tom Ewing and forced a "pledge" from him, making sure the job was done right.[15] If the senator expected the citizens of Lawrence to be comforted, he was mistaken. They, like many other Kansans, had no faith in Ewing or the military and were convinced that the order would not be carried out properly. Besides, they argued, this would not get their property back, nor was it the kind of punishment they had in mind. To a man, they were for going to Missouri and doing the job themselves, recovering their goods and killing off any Rebel or so-called Union man who claimed differently. When the point was raised that the military would never condone such an invasion, emotions were murderous.

On his journey back from the border, Lane had a chance to sound the opinions of many and knew well that the feeling expressed here at Lawrence was general elsewhere. Kansas demanded blood— Missouri blood—and the people were going there to get it under anyone who cared to take them. And so rather than stay at home and defend an unpopular cause, Lane changed course on the spot and in a few seconds became the leading advocate for the invasion of western Missouri. But as was the case with any of the senator's actions, there was more to it than that. There were political considerations as well. As a rival for the senate, Thomas Ewing, Jr., was finished. But John Schofield was another matter. Impediment that he was to the radical takeover of Missouri, if President Lincoln could be shown by a great popular uprising the universal contempt and lack of confidence in the St. Louis general, it stood to reason that he would be replaced. If this came to pass, Lane would very quickly have a mightier say, perhaps the mightiest say in the West. And so while the senator preached invasion on the one hand, he was careful to rail at the moderate Schofield on the other, painting him as the man most responsible for the Lawrence bloodbath.

With little sleep and less rest, yet spurred by the possibilities, James Lane adjourned the meeting and raced off to Leavenworth to fire support for the plan.

Watching as the senator left, a bitter, very bitter Charles Robinson had no doubts whatsoever as to who was "most responsible" for all the ills along the border. And it wasn't Thomas Ewing, John Schofield, or even William Quantrill!

As was the case up and down the border, Leavenworth was a hive of excitement and fear, for it was fully expected that when the next blow fell it would fall nowhere but there. Every day new and graphic horror stories from Lawrence set nerves on edge. The presence of Lane did nothing to calm the situation. Stalking here, then there, blasting "Skowfield" in one breath, drawing lurid scenes of Lawrence in the other, the senator found an audience on every corner. "Think of riding down the streets, and seeing a hundred and fifty of your fellow-citizens cooked—literally cooked—on the sidewalk."[16]

Early the following evening, August 27, while hundreds of militiamen nervously patrolled the outskirts, the largest, most riotous crowd in Kansas history came together in front of the Mansion House. Sharing the podium were Mayor Anthony, Charles Jennison, George Hoyt, and other well-known radicals. Each in turn regaled the torch-lit audience—estimated at 10,000—hour upon hour, calling loudly for the destruction of western Missouri and ritually beheading Ewing and Schofield. But everyone, though warm to the others, had come for the top bill, the master himself, to learn of his plans for the invasion of Missouri and, incidentally, to be thoroughly entertained in the process. Lane did not disappoint. For two hours the audience stood riveted, looking up with "open mouths" as the senator delivered his speech from the balcony, animated as always, removing one article of clothing, then another, warming to the crowd as they in turn were fired to a frenzy.

> Extermination—I repeat here, that for self-preservation there shall be extermination of the first tier of counties in Missouri, and if that won't secure us, then the second and third tier, and tier on tier, till we are secure. [Uproarious cheers] Oaths of allegiance! Great God!
> What was Schofield doing while the fiends were murdering the citizens of Lawrence? He was administering oaths of allegiance to their companions in Missouri, trying to woo them back to their allegiance, instead of killing them. . . . I take the ground here of vengeance for blood and devastation for safety.

Finally, when the crowd was "boiling over," the senator closed by calling on 5,000 men to prepare for what had to be done—to march over the line with him and scorch Missouri black with fire and sword. A thunderous roar and ovation went up, rattling the windows of Leavenworth: *Burn them over! Kill every living thing! Make a desert and call it peace!* Voices from the frenzied mob assured Lane that twice the number of men asked for could be raised. At last, with the invasion set to start from Paola on September 8, the tumultuous throng broke into the night convinced that the problem on the border would be settled in a very short time.[17]

Even before the Leavenworth meeting made blood its abiding aim, there had been hints of what might lay ahead for western Missouri.

Following the pursuit of Quantrill, hundreds of angry Kansans had lingered briefly and crashed through the border region. And partly in frustration and partly for old motives' sake these men had turned savagely on the people, those whose simple proximity to Quantrill's route was itself grounds for suspicion. Any group of men, or women for that matter, caught in the Union net were considered fair game. Some were arrested and hauled to jail while not a few were killed. Anyone found by George Hoyt and his Red Legs wearing a new shirt or hat or riding a good horse was lynched on the spot.[18]

That evil-looking, evil-acting men like Lane, Jennison, and Anthony flew about threatening extermination was one thing and would always be enough to pump fear into the hearts of men across the line no matter when it came. But suddenly, after the massacre at Lawrence and the meeting at Leavenworth the threats never seemed more ominous, with all of Kansas apparently poised to sweep into Missouri and have a serious go at wholesale slaughter. Mayors, senators, and congressmen were stumping hardest for it; prominent radicals and editors everywhere appeared to glory in it; the leading military men, even if they were disposed to do so, seemed incapable of preventing it; and at the moment there appeared to be no one on earth willing or daring enough to raise a hand against it.

"We are drifting between Scylla and Charybdis!" one frightened man wrote. "Who has the foresight and the will to save us?"[19]

On Monday, the last day of August 1863, John Schofield and members of his staff climbed aboard a special westbound train waiting at the St. Louis station. Schofield had hoped that the long trip wouldn't be necessary, and at first it seemed that it might not. Shortly after the massacre, even by the banks of the Mississippi, the young general felt the waves for retribution come rolling in from Kansas. Responding to a request from Thomas Carney for a stand of arms, Schofield agreed; in return he asked the governor to do his utmost to check the invasion movement before it got out of hand. "I hope," he continued to Carney, "a few day's reflection will show the popular leaders of Kansas the folly and wickedness of such measures of retaliation." Carney's response was encouraging. Also, considering the heap of abuse, Ewing had done well enough. His troops had fanned out to watch ferry crossings, and to help with the difficult days ahead two fresh regiments were moving up to the border.[20] But things simply had not gone as hoped.

Just prior to the Leavenworth meeting Schofield had wired the Kansas leaders cautioning them that, excited though they justly were, any move over the line was strictly forbidden. That night when the telegram was read aloud in Leavenworth, it was unanimously shouted down by the crowd. And the next morning Ewing himself showed signs of stress when he wired St. Louis stating that Lane had offered him sole control of the expedition to Missouri. The leaders "would place themselves under my orders," he said. "I have but little doubt I will be able to control matters to prevent any considerable acts of retaliation." If General Ewing had "little doubt," John Schofield had more than enough. Again he was forced to state the government's position. In turn, and "in the present state of feeling," Ewing himself worried about the reliability of his troops at stopping an invasion, torn as they were with Rebels to their back and radicals to their front.[21] Concern was greatest at Leavenworth, however, where Dan Anthony was doing all he possibly could to twist the knife in Ewing and get himself and a mob over the river.

And when Ewing, feeling terribly isolated, sought the aid of Governor Carney, it was in the eyes of all the ultimate sign of weakness since the two were well-known political foes. Thus, one week after the massacre at Lawrence, with "unprincipled leaders," as Schofield termed them, seeking to "fan the flame . . . and goad the people to madness," it appeared that the border, despite best efforts, would soon be consumed by fires beyond control.[22] And so to Schofield's mind there remained but one thing to do. Sometimes words on telegrams were not enough and only flesh and blood would do. And as the cars clattered away from the St. Louis station they were taking west not only the commander of the department—cold comfort, for John Schofield entertained no illusions about his popularity in Kansas—but were also, in his person, taking west all the authority vested in him by the commander in chief. His words were the president's.

Although Schofield had no way of knowing, there was at that moment a shift taking place in the minds of many along the border. For some it was subtle, for others sudden, but like Governor Carney all thinking men began to look about themselves and determine in what direction they were heading. Many decided they didn't like the direction, nor who they were going with. Men who had been swept along in the current during the first days of excitement and who might have otherwise been carried on and on to the falls, recoiled to find themselves keeping company with James Lane. Long ago they had learned that when Lane sailed one way, then this was reason aplenty for an intelligent and honest man to sail the other. The editor of the *Leavenworth Daily Times* had always known this and was one of the first to urge caution. "The storm-cloud that now hangs with such black and threatening fury over this ill-fated border, must be guided with a wise and an iron hand, or it will burst upon us, involving *all* in one common ruin." And the editor let it be known that the "iron hand" he had in mind was not that of the demagogue Lane, ruefully adding that the jayhawker would not even be around to agitate and boast of heroics but for his "lucky star and a neighboring cornfield."[23]

"Whenever one of those Lawrence murderers is caught," echoed another man, "let him hang until the buzzards fat on his carcass. But let us not imitate his barbarous example by an indiscriminate butchery of innocent persons."[24]

As ever, Lane turned a shrewd eye to all forms of criticism. To keep the pressure building and the Paola movement burning he called for yet another meeting at Leavenworth, scheduled for September 2.

By the first of September, little had changed in Lawrence since the weekend of the attack. A few individuals, then a few more had cleared the debris sufficiently to begin rebuilding, but it was a slow, painful process, and between staying clothed and fed and guarding the town, no real headway was made. Happily, work on the new bridge continued. And to ease the housing shortage there was talk of hauling the old proslavery Legislative Hall from Lecompton to the town. Both Hovey Lowman and John Speer began stirring to revive their newspapers. "Lawrence is not to 'wink out,' " wrote Speer, with more defiance than reason. "We have a glorious record; and a destiny. We are to be one of the largest cities west of the Missouri. There is no possibility of mistaking that."[25]

One of those who felt as Speer did was Peter Ridenour. On the Monday after the raid he began the long climb back. With what little money remained the grocer hired several blacks to clear the ash and debris from the store cellar. To the rear of the gutted building stood a corncrib untouched by the raiders; here Ridenour set up shop, throwing a lean-to on the side and planting a U.S. flag atop it all. The once-wealthy merchant then began selling the only thing in stock— salt. Taking a few dollars aside for expenses, he used the rest to pay as much to Eastern creditors as possible, which came as a shock to those who had read the names *Ridenour* and *Baker* among the list of dead. And because of the gesture and R & B's past honesty, letters from the East arrived in turn, telling Ridenour that his rating, despite his poverty, was still sound. Supplies did come in bit by bit and the tiny profits were used to pay for labor and material on the new store—a hod of bricks, a keg of nails, a load of boards—or to purchase a few more items to stock the corncrib.

Rising with the sun, clearing the rubble, waiting on customers with soot-smeared face and hands, still Peter Ridenour was never so tired at day's end that he could not return to the bedside of his friend. And to his great relief, he watched as Harlow Baker's condition improved with each passing day. Although his partner could speak, he still suffered much, and little was said between the men, and not a word about the business. Then one evening, quite unexpectedly, Baker looked up at his old friend and smiled. "Now, tell me what you are doing," he whispered. From that moment on, the last doubt vanished and Peter Ridenour knew they had won. The bond would not be broken.[26]

Money and supplies began to reach Lawrence in greater amounts. Although the East rose to the crisis, Leavenworth continued to give and do the most by far. Funds there were solicited anew and the machines of hastily formed sewing circles whirred night and day, stitching out clothes, sheets, and pillows. But the catastrophe was great, the resources of the state limited.

"For God's sake," wrote a citizen of Leavenworth to a wealthy Chicago friend, "This is no 'shrieking Kansas cry.' " Having just returned from Lawrence he could vouch for that. The Kansan beseeched his friend to send as much clothing as possible for, he said, the survivors were almost naked.[27] And for the people of Chicago the tragic stories of the past two weeks suddenly became much more than black ink and statistics when a host of widows and orphans stopped for a day in the town. The women, noted a journalist, were "exceedingly painful to behold." They were "pale and haggard, as if just risen from a long illness, with an expression of terror and fright. . . . They seemed to tremble at every slight noise."[28]

Like this pathetic group, hundreds more with no recourse were compelled to return to families in the East. Although only half the original population remained in Lawrence, recovery did continue. And with most admitting that a terrible mistake had indeed been made, Sallie Young returned from Fort Leavenworth, free of all charges.

Early on Wednesday, September 2, John Schofield stepped off the ferry and walked up through the streets of Leavenworth. Behind followed an impressive staff, gold and silver glittering on blue coats, revolvers on hips. Entering the Planter's Hotel the officers from St. Louis got down to business.

JOHN SCHOFIELD
(courtesy of the National Archives).

Schofield first spoke with Governor Carney and his aides. Once more the governor pledged his support and determination to reestablish peace on the Kansas-Missouri line. Satisfied, the general then "asked and obtained" a long interview with his most bitter accuser, James Lane. Coming to the point, he asked Lane about the Paola movement and his plans for September 8. Speaking in his own inimitable way, the senator rehashed his views, the views of Kansas, so he said, the determination of the people to march from Paola to Missouri and make a "desert waste." Little or nothing could prevent the inevitable, he added, and a prudent man wouldn't try. Unimpressed, the general replied that no unauthorized force would enter Missouri.

Surprised at Schofield's inner toughness, Lane tried to strike a sly deal, offering to the hard-smoking general—the man he was hoping to see unemployed within a fortnight—a position as supervisor of the Paola affair. If the general would oversee the operation then not only would he gain grace with Kansans, but he would also be on the spot to judge how the thing was handled, or so the reasoning went. John Schofield was no fool. And he had not traveled all the way from St. Louis just to hear this. To accept the offer, unthinkable as it was, would temporarily salve Kansas but place the blame firmly on his shoulders should pillage and murder erupt. To refuse, as Lane knew he must, would set him at odds with not only Kansans but radicals everywhere, and the senator would use it for all it was worth. Again the general's response was a flat no.

Lane continued the argument and tried to bargain but Schofield, not swayed in the least, only shook his head. No mob, under any circumstances, would cross the line, and now the senator from Kansas knew it! Lane warned the commander to consider what he had just said and digest it slowly, for if he persisted in his refusal to allow Kansans the "right" to search for their property, he would lay the case at the feet of his close friend and confidant, President Abraham Lincoln. With that the stormy duel ended. And John Schofield, facing down one of the most powerful men in America, had not budged an inch.[29]

That evening as promised Jim Lane delivered his second speech in less than a week. As before he spoke to a large audience in front of the Mansion House. Once more the senator called on the people to rise up and march on Missouri, assuring the crowd that the military would not interfere; on the contrary, he said, they would even cooperate with the expedition. The speech rambled on in a similar vein, Lane touching upon politics and himself, railing into the night against Missouri and treason.[30]

On the day following his joust with Lane, General Schofield steamed downriver and met with Thomas Ewing. The two men discussed at length the crisis along the border and the best means of dealing with it. Just speaking with a few leaders was not enough, they agreed, and so the generals issued a proclamation, spelling out in black and white the government's position. "No armed bodies of men," ran the decree, "will be permitted, under any pretext whatever, to pass from one State to the other."[31] The statement was brief, yet clear; how the majority of Kansans would react remained to be seen.

When the dawn of September 8 came, the date appointed for the invasion of Missouri, dark and heavy skies hung low over the border. Throughout the morning men continued to arrive in Paola, a place that had seen its share of excitement in the past two weeks. One hundred blacks were on hand, and even some women joined the crowd. Although the gathering was large for such a small town, it was not the 5,000 men asked for, certainly not the 10,000 promised. But everyone agreed that if the turnout was disappointing, their numbers were still more than enough, and just as important, the spirit of vengeance was very much alive.

Then as promised, and with a claque at his coattails, James Lane stalked through the crowd and mounted the stage. "I know not what course others may pursue," the senator began, "but as for me, I don't intend to leave this town until I have indemnity for the past, and security for the future."

With that the clouds broke open and the rain came down in a roar. As the drenched crowd gathered about the speaker's stand, Lane began a rant that continued in the deluge for three solid hours. Unlike the Leavenworth harangues, however, talk of invasion was noticeably lacking. The few times he alluded to it his speech was halted by loud applause, which only caused the senator to quickly shift to slavery, Schofield, or Quantrill.

"Why the devil don't Schofield go after him, and if he can't catch him, why don't he let us? We are entitled to protection. . . . We've got the brains on Schofield, big! I don't pretend to hold Old Abe responsible for the acts of Schofield; I hold that officer himself responsible, and I don't think another man so deficient and wanting in brains as Schofield could be found."

"Let's go to Missouri," came an impatient voice over the pounding rain. "Down with Schofield and Ewing."[32]

But other than this, little occurred save Lane telling the waterlogged crowd that Schofield would not grant them the right to enter

Missouri. And with that the meeting wound down by tamely passing resolutions. Thus, as the dispirited men splashed back home, the much-vaunted expedition to Missouri came to an end. Undoubtedly, a number of fair-weather soldiers were kept away by rain and muddy roads. A far greater number, however, had indeed taken a "sober second thought," and when their anger cooled sufficiently it was easy to see the truth of the matter—that Generals Schofield and Ewing, along with nearly all Kansans, were striving to achieve the same goal: an end to the border war. But probably most bitter and embarrassing of all, especially for those swept right into Paola, was the dawning that once more they had been diced up and skewered for yet another political barbecue.

Even as excitement swirled in Kansas over the Paola movement, just east of the line the gears of Order No. 11 were grinding on and hurling the people from the land. At first the evacuation had been hesitant; some who left early returned again and again to haul away possessions. But as the deadline drew nigh, the trickle of refugees on the roads soon became a swift stream. Most packed what little they owned into broken-down wagons and once-splendid carriages, hitched a mule with washboard ribs, took a backward glance, and left their homes forever. The journey alone would have been enough. But there were other hazards. Ewing's men, composed almost entirely of Kansas troops, were on the roads too, waiting at fords and crossroads, ensuring that the order was obeyed, searching for weapons and other contraband. Many showed only a thimble of restraint and seized the chance to punish their old foes and steal what little remained. A number didn't even wait for the Missourians to clear their dwellings, but burst in, pushing and shoving, looting and setting fires. To protest was to invite a drawn pistol, a beating, or worse. Some were arrested and thrown into prison and never heard from again, whereas others showed up days later, floating face down in the Missouri.[33]

Near Lone Jack, shortly before the deadline, a group was loading the last of its belongings, "straining every nerve" to escape the doomed region. Just as the people were about to leave, a party of Federals rode up. After interrogating the menfolk, two were allowed to continue with the women and children but six others ranging in age from seventeen to seventy-five were held for further questioning. When the families had gone about a mile, shots were heard back up the road. Returning to the area, six bodies were found sprawled on the grass, "shockingly mangled," some unrecognizably so. The widows could do little more than weep, bury the dead, and hurry in their

SELF-PORTRAIT, BY GEORGE CALEB BINGHAM
*(on loan from the Kansas City Public Library to The Nelson-Atkins Museum of
Art, Kansas City, Missouri).*

flight. "The world will doubtless be told that six more bushwhackers have been cut off," lamented a survivor.[34]

As promised, George Caleb Bingham set to work on his next
painting. Bingham was wealthy, and for him money had ceased to be

a concern in life. Not only was he the most sought after portrait-ist in Missouri but he was also one of the most accomplished landscape artists in America. Unlike his previous works, however, which so vividly expressed his own free spirit and winging opti-mism, Bingham knew that, when completed, the next would be stiff and ugly to behold; in creating it each stroke of the brush would be a bitter, painful reminder of a deep and personal tragedy. Passing along the roads of western Missouri, the former Union soldier wit-nessed for himself the suffering and confusion of his beloved coun-trymen. Each cruel scene that met his burning gaze became yet another terrible sketch seared forever in his mind. Eventually, the outline was complete. As for Thomas Ewing, a seat of honor in the painting was being reserved especially for him, and more than ever before the little artist was determined to cast down to "eternal in-famy" the man and the deed, as he had vowed.[35]

But no amount of painting could undo what was already done. By September 9, two weeks after Ewing signed the paper, western Missouri was bleak and silent. Order No. 11 had been carried out, as one officer put it, "to the letter." By day the smoke hung thick in the air, and at night the clouds above the border were streaked with red. From that time forth, the region so happy and prosperous prior to the war came to be known as simply "the burnt district."

Some of the people, those who could prove their loyalty, did enter the garrisoned towns or crossed to an uncertain life in Kansas. Those who could not yet were fortunate enough to have relatives elsewhere and the means to get there left with a degree of hope. But for the ma-jority, with little money and nowhere to go, they simply drifted off following others who were going nowhere, subsisting on roots, cracked corn, and green apples. Although begged for, shelter was de-nied at schools and churches.[36] "There come the refugees, take in your clothes," Union women mocked.[37]

One man, viewing the flight from a snug vantage point, laughed at their condition. Scornfully he remarked that the victims were "haggard, woe-begone, melancholy, and of course disloyal." Others had similar comments. Whether these people noticed or not, or whether they cared, the irony of it all was that the same trains, boats, and trails used by the Missourians to flee their state were the same trains, boats, and trails used by Kansans to flee theirs.[38]

In a letter to John Schofield dated the last of August 1863, General Ewing sized up the situation in the West as he saw it and amplified on his recent Order No. 11. The message had ended on a cautious but positive note: "The execution of these orders will possibly lead to a still fiercer and more active struggle . . . but will soon result, though with much unmerited loss and suffering, in putting an end to this savage border war."[39]

If Thomas Ewing could somehow look far away into the peaceful distance to a time when "this savage border war" would at last be ended, Kansans could not. They saw only the grim here and now and the "fiercer struggle" that yet lay ahead. Even with two additional regiments and the border patrols doubled, the general feeling was that no force known could keep Quantrill out of Kansas if he had a mind to come.

"Never," noted an observer, had he "seen the people—the lion-hearted courageous men and women of Kansas—so thoroughly disheartened."[40] "They have lost all confidence," said another. And now, with the guerrillas undoubtedly more vengeful than ever before, the horizon in Kansas never looked blacker. Every shifting breeze carried its alarm. Quantrill was said to be here—pillaging and murdering near Fort Scott to the south, then there—leading a thousand men toward Leavenworth in the north. He was moving south to "kill, burn, and plunder everything," while at the same time he was marching west to finish off Olathe. Osawatomie was on fire. Endless knots of his men were filtering up the Marais des Cygnes Valley to form and fall on a town in the rear. Again he was going south but at Elwood in the north there was wild panic. "Look Out," warned an excited editor. "Where the blow will fall, nobody can tell."[41]

All business ground to a halt. And while their fields went to rot, local militias, exhausted and stretched to the limit, marched and patrolled day and night. "I wish to God, Quantrell was on the Union side!" one militiaman burst out.[42]

Terrified families from the border streamed into the larger towns while others fled far to the interior. Many gave up the state entirely. Some stubborn individuals did remain, however, determined to hold their hard-won farms to the last. But it wasn't for long. As the final act of Order No. 11 was being played out in Missouri, a rumor swept into Kansas like a whirlwind, causing a "perfect stampede," emptying farms and villages, and completely clearing the land. An edict had been issued by Quantrill himself, so it went, requiring all Union citizens in the border counties south of the Kaw to be off the land within fifteen days. He and his men were surely coming, the report continued, and any man found in the restricted zone who could not prove his loyalty to the Confederacy must certainly know the rest!

Unlike Ewing's order, no troops were on hand to force Kansans from the border. But like their neighbors across the line, the people of the state went just as swiftly, just as surely.[43]

Then, with a strip of desolation fifty miles wide, an eerie calm settled over the western border. "The stillness," wrote Ewing, "is like that which preceded the Lawrence raid."

"No sign of Quantrill," came the report from Lexington in the north.

"Still as death. . . . They have mysteriously disappeared," echoed the eastern district. To the south, the word was the same with no Rebels seen in any sector. But they were there, and from some of his best spies Ewing soon knew where.[44]

Suddenly, in mid-September Ewing sprang the trap. With hundreds of troops posted to guard the passes leading south, thousands more swarmed in from the north for a sweep up the Sni Valley. The general's plan was simple, yet direct: First, press the guerrillas so vigorously, so relentlessly that a club and claw fight to the finish would be their only option, and second, flush those who survived to the south for a slaughter on the prairie beyond. The core of the hunt was Col. William Weer's Tenth Kansas, just returned from Ohio and the successful chase of the raider John Morgan. Perhaps one of the best antipartisan men in the country, the colonel knew all the tricks. And as he moved up the Sni, Weer had a man on his left flank who understood the "habits of the animal" better than any, Charles Coleman. Also participating was Bazel Lazear and his Missouri militia, who, on that hot afternoon by the banks of Big Creek, had come within a hair of making much of the Sni campaign unnecessary. With almost a thousand men, Colonel Lazear eagerly joined the hunt. "If we could only succeed in catching Quantrill," he excitedly wrote his wife, "that would put the cap-sheaf on for us."[45]

Almost immediately Coleman struck home. He and his company surprised a large band of bushwhackers, killed two, captured forty horses, and destroyed a large amount of equipment. The rest were driven ahead. Lazear had a similar success. There were more clashes and more Rebels slain. As the last days of September slipped by and the net closed tighter on the Sni, Ewing sent a hasty reminder to his troops at the southern passes to get ready. Never in the history of the border war had such an operation taken place, and with Weer, Lazear, and Coleman in the brush there was a feeling in the air that the time had finally arrived. And if officers were guarded in their words, others were not.

"With a large force of experienced border fighters now on his track," one man predicted, "his escape is hardly possible."

"They cannot run far now."[46]

Far to the south, James Blunt lounged comfortably in his parked buggy, "enjoying a quiet smoke," a five-gallon demijohn of brandy by his side. It was a sunny autumn day in southeast Kansas and the general was on the road to Arkansas. Although he was hoping to make a "quick trip," at the moment Blunt sat waiting for the rest of his column to close up before going into the Union fort at Baxter Springs, a mere stone's throw away. In addition to the eight wagons that composed his train, there were staff officers, civilians, Blunt's brass band, and regular soldiers acting as escort—over one hundred men in all.

After a wait of fifteen minutes the stragglers joined and the order to march was given. But just then, a short distance to the east, a large body of men were spied emerging from the woods. As the blue-clad riders were forming into a wide front, the Federal column halted to watch. Everyone, including the commanding general, assumed that these were troops from the fort beginning daily exercises. In a few moments the riders advanced.

Five minutes later James Blunt was several miles away lashing a fleet horse over the open prairie—hatless, saberless, no cigar, no brandy. Behind him, as the dust settled, the wagon train was ablaze and most of his men lay scattered about the road, each with a neat black hole burned into his head.[47]

Word traveled slower this time, back up the lonely Fort Scott Road with survivors; from there by couriers along the state line—the Trading Post, Aubrey, Kansas City, upriver to Leavenworth; by telegraph from here, across Missouri, fanning out until word had finally spread. "QUANTRILL AGAIN!"

That same day, as the corpses were being laid out for burial in the south, far to the north in Lawrence spades were also turning the earth. Two more bodies were pulled from a well.[48]

JAMES BLUNT
(courtesy of the Kansas State Historical Society).

I I

WHEN PATHS JOIN

"Such is the excitement and terror of the people caused by last year's experience," wrote editor Hovey Lowman, "that the report 'they are coming,' will create almost as much consternation as if they were upon us."[1]

And that spring, 1864, like a gathering black cloud on a clear southern horizon, they were coming. All reports arriving from the south, and there was a storm of them, indicated that Quantrill, Todd, and Anderson had broken winter camp in Texas and were weaving their way north with hundreds—some said thousands—of followers. Frantic efforts to intercept and slow their progress were to no avail. Finally, in early May the guerrillas reached their Sni and Blackwater lairs. The nightmare began anew. For Missouri it proved the bloodiest, most ferocious summer of the war. Seldom did an hour pass without death and destruction. Reckless Federal patrols led by green officers stumbled into ambush and were annihilated; steamboats were riddled with rifle fire; railroad and stage lines stopped running; towns were captured; nightly, homes and barns shot orange sparks heavenward while in the fiery glow owners were beaten, tortured, or killed.

"The very air seems charged with blood and death," wailed a Kansas City journalist. "Pandemonium itself seems to have broken loose, and robbery, murder, . . . and death runs riot over the country."[2]

Understandably, such savagery and strife across the line kept Kansas churning in dreadful anticipation. Awesome though it was, Kansans viewed the renewal of the vicious war in Missouri as merely a prelude of things to come, for there were no doubts in that state about the bushwhackers' ultimate ambition. Consequently, each city, town, and farm suffered its share of terror during the panic of 1864. And although each bloodcurdling report proved in the end a false alarm, it mattered naught to Kansans. "We must take all these reports with many grains of allowance," warned one high-ranking officer, "but there must be some fire where there is so much smoke."[3]

When the spring sun rose on Lawrence that year, it unveiled a transformation quite unlike anything seen in the brief history of Kansas. The most obvious change was Camp Lookout. Glowering over the wide valley the outpost crowning Mount Oread surveyed all movement on the roads leading into town. Built of rough, heavy logs, the stockade also housed several big cannons, which glared menacingly from the gunports. Fifty men ate, slept, lived in the fort night and day, without exception.

Below Mount Oread, carving the city up like a gigantic jigsaw puzzle, stretched a system of trenches, pits, and breastworks capable of containing hundreds of men. Down Massachusetts Street two solid blockhouses anchored the heart of town. Others were scattered about at key points. Eight men remained at each bastion continually, four inside, four out. Five companies of city militia marched and drilled more often than not and stood ready at a moment's notice. Although armed by the state, one dissatisfied company bought the best repeating rifles available. Every able-bodied man belonged to the militia. Exemptions were few. Two companies of U.S. regulars also guarded the town permanently.

Scouts ranged the countryside, patrolling the Santa Fe Road from the border west as far as Council Grove. Strangers crossing the earthworks by day were questioned and watched, sometimes roughed up and arrested, and no one entered the town at night without being stopped. Failure to do so could mean death.[4] Forts, cannons, drums, bugles, pickets, scouts, signs, and countersigns—in six months the place had become one of the most fortified towns in the West. Lawrence was a citadel.

And when the people weren't working on the defenses or standing guard or watching strangers, visitors, and very often one another, they were busy rebuilding their town. Blackened lots on broad Massachusetts Street began to sprout new shops and stores, some raised by former merchants, some by new. Homes were also rising, grander and more ornate than ever. Altogether over one hundred and fifty various buildings had been constructed since the raid, including more than a score on the opposite side of the river. There were other improvements as well.

Spanning the Kaw, the new wooden bridge connected the two sections of town, making the cumbersome ferry all but obsolete. Beyond, grading for the long-awaited Pacific Railroad had been completed to Lawrence; citizens eagerly watched for smoke from the first locomotive. And the telegraph had reached town: overnight Lawrence found itself only a finger tap away from the thoughts of Chicago, New York, and Boston; more important, at least while the war lasted, Lawrence also had instant contact with Leavenworth, Kansas City, and Olathe. There was a modest immigration to the city as well, which eased the labor shortage. The influx of eligible males also did much to put sparkle into the lives of a large number of widows and maturing young women. And for the town as a whole the arrival of new faces was a spectacle that was bound to boost sagging spirits, for it was reassuring to know that others felt so confident in Lawrence that they were actually willing to move there.

The work went on without letup. Sawmills ran night and day and the sounds of the hammer and trowel were notes both constant and comforting. Optimism soared as the paint dried on each new shining home, and each proud store shingle signaled business as usual. "If Quantrell will let us alone, the anniversary of his butchery will see Lawrence fully revived," waxed John Speer in his new paper, the *Kansas Tribune*.[5]

Whether intended or not Speer expressed a sentiment that, despite outward appearances, always ran deep and would remain the dominant theme of day-to-day thought—Quantrill. Although Lawrence was a fortress and through hard work and courage had made itself invulnerable to guerrilla raids, no one truly believed in its safety. The general mood in town was "it can be done again," as Hovey Lowman noted. "Such great crimes . . . seldom repeat themselves. Civilization don't crimson its pages with such an awful deformity but rarely. We trust in God it may never happen again. To guard against it, we must watch without ceasing. Eternal vigilance alone is our protection."[6]

Every man, regardless of occupation, went to work each day with a musket on his arm and at least one revolver under his coat. An accidental discharge of a gun or a rider galloping through the streets at night was more than enough to rally the militia, and when the sawmill whistle went off one dark morning the entire town flew to the alarm. Later it was discovered the whistle had simply been stuck, and everyone laughed in relief. But these same people jumped just as quickly at the next alarm and the next.[7]

June and July came and went with similar panics, but other than the terrifying rumors, nothing whatsoever was heard of Quantrill. Nevertheless work on the fortifications continued, and as the anniversary of the raid approached, three additional cannons plus hundreds of extra troops and militiamen arrived.[8] But except for one more nervous day and one more sleepless night, Sunday, August 21, 1864, passed without incident.

Then in September a telegram arrived that sent a cold, violent shiver through the town. Quantrill had finally been captured. Arrested as a spy in Indiana, a man fitting his description was currently sitting in an Indianapolis jail cell within days of execution. His name—Charles Hart. Several Missourians had already viewed the prisoner and agreed that he was the man, but to make absolutely certain the Indiana commandant wired Kansas requesting further information. When that message was returned, last doubts were removed. Asking the authorities there to delay execution, a committee of four men, including Peter Ridenour, was quickly appointed to rush east and bring William Quantrill back to Lawrence for trial and punishment. And within forty-eight hours of leaving, the cell door swung open and the Kansans stood staring into the eyes of the prisoner.

A few days later, amid great anticipation, the committeemen returned to Lawrence. To the dismay of the people, however, they came back alone. There were many similarities, argued Ridenour to the incredulous townsfolk, and to be sure it was a terrible, fantastic chain of coincidence, but beyond doubt the Hart of Indiana was not the Quantrill of Kansas. And thus the prayers of thousands went unanswered.[9]

Following the excitement, September faded quietly away. In fact, although Missouri was abroil, and despite the awful alarms, the summer of 1864 had proven the most peaceful and uneventful of the war. But that all began to change when the leaves began to fall.

In mid-September, with his band playing "Dixie," Gen. Sterling Price crossed over from his Arkansas exile and marched into his beloved home state. Behind "Old Pap" followed nearly 12,000 Rebel cavalrymen, Missourians for the most part, many rugged veterans toughened by three years of fighting. Price's objectives were as varied as recruiting men for the drained Confederacy to swaying public opinion in the November elections, but the old general's chief ambition was nothing less than the recapture of Missouri. Initially, his first target was the metropolis of St. Louis.[10]

From his headquarters by the banks of the Mississippi, new Department of the Missouri commander, William S. Rosecrans, sent urgent messages alerting the state and ordering a concentration of troops around St. Louis. Far downriver a small force was standing by, but for the time-being no sufficient body of Union soldiers stood between the Rebel army and St. Louis. If Price moved swiftly he might soon hold the keys to the seventh largest city in America. At the moment only a scratch outfit of 1,000 men could be placed anywhere near Price's advance. But to Rosecrans's mind the sacrifice was necessary, and to buy time this unit was sent forward to try to slow the Rebel host.

At age thirty-three, John Schofield left his St. Louis desk to join William T. Sherman in his epic campaign for Atlanta. Without question the bright, young general was glad to be rid of the hopeless Missouri quagmire. He had tried to find an answer for the "evil on the border," as he called it, but to the best of his abilities he had not. Schofield had survived, however. And although no one in Kansas or Missouri mourned his departure, he left with his reputation intact. Not only had the one-time physics professor shown himself to be a wise and capable administrator, but shortly the record would prove him a valuable field commander as well. Later, success in conflict was crowned in peace when in 1888 John Schofield was appointed commanding general of the United States Army.

During the final days of September the army of Sterling Price marched nearly one hundred miles into Missouri without a trace of Federal opposition. There was even talk of taking the war to Iowa as confidence swelled in the ranks.

Then, on September 26, in the shadow of a towering crag called Pilot Knob, Price suddenly found his path barred. A small Union force had settled in behind earthworks to meet the onslaught. Twice the Rebel general demanded surrender and twice he was refused. Thus Price deployed his thousands and sent them charging against the works, hoping to root the Federals out with as little time lost as possible. But two days of fierce fighting and 1,500 Rebel casualties later, Tom Ewing and his hard-pressed little band still held the pass.

Time had run out, however, and with the railroad to his rear destroyed and hope of reinforcements out of the question, Ewing withdrew his exhausted force and led it away to safety.[11]

As most demanded, as everyone expected, Thomas Ewing by his own request was replaced as commander of the border. By March 1864 he found himself in the District of St. Louis, an area that had been a military backwater and all signs indicated it would remain so until the end of the war. But fate and Sterling Price intervened, and Ewing was given a last opportunity to revive his failing career. After the war, however, and all but friendless, Ewing saw no reason to return to his adopted home in Kansas. Practicing law for a time in Washington, he returned to his native Lancaster, Ohio, and as expected he then set sail on a political voyage worthy of his father.[12] And when he did, his foremost foe was right there, ready and waiting.

"It will be adequate," said George Bingham as he laid down the brush from his latest painting. For five long years the artist had pressed ahead with the huge oil, despite entreaties from friends to let old wounds heal. But Bingham was not like that. The bitter little man meant each and every word that day at the Pacific House, and passing time, if a balm to some, only fueled his determination. His attacks on Ewing were tireless, and when he wasn't exhibiting the monumental work "Order No. 11" or distributing prints of it to Ohio politicians, the Missourian was wielding the pen like a rapier: "Scarcely was the ink dry upon the paper, when like a pack of infuriated and starved bloodhounds they were unleashed and turned loose upon the horror-stricken communities. . . . Never was a robbery so stupendous, more cunningly devised or successfully accomplished, with less personal risk to the robbers."[13]

Much through Bingham's efforts, Ewing's first bid fell short when Ohio leaders failed to back his name for office. But several years later, and with the aid of his illustrious brother "Cump" and old commander Schofield, Ewing fought back and won for himself a seat in Congress. Then began the stretch for the governorship, which in the eyes of all was the next stepping-stone to the White House in 1880. But once again and with renewed vigor Bingham and other Missourians rose to the attack. More copies of "Order No. 11" were circulated; essays increased in virulence. Finally, when the crucial votes for governor were counted Thomas Ewing had fallen by a 3-percent margin. And with that the political dreams of a lifetime ended.

Years later, talking with a visitor in his New York law office, the aging man reminisced about his life in Kansas, the war, and George C. Bingham. "I suppose my military order changed the lives of a lot of people," he confided. "It changed mine, I know."

"You might have been President of the United States or should I say now, an ex President?"

Ewing sat quietly, listening, contemplating the words. "It is in the past now," he finally answered, "but I sometimes wonder if I had not issued that order . . . what might have happened."

ORDER NO. 11, BY GEORGE CALEB BINGHAM
(courtesy of the State Historical Society of Missouri, Columbia).

Crossing to his downtown office on January 21, 1896, Thomas Ewing, Jr., was struck by a streetcar and died from injuries a few hours later. He was sixty-six.[14]

The Battle of Pilot Knob dashed whatever hope Sterling Price had of capturing St. Louis. Two days had elapsed, two precious days that gave Union forces in Missouri the much-needed margin to work with. Consequently, when Price's army left the battlefield it marched not north toward St. Louis, but west toward the Kansas border. And as it did large numbers of guerrillas came out of the woods to ride along. The sight of these half-wild creatures was a jolt to regular soldiers and a graphic, sickening comment on the condition of the war in Missouri. Proudly displayed around the necks of their horses or dangling from bridles were trophies of human ears and freshly torn scalps.[15]

On September 27, 1864, Bill Anderson, George Todd, and several hundred bushwhackers swarmed in and around the village of Centralia, Missouri. The day was hot, the whiskey plentiful. Shortly before noon a train pulled into the station. Among the passengers were more than twenty Union soldiers, many returning home on leave from Georgia. These helpless men were taken from the car, hustled to a nearby wall, and then, despite pleas for mercy, shot.

Not long after the Rebels left, a patrol of over one hundred raw militiamen rode into Centralia and started off on the trail at once. After a short ride the militia found itself on a small hill. And suddenly, as if arisen from hell, the land all about them was ringed with the most experienced killers in the West. Surrounded, outnumbered, frightened, the issue was never in doubt. Anderson charged, then Todd, and after a harmless volley by the militia the great slaughter began. Those who died quickly were blessed. Those who surrendered suffered most. When Federal troops arrived the following day they were overwhelmed by the scene spread about them. "The war has furnished no greater barbarism," muttered a stunned Union general.[16]

Legend has it that when the last knot was added, the silk cord carried by Bill Anderson had fifty-three tied into it. The first fourteen were knotted at Lawrence. "I have fully glutted my vengeance. I have killed many. I am a guerrilla."[17]

One month after Centralia, with two musket balls in the back of his head, Bill Anderson at age twenty-five was dead. At twenty-four, so too was George Todd. And soon, many more young men would join them. Their fight for Missouri was over.

In five smoke-filled days, from the nineteenth of October 1864 to the twenty-third, the Civil War on the border effectively came to an end. During that time the Rebel army under Sterling Price engaged the combined might of Kansas militia and Union regulars, and after several bloody assaults near Kansas City the climactic Battle of Westport was fought. The result sent Price reeling south in total retreat. As the beaten Confederates fled down the state line with the Federals hard at their heels, there was no chance to go further into Kansas and gather the military stores so desperately needed. Nor did Missouri soldiers find the time to go and get "their things." It was enough to escape. And escape they did—down the desolate border, through southern Missouri, with hunger and death stalking every mile of the way. By early November Price's army of "half-starved bushwhackers and brutish vagabonds" crossed the Arkansas River never to return.[18]

With rousing cheers and notes of "When Johnny Comes Marching Home" filling the crisp autumn air, the Lawrence militia crossed the new bridge looking every inch the conquering heroes. And for their role in routing Price they received a welcome befitting such. Grown men ran to the bridge "like a lot of school boys let loose." There were speeches, toasts, and tears, much thanksgiving, and much pride in a common effort.

Hardly had the sounds of victory faded when a new reason to shout spread through the city. On November 26, workmen drove the last spike at Lawrence of the long-awaited Pacific Railroad. "Today we bid farewell to the past," announced a local speaker, "today we emerge into a new life."[19]

Although he held minor positions and was active locally, the flame for high office never quite died in Charles Robinson. More than a decade after the bond scandal and his impeachment, Robinson again sought the public eye. And for the moment it seemed as if healing time had wiped much of the stain from his name for, and probably much to his surprise, the former governor was elected to a term in the state senate. Later, however, the sand castle crumbled when he was denied a seat in Congress. No one had really forgotten his earlier disgrace, and when the real test came Robinson was soundly defeated in a race for the governorship. Once more, broken and alone, the Father of Kansas retired to his new home across the river while the sweep of events moved on without him.[20]

To his dying day, Charles Robinson, the only Lawrence man to view the massacre from beginning to end, felt that his archenemy James Lane was in some satanic way connected with it. Of course it was just a feeling. There existed no hard evidence to support such a claim and thus the governor kept his beliefs largely to himself. In his blinding hatred, however, Robinson firmly believed that Lane was willing and able to engineer such a scheme. And that the senator would stop at nothing to attain a goal, alas, the former governor knew all too well.[21]

But whether Charles Robinson was right or whether he was wrong the world would never know. Depressed over his waning support among the radicals of Kansas, discouraged at his inability to stay atop the tiger, one year after war's end Jim Lane stuck a pistol in his mouth, then squeezed the trigger. "His suicide," wrote a friend to Robinson, "was his own verdict on his life & actions."[22]

On April 10, 1865, Lawrence was "electrified" by word of Lee's surrender. Instantly, despite the rain and mud, people ran to the telegraph office to learn more. "Soon crowds gathered in the streets, and cheer after cheer went up in every direction. All was hilarity and excitement." There were parades and music and singing into the evening, and that night bonfires and rockets painted the sky.[23] The celebration really didn't stop for the entire week when the war was ending everywhere. There was peace and then there was much more to be happy about, for Lawrence was well along the road to recovery.

To anyone returning since the raid—and there were many coming back now that it was safe to do so—the town was a far cry from the blackened shell they had fled. Proud citizens were forever counting their achievements: "Fourteen places where groceries and provisions are sold, five livery stables, two milliner shops, two daguerrian artists, two lumber yards, two banks, two jewelers, two harness shops, eight saloons, one foundry and machine shop, four flour mills, one brewery, three hotels," and on and on. Then there were the tireless sawmills whirring day and night, devouring whole forests to keep pace with demand. Over three hundred and fifty homes stood in Lawrence, and across the river a hundred more had risen since the raid. But even these impressive figures were not enough. More homes were needed, homes for new arrivals.

They came by the hundreds after the war. The flow was so swift, in fact, that almost overnight the old-time residents became a minority. And with each new face the collective memory of Lawrence unavoidably grew a little fainter. Most latecomers actually knew little about the town's history; except for the blockhouses and maze of trenches, vestiges of the famous raid were fast disappearing. Few would have guessed when talking to him over the counter of his store that at one time Harlow Baker had been so riddled with bullet holes that he was twice passed over for dead. Or that the quiet lady librarian had been widowed one morning before she had cleared the sleep from her eyes. Or that the church where they now heard the Reverend Cordley's sermons was once littered with bodies and used as a morgue. Or that the same brushy ravine where little boys played and chased frogs had once been crowded with scores of terrified men whose sole hope for survival lay in choking back tears and clinging to its steep banksides.

With each day that passed, there was less to remind. Soon tall rows of buildings, larger and sturdier than before, again walled Massachusetts Street, creating one unbroken line of business and trade. The limits of the city expanded and reached out along the old California Road, sprawled around and over Mount Oread, and edged up to the new state university that crowned its top. And shortly, the crumbling blockhouses were torn down and the trenches covered over with lawns and gardens.

William Quantrill never attempted another raid into Kansas. He really didn't need to. By the summer of 1864 his giant, dark shadow crossed and recrossed the border as surely as if he cast it himself, and in his or her mind some Kansan somewhere saw him each and every hour of each and every day. He was said to have been almost everywhere and yet he was nowhere. It was only when frightened, running people finally slowed to a walk and began looking about that they discovered to their amazement he existed in these places through the mind alone. "We hear nothing of Quantrill," was the last word when hysteria had crested. And that was the story for the remainder of the war. "We hear nothing of Quantrill."[24]

There are a number of possible reasons why the enigmatic Ohioan left the war when he did. Certainly, William Quantrill's purpose for war lay west of the state line. And undoubtedly, he above all saw the madness of attempting another raid into Kansas. Before 1863 the risks had been great enough; after the raid on Lawrence, however, although Kansans refused to believe it, to get into the state and out again had become an impossibility, and any force attempting it would have certainly faced destruction. There is also the likelihood

LAWRENCE REVIVED: LOOKING NORTH ON MASSACHUSETTS STREET
(courtesy of the Kansas State Historical Society).

that Quantrill, the refined former schoolteacher, had no stomach for the brutal savagery that later shamed the fighting in Missouri and the ugly games played with fervor by both sides.

But perhaps the best reason for his sudden departure from the war was given by Quantrill himself. After his triumphant return to Lawrence, his "greatest exploit," he mentioned to someone that morning that for him there was no more aim in life. His goal was reached; he was now "ready to die."[25] He had destroyed Lawrence and by so doing accomplished that which others had threatened but been unable to do for almost a decade.

"And not one of us has ever regretted that we were in it," announced one raider long after the war. "We are proud that we were able to revenge our fathers and mothers and sisters."[26]

And so it was. On one side of the border he was a hero, a cavalier, an avenging angel.

> Hurrah for Quantrell . . .
> And all [his] bravest men.
> God may they save our country yet
> From those foes they do offend.[27]

Yet a few yards west of that same line, his memory burned like white iron: "Butcher"; "Monster"; "He comes from the dregs of a degraded population. He cannot write his name. . . . He seldom washes his hands or changes his shirt. He . . . lives in wretchedness, squalor and crime."[28] Whatever the mood, Kansas had quaffed from the cup of war, and for that state, William Quantrill had proven the bitter red wine. On May 10, 1865, near Bloomfield, Kentucky, one of the last skirmishes of the Civil War took place. Several weeks later, at a military hospital in Louisville, the quiet, mysterious man with the strange-sounding name closed his eyes forever. He was twenty-seven.

Not long after the massacre, the Reverend Richard Cordley had written how time would soon erase "the real marks of Quantrell's steps." And in a sense this was true. With an energy and determination that seemed to defy the purely materialistic, the people reconstructed their town, laboring day and night, lending more than a willing hand to one another when their own task was complete, working to the point of exhaustion as if fleeing from a moment in history they chose to forget. Their success was remarkable. Several years afterward the visitor to Lawrence would be hard pressed to discover an outward trace of the raid. These "marks," as the Reverend Cordley once knew them, were gone forever.

But long after the raid, when Lawrence was transformed into a city of paved streets lined with gas lamps, a hive of trade and learning in the state, a garden spot of spreading Dutch elm and sweet-smelling lilac, even then, the invisible marks lingered. The afflictions of the mind, the mysterious ailments that the Reverend Cordley hardly understood and the likes of which words had not yet come to describe; the psychosis, the paranoia, the recurring visions of a peaceful morning shattered by fire and death; the nightmares on sultry summer nights when the moon waxed and waned and the air was as still as a hush—these marks remained and continued to linger until the last aged survivor was laid to rest.

And as for Quantrill's "steps," unwittingly, unavoidably, the kindly, white-haired minister, his fellow townsmen, and others along the border enshrined these for generations to come. They exist today and they exist in many places; in a forgotten, shady grove of western Missouri; on a treeless, sunbaked Kansas plain; by the quiet banks of a meandering river; wherever his enemies were unsuspecting, rash, or bold, there the path of Quantrill winds. But always in the end the paths join and lead to the same spot, to the grassy hill overlooking the beautiful valley, to the graveyard where the victims of the Lawrence Massacre were laid, down to the bone-white and wind-smoothed headstones, down to Quantrill's footsteps.

NOTES

KHC *Kansas Historical Collections,* 1887–1933
KHQ *Kansas Historical Quarterly,* 1933–78
LKSHS Library of the Kansas State Historical Society, Topeka
MHR *Missouri Historical Review*
OR *War of the Rebellion: Official Records of the Union and Confederate Armies.*
  128 vols. Washington, D.C.: Government Printing Office, 1880–1901.
WHQ *Westport* (Missouri) *Historical Quarterly*

1. Old Scores

1. *OR,* 22, 1:587–88; William Elsey Connelley, *Quantrill and the Border Wars,* 2d ed. (1909; reprint, New York: Pageant, 1956), 313–15.

2. George W. Martin, "The First Two Years of Kansas," *KHC* 10 (1907–8): 138.

3. Ibid.

4. *Lawrence Herald of Freedom,* Mar. 10, 1855.

5. Sara T. D. Robinson, *Kansas: Its Interior and Exterior Life* (Boston: Crosby, Nichols and Co., 1857), 221.

6. *Lawrence Herald of Freedom,* Jan. 12, 1856.

7. *Leavenworth Daily Times,* Jan. 30, 1861.

8. Joseph G. Gambone, "Economic Relief in Territorial Kansas, 1860–1861," *KHQ* 36 (Summer 1970): 149–50.

9. Hildegarde Rose Herklotz, "Jayhawkers in Missouri, 1858–1863," *MHR* 18 (Oct. 1923): 71–72, 74; *Atchison Freedom's Champion,* Jan. 25, 1862; Stephen Z. Starr, *Jennison's Jayhawkers* (Baton Rouge: Louisiana State Univ. Press, 1973), 94–113.

10. W. A. Mitchell, "Historic Linn," *KHC* 16 (1926): 654; Michael Fellman, *Inside War: The Guerrilla Conflict in Missouri During the American Civil War* (New York: Oxford Univ. Press, 1989), 188.

11. Lew Larkin, *Bingham: Fighting Artist* (St. Louis: State, 1955), 144.

12. Albert Castel, *A Frontier State at War: Kansas, 1861–1865* (Ithaca, N.Y.: Cornell Univ. Press, 1958), 45; *Lawrence Kansas State Journal,* Jan. 30, 1862 (hereafter cited as *Lawrence Journal*); Edgar Langsdorf, ed., "The Letters of Joseph H. Trego, 1857–1864," *KHQ* 19 (Aug. 1951): 299.

13. *Atchison Freedom's Champion,* Jan. 25, 1862.

14. Ibid., Oct. 12, 1861.

15. A. T. Andreas, *History of the State of Kansas* (Chicago: A. T. Andreas, 1883), 2:669; *OR*, 3:468–69.

16. *Lawrence Republican*, Jan. 23, 1862.

17. Darrell Garwood, *Crossroads of America: The Story of Kansas City* (New York: W. W. Norton, 1948), 51–55; William Elsey Connelley, *History of Kansas, State and People* (Chicago: American Historical Society, 1928), 2:632–34; William Elsey Connelley, *The Life of Preston B. Plumb, 1837–1891* (Chicago: Brown and Howell, 1913), 146–49.

18. *Kansas City* (Mo.) *Daily Western Journal of Commerce*, Aug. 15, 1863 (hereafter cited as *Kansas City Daily Journal*).

2. The Dead Men

1. *Kansas City Daily Journal*, July 17, 1863.

2. *Oskaloosa Independent*, Aug. 15, 1863.

3. *OR*, 22, 1:580, 589.

4. *Council Grove Press*, June 22, 1861.

5. *Leavenworth Daily Times*, May 31, 1862; *Kansas City Daily Journal*, July 11, 1862; *Emporia News*, May 17, 1862; William Elsey Connelley Papers, box 13, LKSHS, interview with B. F. Munkers, July 7, 1910.

6. *Kansas City Daily Journal*, Aug. 2, 7, 1863; Connelley, *Kansas*, 2:636–37; Garwood, *Crossroads*, 54.

7. Lela Barnes, ed., "An Editor Looks at Early-Day Kansas: The Letters of Charles Monroe Chase," *KHQ* 26 (Summer 1960): 118, 124–25; George Walton, *Sentinel of the Plains: Fort Leavenworth* (Englewood Cliffs, N.J.: Prentice-Hall, 1973), 129.

8. *Kansas City Daily Journal*, Mar. 31, 1863; *Lawrence Journal*, Apr. 2, 1863.

9. *Kansas City Daily Journal*, June 19, July 9, 1863; *Oskaloosa Independent*, June 27, 1863; W. S. Burke, *Military History of Kansas Regiments* (Leavenworth: W. S. Burke, 1870), 276–77.

10. Cole Younger, *The Story of Cole Younger, by Himself* (1903; reprint, Provo, Utah: Triton, 1988), 7–8; A. Birdsall, *History of Jackson County, Missouri*, 2d ed. (1881; reprint, Kansas City, Mo.: Ramfre, 1966), 272; Larkin, *Bingham*, 143; Richard S. Brownlee, *Gray Ghosts of the Confederacy* (Baton Rouge: Louisiana State Univ. Press, 1958), 61.

11. *Kansas City Daily Journal*, Aug. 15, 1863.

12. Ethylene Ballard Thruston, "Captain Dick Yeager—Quantrill Man," *WHQ* 4, no. 1 (June 1968): 3; Albert N. Doerschuk, "Extracts from War-Time Letters, 1861–1864," *MHR* 23 (Oct. 1928): 100.

13. Ed Blair, *History of Johnson County, Kansas* (Lawrence: Standard, 1915), 140–44; David Hubbard, "Reminiscences of the Yeager Raid," *KHC* 8 (1903–4): 168–71.

14. Thruston, "Yeager," 3.

15. Connelley, *Quantrill*, 315, 323; Quantrill Scrapbook, LKSHS, 2:130–31.

16. *OR*, 22, 1:585, 589.

17. *Oskaloosa Independent*, Aug. 15, 1863; Quantrill Scrapbook, LKSHS, 2:130–31.

18. "Statement of J. A. Pike," *KHC* 14 (1915–18): 313–14; *OR*, 22, 1:589.

3. The "Live" Man

1. *OR*, 22, 1:585–86.

2. Ibid., 589–90.

3. Ibid., 825.

4. *Lawrence Journal*, May 1, 1862; *Olathe Mirror*, Mar. 20, 1862.

5. *Dictionary of American Biography* (hereafter *DAB*), s.v. "Ewing, Thomas."

6. Thomas Ewing, Jr., Private Papers, 1856–1908, LKSHS.

7. Don W. Wilson, *Governor Charles Robinson of Kansas* (Lawrence: Univ. Press of Kansas, 1975), 73; Larkin, *Bingham*, 207–8.

8. *DAB*, s.v. "Ewing, Thomas"; Elvid Hunt, *History of Fort Leavenworth, 1827–1927* (Fort Leavenworth, Kans.: The General Service Schools Press, 1926), 120.

9. *Kansas City Daily Journal*, June 17, 1863; *Kansas City Weekly Western Journal of Commerce*, June 20, 1863 (hereafter cited as *Kansas City Weekly Journal*).

10. *Oskaloosa Independent*, June 27, 1863.

11. *Kansas City Daily Journal*, June 30, 1863.

12. Ann Davis Niepman, "General Orders No. 11 and Border Warfare," *MHR* 66, no. 2 (Jan. 1972): 192.

13. *OR*, 22, 1:581, 584.

14. Ibid., 579.

15. Allan Nevins, *Ordeal of the Union* (New York: Scribner's, 1971), 7:170.

16. *OR*, 22, 2:428–29.

17. James L. McDonough, "And All for Nothing—Early Experiences of John M. Schofield," *MHR* 64, no. 3 (Apr. 1970): 306–7.

18. John M. Schofield, *Forty-six Years in the Army* (New York: Century, 1897), 69.

19. James L. McDonough, *Schofield: Union General in the Civil War and Reconstruction* (Tallahassee: Florida State Univ. Press, 1972), 44; Schofield, *Forty-six Years*, 70–71.

20. Schofield, *Forty-six Years*, 78; McDonough, *Schofield*, 54.

21. *OR*, 22, 1:579, 584.

22. *Oskaloosa Independent*, Aug. 15, 1863.

23. *Kansas City Daily Journal*, June 25, 1863.

24. *Kansas City Weekly Journal*, July 4, 1863; *Oskaloosa Independent*, July 4, 1863.

25. *Kansas City Daily Journal*, Aug. 2, 5, 1863.

26. *OR*, 22, 1:580, 585–87, 589–90.

27. Ibid., 580–81.

4. The Darkest Hour

1. *OR*, 22, 1:583.

2. Ibid., 580–82; Connelley, *Kansas*, 2:642.

3. Richard Cordley, *History of Lawrence, Kansas* (Lawrence: E. F. Caldwell, 1895), 182.

4. *Lawrence Journal*, May 9, 1861.

5. Ibid., May 16, 1861.

6. *Lawrence Republican*, May 23, 1861.

7. Ibid., Mar. 7, June 27, 1861.

8. *Lawrence Republican*, Jan. 31, 1861; *Lawrence Journal*, Aug. 8, Dec. 5, 1861.

9. Ibid., Apr. 17, 1862.

10. Ibid., Apr. 3, 10, 1862; Theodore Gardner, "The First Kansas Battery," *KHC* 14 (1915–18): 259.

11. *Lawrence Journal*, Jan. 9, 1862.

12. Nevins, *Ordeal of the Union*, 6:371; *Lawrence Republican*, Sept. 19, 1861; Cordley, *Lawrence*, 182, 184.

13. *Lawrence Journal*, June 13, 1861, Dec. 11, 1862.
14. *Lawrence Republican*, Sept. 18, 1862.
15. *Lawrence Journal*, Sept. 18, 1862.
16. *Atchison Freedom's Champion*, Oct. 25, 1862.
17. *Lawrence Republican*, Oct. 23, Nov. 6, 1862.
18. Ibid., Oct. 23, 1862.
19. *Lawrence Journal*, Nov. 6, 1862; *Lawrence Republican*, Nov. 6, 1862.
20. *Lawrence Journal*, May 7, 1863.
21. Ibid., May 14, 1863.
22. Ibid.
23. Ibid., May 21, 1863.
24. Ibid., June 25, 1863; Connelley, *Kansas*, 2:657–58.
25. Andreas, *History of Kansas*, 2:321.
26. Ibid.
27. *Lawrence Journal*, July 2, 1863.
28. Ibid., June 25, 1863.
29. Ibid., July 30, 1863.
30. Quantrill Scrapbook, LKSHS, 1:92.
31. *Lawrence Journal*, Aug. 6, 1863.
32. Ibid.; Andreas, *Kansas*, 1:321.
33. *Lawrence Journal*, Aug. 6, 1863.
34. Douglas County Scrapbook, LKSHS, 4:18.
35. Quantrill Scrapbook, LKSHS, 1:91–92; *Leavenworth Daily Times*, Sept. 6, 1863.
36. *Lawrence Journal*, Aug. 13, 1863.
37. Andreas, *Kansas*, 1:321; *OR*, 22, 1:579.
38. Andreas, *Kansas*, 1:321.
39. Connelley, *Quantrill*, 324.

5. The Fairest City

1. *OR*, 22, 1:590.
2. G. W. Brown, *Reminiscences of Gov. R. J. Walker* (Rockford, Ill.: G. W. Brown, 1902), 19.
3. *Lawrence Journal*, Apr. 16, 1863.
4. Ibid., May 9, 1861; H. D. Fisher, *The Gun and the Gospel* (Chicago: Kenwood, 1896), 156–57, 167–70, 185–86.
5. Andreas, *Kansas*, 1:323.
6. Connelley, *Quantrill*, 337–40.
7. *Lawrence Journal*, June 25, 1863.
8. Peter D. Ridenour, *Autobiography of Peter D. Ridenour* (Kansas City, Mo., 1908), 144–47, 183; James Horton, "Peter D. Ridenour and Harlow W. Baker, Two Pioneer Kansas Merchants," *KHC* 10 (1907–8): 601–2.
9. Martha B. Caldwell, "The Eldridge House," *KHQ* 9, no. 4 (1940): 362–63; (Topeka) *Kansas State Record*, Aug. 26, 1863; Douglas County Scrapbook, LKSHS, 3:161; "Sallie Young and Quantrell," by Alex E. Case, Learned Scrapbook, Kansas Collections, Spencer Library, University of Kansas, Lawrence, vol. 4 (1863).
10. *DAB*, s.v. "Robinson, Charles"; Letter, A. A. Lawrence to Chas. Robinson, Jan. 31, 1856, Papers of Charles and Sara T. D. Robinson, 1834–1911, LKSHS.

11. Robinson, *Kansas,* 123.
12. Ibid., 325-26.
13. *DAB,* s.v. "Robinson, Charles."
14. Letter, Charles to Sara Robinson, June 17, 1861, Robinson Papers, LKSHS.
15. *Oskaloosa Independent,* June 5, 1861.
16. *OR,* 3:468-69.
17. *Leavenworth Daily Conservative,* Sept. 3, 23, 1863.
18. *Lawrence Republican,* June 5, 1862.
19. Castel, *Frontier State,* 21.
20. Alice Nichols, *Bleeding Kansas* (New York: Oxford Univ. Press, 1954), 42.
21. Jay Monaghan, *Civil War on the Western Border, 1854-1865* (Boston: Little, Brown, 1955), 31.
22. Edgar Langsdorf, "Jim Lane and the Frontier Guard," *KHQ* 9 (Feb. 1940): 22-23.
23. *OR,* 3:455, 490.
24. *Lawrence Republican,* Oct. 3, 1861; *OR,* 3:196; Castel, *Frontier State,* 54; *Leavenworth Daily Times,* Nov. 12, 1863.
25. Henry E. Palmer, "The Black Flag Character of the War on the Border," *KHC* 9 (1905-6): 457; *Lawrence Republican,* Oct. 3, 1861; *Atchison Freedom's Champion,* Nov. 23, 1861; Albert Castel, "Kansas Jayhawking Raids into Western Missouri in 1861," *MHR* 54, no. 1 (Oct. 1959): 4.
26. *Leavenworth Daily Times,* Nov. 16, 1861.
27. *Lawrence Republican,* Jan. 9, 1862.
28. *Lawrence Journal,* Oct. 17, 1861.
29. *Leavenworth Daily Times,* Oct. 9, 1861.
30. Cordley, *Lawrence,* 190-91.
31. *OR,* 22, 1:585-86, 589-90.

6. Vengeance in My Heart

1. Connelley, *Quantrill,* 324-25; *OR,* 22, 1:583; Andreas, *Kansas,* 1:321; Kansas Scrapbook, LKSHS, 9:79.
2. *Olathe Mirror,* Dec. 19, 1861.
3. *Lawrence Journal,* July 31, 1862.
4. Blair, *Johnson County,* 196-98; *Lawrence Republican,* Sept. 11, 1862; *Lawrence Journal,* Sept. 11, 1862.
5. *OR,* 13:803.
6. Connelley, *Quantrill,* 200.
7. Ibid., 227-28, 230-31, 234; *Leavenworth Daily Conservative,* Mar. 13, 22, 1862.
8. *Lawrence Republican,* Mar. 13, 1862.
9. *Liberty* (Mo.) *Tribune,* March 21, 1862; Brownlee, *Gray Ghosts,* 64; *Kansas City Daily Journal,* Mar. 18, 23, 1862; Birdsall, *Jackson County,* 472.
10. Connelley, *Quantrill,* 241-43; Joyce Farlow and Louise Barry, eds., "Vincent B. Osborne's Civil War Experiences," *KHQ* 20, no. 2 (May 1952): 127-28.
11. Albert Castel, *William Clarke Quantrill: His Life and Times* (New York: Frederick Fell, 1962), 77-80.
12. Ibid., 82-83.
13. *Kansas City Daily Journal,* July 13, 14, 1862; Barnes, "An Editor Looks," 124.
14. *Leavenworth Daily Times,* June 28, 1862.

15. *Leavenworth Daily Conservative*, Aug. 2, 5, 1862.

16. Castel, *Quantrill*, 88–92.

17. Brownlee, *Gray Ghosts*, 99.

18. *Leavenworth Daily Times*, Aug. 19, 26, 1862.

19. *Leavenworth Daily Conservative*, Aug. 23, 1862.

20. Blair, *Johnson County*, 164–65; Connelley, *Quantrill*, 275; *Olathe Mirror*, Oct. 25, 1862.

21. Castel, *Quantrill*, 100.

22. *Leavenworth Daily Times*, Sept. 18, 1862.

23. *Lawrence Journal*, Sept. 11, 1862.

24. *Wyandotte Commercial Gazette*, Sept. 13, 1862; Connelley, *Quantrill*, 282.

25. *Atchison Freedom's Champion*, May 30, 1863.

26. *Boston Daily Advertiser*, Aug. 24, 1863.

27. Garwood, *Crossroads of America*, 50–51.

28. *Leavenworth Daily Conservative*, Aug. 14, 1863.

29. George Miller, *Missouri's Memorable Decade, 1860–1870* (Columbia, Mo: E. W. Stephens, 1898), 76.

30. Quantrill Scrapbook, LKSHS, 1:186.

31. Connelley, *Quantrill*, 62, 64–66.

32. Castel, *Quantrill*, 26.

33. Connelley, *Quantrill*, 77–82.

34. Ibid., 89–91, 95.

35. Ibid., 114–15.

36. Henry Earle Riggs, *Our Pioneer Ancestors* (Ann Arbor, Mich., 1942), 204; Kansas Scrapbook, LKSHS, "L," 5:131.

37. Connelley, *Quantrill*, 154–59; John J. Lutz, "Quantrill and the Morgan Walker Tragedy," *KHC* 8 (1903–4): 324–26.

38. "The Lawrence Raid," William H. Gregg Manuscript, LKSHS, 3.

39. Connelley, *Quantrill*, 331.

40. Ibid., 328.

41. Andreas, *Kansas*, 1:321.

42. Connelley, *Quantrill*, 94–95, 101–2, 125.

7. Death in My Hand

1. H. E. Lowman, *Narrative of the Lawrence Massacre* (Lawrence: State Journal, 1864), 49.

2. Andreas, *Kansas*, 1:321–22.

3. Lowman, *Narrative*, 49.

4. Russell E. Bidlack, ed., "Erastus D. Ladd's Description of the Lawrence Massacre," *KHQ* 29, no. 2 (Summer 1963): 116.

5. Andreas, *Kansas*, 1:322.

6. Lowman, *Narrative*, 49–50.

7. Quantrill Scrapbook, LKSHS, 2:199; Lowman, *Narrative*, 52; John C. Shea, *Reminiscences of Quantrell's Raid* (Kansas City, Mo.: Isaac P. Moore, 1879), 24.

8. Richard Cordley, *Pioneer Days in Kansas* (Boston: Pilgrim, 1903), 179.

9. R. G. Elliott, "The Quantrill Raid as Seen from the Eldridge House," *KHC* 2 (1920): 188–89.

10. Lowman, *Narrative*, 53–55.

11. Quantrill Scrapbook, LKSHS, 2:1; Lowman, *Narrative*, 55; Shea, *Reminiscences*, 20.

12. Shea, *Reminiscences*, 21; Quantrill Scrapbook, LKSHS, 1:17.

13. Andreas, *Kansas*, 1:322; *Kansas City Daily Journal*, Aug. 25, 1863.

14. Lowman, *Narrative*, 50.

15. *Boston Daily Post*, Sept. 2, 1863; *Leavenworth Daily Conservative*, Aug. 24, 1863; Lowman, *Narrative*, 57, 82; Quantrill Scrapbook, LKSHS, 1:17.

16. Andreas, *Kansas*, 1:322.

17. Mrs. R. C. Dix, "Quantrill's Raid—An Eyewitness Account," *WHQ* 1, no. 1 (May 1965): 8–11; *New York Daily Times*, Aug. 30, 1863; Elliott, "Quantrill Raid," 194.

18. Andreas, *Kansas*, 1:322; Elliott, "Quantrill Raid," 188; Cordley, *Lawrence*, 211–12.

19. Andreas, *Kansas*, 1:322.

20. Lowman, *Narrative*, 71–72.

21. *New York Daily Times*, Sept. 4, 1863; John I. Speer, *The Life of Gen. James H. Lane* (Garden City, Kans.: John Speer, 1896), 265–66; *Leavenworth Daily Times*, Aug. 23, 1863.

22. Andreas, *Kansas*, 1:322; *New York Daily Times*, Aug. 30, 1863; *Leavenworth Daily Times*, Aug. 23, 1863; Cordley, *Lawrence*, 212; *Manhattan Independent*, Sept. 28, 1863; Lowman, *Narrative*, 61–62; Douglas County Historical Society Files, box 5, folder 15, p. 3, Kansas Collection, Spencer Library, University of Kansas, Lawrence.

23. Andreas, *Kansas*, 1:322.

24. Quantrill Scrapbook, LKSHS, 1:67–71.

25. Lowman, *Narrative*, 70.

26. Andreas, *Kansas*, 1:323; Quantrill Scrapbook, LKSHS 1:73; Riggs, *Pioneer Ancestors*, 205.

27. Elliott, "Quantrill Raid," 191; Riggs, *Pioneer Ancestors*, 206; *Leavenworth Daily Conservative*, Aug. 24, 1863.

28. Lowman, *Narrative*, 50–51, 82–84; Shea, *Reminiscences*, 4; Elliott, "Quantrill Raid," 187.

29. Fisher, *The Gun and the Gospel*, 185–93.

30. Ibid., 186–87; Quantrill Scrapbook, LKSHS, 1:75.

31. Andreas, *Kansas*, 1:322.

32. Ibid., 323; Shea, *Reminiscences*, 23.

33. Andreas, *Kansas*, 1:322; Lowman, *Narrative*, 88.

34. Andreas, *Kansas*, 1:323; John Speer, "The Burning of Osceola, Mo., by Lane, and the Quantrill Massacre Contrasted," *KHC* 6 (1897–1900): 311; John M. Peterson, ed., "Letters of Edward and Sarah Fitch, Lawrence, Kansas, 1855–1863, Part II," *Kansas History* 12, no. 2 (Summer 1989): 96, 100.

35. Quantrill Scrapbook, LKSHS, 1:57.

36. Andreas, *Kansas*, 1:322–23; *New York Daily Times*, Sept. 4, 1863.

37. Cordley, *Lawrence*, 224–26.

38. Shea, *Reminiscences*, 11; Barnes, "An Editor Looks," 147.

39. Shea, *Reminiscences*, 16.

40. Ibid., 17–19; Cordley, *Lawrence*, 217.

41. Lowman, *Narrative*, 62–63.

42. *New York Daily Times*, Sept. 4, 1863; *Kansas City Daily Journal*, Sept. 27, 1863; Fisher, *The Gun and the Gospel*, 194–98; *Leavenworth Daily Conservative*, Oct. 6, 1863.

43. Ridenour, *Autobiography*, 167; Speer, "Burning of Osceola," 311; Andreas, *Kansas*, 1:323.

44. Speer, "Burning of Osceola," 310–11; Andreas, *Kansas*, 1:323; Shea, *Reminiscences*, 7.

45. Lowman, *Narrative*, 84.

46. *Lawrence Daily Journal-World*, Aug. 21, 1924; Lowman, *Narrative*, 91; Shea, *Reminiscences*, 24.

47. Cordley, *Pioneer Days*, 181–82.

48. Bidlack, "Ladd's Description," 118.

49. Douglas County Scrapbook, LKSHS, vol. 7, from *Dodge City Globe*, Mar. 29, 1939; Ridenour, *Autobiography*, 183–85.

50. *Leavenworth Daily Conservative*, Aug. 24, 1863.

51. Lowman, *Narrative*, 93; Cordley, *Lawrence*, 216.

52. Lyon County Scrapbook, LKSHS, 4:275–76.

53. Lowman, *Narrative*, 63.

54. Elliott, "Quantrill Raid," 183; Andreas, *Kansas*, 1:321; Barnes, "An Editor Looks," 147.

55. Cordley, *Pioneer Days*, 182–83; *Leavenworth Daily Conservative*, Oct. 6, 1863; Shea, *Reminiscences*, 21–22; Quantrill Scrapbook, LKSHS, 1:18; *Lawrence Daily Journal-World*, Aug. 21, 1924.

56. Riggs, *Pioneer Ancestors*, 207–8: Elliott, "Quantrill Raid," 191–92.

57. *Wyandotte Commercial Gazette*, Sept. 12, 1863.

58. Cordley, *Lawrence*, 239.

59. Ibid., 234.

60. *Leavenworth Daily Times*, Aug. 23, 1863; Shea, *Reminiscences*, 22; Lowman, *Narrative*, 90.

61. Quantrill Scrapbook, LKSHS, 1:18, and 2:193; *Junction City Smoky Hill and Republican Union*, Aug. 29, 1863.

62. Quantrill Scrapbook, LKSHS, 2:193; Riggs, *Pioneer Ancestors*, 209.

63. Lowman, *Narrative*, 66–67.

64. Elliott, "Quantrill Raid," 196.

65. Riggs, *Pioneer Ancestors*, 209; Elliott, "Quantrill Raid," 193.

66. Cordley, *Lawrence*, 228; Quantrill Scrapbook, LKSHS, 1:51.

67. Cordley, *Lawrence*, 239.

68. Douglas County Scrapbook, LKSHS, 4:19.

8. The Heathen Are Come

1. Andreas, *Kansas*, 1:323.

2. Cordley, *Lawrence*, 239.

3. *New York Daily Times*, Sept. 4, 1863.

4. Quantrill Scrapbook, LKSHS, 1:19.

5. Ridenour, *Autobiography*, 172; Connelley, *Quantrill*, 275.

6. Genevieve Yost, "History of Lynchings in Kansas," *KHQ* 2, no. 2 (May 1933): 187–88; Barnes, "An Editor Looks," 144–45; *New York Daily Times*, Sept. 4, 1863.

7. Shea, *Reminiscences*, 4, 22.

8. Letter, F. L. Pilla to "Dear Brother," Sept. 21, 1863, Kansas Collections, Spencer Library, University of Kansas, Lawrence.

9. Andreas, *Kansas*, 1:323; Cordley, *Lawrence*, 240.

10. *Lawrence Daily Journal-World*, Feb. 7, 1939.

11. Horton, "Two Pioneer Kansas Merchants," 602–6; Ridenour, *Autobiography*, 166, 177, 183–85.

12. Cordley, *Lawrence*, 241–42.

13. Connelley, *Quantrill*, 387; Cordley, *Lawrence*, 240; Douglas County Scrapbook, LKSHS, 4:19; Peterson, "Letters of Edward and Sarah Fitch," 97.

14. Cordley, *Lawrence*, 218.

15. *Lawrence Daily Kansas Tribune*, Apr. 30, 1864.

16. Riggs, *Pioneer Ancestors*, 212.

17. Lowman, *Narrative*, 67.

18. *Boston Daily Post*, Aug. 31, 1863.

19. Cordley, *Lawrence*, 248–49; Fisher, *The Gun and the Gospel*, 202–4.

20. Bidlack, "Ladd's Description," 120; Alan Conway, ed., "The Sacking of Lawrence," *KHQ* 24, no. 2 (Summer 1958): 150.

9. The Chase

1. *OR*, 22, 1:590.

2. Connelley, *Kansas*, 2:640–42.

3. *OR*, 22, 1:581, 585–87, 589; *Leavenworth Daily Conservative*, Aug. 27, 1863.

4. *OR*, 22, 1:580; Connelley, *Kansas*, 2:641.

5. *OR*, 22, 1:582.

6. *Leavenworth Daily Times*, Aug. 27, 1863.

7. Connelley, *Kansas*, 2:641; *Kansas City Daily Journal*, Aug. 26, 1863.

8. Speer, *Lane*, 267; Garwood, *Crossroads*, 57; *OR*, 22, 1:592.

9. *OR*, 22, 1:590; Kirke Mechem, "Letters of Julia Louisa Lovejoy, 1856–1864," *KHQ* 16, no. 2 (1948): 195–96; Connelley, *Kansas*, 2:641.

10. Castel, *Quantrill*, 137–38.

11. Speer, *Lane*, 267–69; Connelley, *Kansas*, 2:641–42; *OR*, 22, 1:592, 589–90.

12. Connelley, *Kansas*, 2:643; Speer, *Lane*, 268; *OR*, 22, 1:580, 590.

13. *OR*, 22, 1:582.

14. *Leavenworth Daily Conservative*, Aug. 22, 1863.

15. *OR*, 22, 1:583; William E. Unrau, ed., "In Pursuit of Quantrill," *KHQ* 39, no. 3 (Autumn 1973): 386.

16. Blair, *Johnson County*, 224.

17. Andreas, *Kansas*, 2:880; Connelley, *Kansas*, 2:643; *OR*, 22, 1:581.

18. *OR*, 22, 1:585–87.

19. Ibid.; Andreas, *Kansas*, 2:880; Connelley, *Kansas*, 2:643.

20. Connelley, *Kansas*, 2:643; *OR*, 22, 1:592.

21. *OR*, 22, 1:585–87; Connelley, *Kansas*, 2:643–44; Andreas, *Kansas*, 2:880.

22. (Topeka) *Kansas State Record*, Sept. 2, 1863.

23. *OR*, 22, 1:589.

24. Ibid., 581–82.

25. *Council Grove Press*, Sept. 14, 1863.

26. *OR*, 22, 1:581–82.

27. Andreas, *Kansas*, 2:880.

28. Connelley, *Kansas*, 2:641, 644; *OR*, 22, 1:582; Unrau, "Pursuit," 386.

29. *OR*, 22, 1:582.

30. Ibid., 581, 589.

31. "J. A. Pike," 312.

32. OR, 22, 1:582; Unrau, "Pursuit," 386–88; Leavenworth Daily Times, Aug. 27, 1863.

33. (Topeka) Kansas State Record, Sept. 2, 1863; OR, 22, 1:582.

34. OR, 22, 1:587–88, 591.

35. Ibid., 586–87, 589.

36. New York Daily Times, Sept. 4, 1863.

37. Connelley, Quantrill, 418.

10. This Savage War

1. OR, 22, 1:576.

2. Ibid., 580–81; Leavenworth Daily Times, Aug. 26, 1863; Leavenworth Daily Conservative, Aug. 28, 1863; Council Grove Press, Sept. 7, 1863.

3. OR, 22, 1:576.

4. Larkin, Bingham, 184; William E. Connelley, ed., "The Civil War Diary of John Howard Kitts," KHC 14 (1915–18): 319.

5. New York Daily Times, Aug. 27, 1863.

6. OR, 22, 2:472–73.

7. Ibid.

8. Ibid.

9. OR, 22, 1:584–85.

10. Ibid., 584.

11. Larkin, Bingham, 198–206.

12. Barnes, "An Editor Looks," 148.

13. Cordley, Lawrence, 241.

14. Barnes, "An Editor Looks," 148; New York Daily Times, Sept. 4, 1863; Connelley, Kansas, 2:658.

15. Boston Daily Advertiser, Aug. 27, 28, 1863.

16. New York Daily Times, Sept. 6, 1863.

17. Leavenworth Daily Conservative, Aug. 28, 1863; Barnes, "An Editor Looks," 148–49; Boston Daily Advertiser, Aug. 31, 1863.

18. OR, 22, 1:587–88; Leavenworth Daily Conservative, Sept. 25, 1863; Leavenworth Daily Times, Aug. 27, 1863.

19. Leavenworth Daily Times, Aug. 28, 1863.

20. New York Daily Times, Sept. 4, 13, 1863; (Topeka) Kansas State Record, Sept. 9, 1863.

21. OR, 22, 2:490; History of Clay and Platte Counties, Missouri (St. Louis: National, 1885), 238–40.

22. Letter, Thomas Ewing to Gov. Th. Carney, Aug. 27, 1863, Thomas Ewing, Jr., Papers, LKSHS; Schofield, Forty-six Years, 80–81.

23. Leavenworth Daily Times, Aug. 26, 28, 1863.

24. Barnes, "An Editor Looks," 148–49.

25. (Topeka) Kansas State Record, Sept. 2, 1863.

26. Ridenour, Autobiography, 176, 179; Horton, "Two Pioneer Kansas Merchants," 606–7.

27. New York Daily Times, Aug. 31, 1863.

28. Ibid., Sept. 6, 1863.

29. Schofield, Forty-six Years, 80–82; New York Daily Times, Sept. 9, 1863; OR, 22, 1:573–74.

30. Schofield, *Forty-six Years*, 81; *Leavenworth Daily Times*, Sept. 3, 1863.

31. *Leavenworth Daily Conservative*, Sept. 5, 1863.

32. *New York Daily Times*, Sept. 16, 1863; *Leavenworth Daily Conservative*, Sept. 11, 1863.

33. Larkin, *Bingham*, 210–11, 217; Martin Rice, *Rural Rhymes, and Talks and Tales of Olden Times* (Kansas City, Mo., 1882), 117; *Kansas City Weekly Journal*, Sept. 19, 1863.

34. *Charleston Daily Mercury*, Oct. 17, 1863.

35. Garwood, *Crossroads*, 74; Larkin, *Bingham*, 221.

36. Larkin, *Bingham*, 215–16; Rice, *Rural Rhymes*, 117–19; *Clay and Platte Counties*, 238; Castel, *Quantrill*, 145–46.

37. Niepman, "General Orders No. 11," 202.

38. *Leavenworth Daily Times*, Sept. 11, 1863.

39. *OR*, 22, 1:585.

40. *New York Daily Times*, Sept. 16, 1863.

41. *Kansas City Weekly Journal*, Sept. 19, 1863.

42. *Lawrence Journal*, Oct. 8, 1863.

43. *OR*, 22, 2:538; *Leavenworth Daily Conservative*, Sept. 8, 1863.

44. *OR*, 22, 2:518, 524, 566, 568.

45. Ibid., 611; *New York Daily Times*, Oct. 3, 1863; Vivian Kirkpatrick McLarty, ed., "The Civil War Letters of Colonel Bazel F. Lazear," *MHR* 44, pt. 2 (July 1950): 393.

46. *New York Daily Times*, Sept. 6, 24, 1863; *Kansas City Weekly Journal*, Sept. 26, 1863.

47. *Charleston Daily Mercury*, Dec. 5, 1863; Castel, *Quantrill*, 150–52; *OR*, 22, 1:690–98, 700–701.

48. *Kansas City Daily Journal*, Oct. 8, 1863.

11. When Paths Join

1. *Lawrence Journal*, May 5, 1864.

2. Castel, *Quantrill*, 181–82.

3. *OR*, 34, 4:417.

4. *Lawrence Daily Kansas Tribune*, Mar. 29, Apr. 29, July 14, 1864; Cordley, *Lawrence*, 251–52, 255; Ridenour, *Autobiography*, 185–86; *Kansas City Daily Journal*, Sept. 8, 13, 1864.

5. *Lawrence Daily Kansas Tribune*, May 3, 1864.

6. *Lawrence Journal*, May 5, June 23, 1864.

7. Cordley, *Lawrence*, 255.

8. *Lawrence Journal*, Aug. 4, 11, 1864.

9. Horton, "Two Pioneer Kansas Merchants," 609–11.

10. Albert Castel, *General Sterling Price and the Civil War in the West* (Baton Rouge: Louisiana State Univ. Press, 1968), 204–5; Robert L. Kerby, *Kirby Smith's Confederacy* (New York: Columbia Univ. Press, 1972), 335–36; Richard S. Brownlee, "The Battle of Pilot Knob," *MHR* 59, no. 1 (October 1964): 10.

11. Castel, *Price*, 209–17; Edwin C. McReynolds, *Missouri: A History of the Crossroads State* (Norman: Univ. of Oklahoma Press, 1962), 253.

12. Nevins, *Ordeal of the Union*, 8:330–31.

13. Larkin, *Bingham*, 245, 260, 294.

14. Ibid., 242–329.

15. *OR*, 41, 3:900.

16. Thomas Goodman, *A Thrilling Record*, 2d ed. (1868; reprint, Maryville, Mo.: Rush, 1960), 22–24, 31–33; *OR*, 41, 3:455.

17. Brownlee, *Gray Ghosts*, 201; Garwood, *Crossroads*, 54, 57.

18. *OR*, 41, 4:356, 496.

19. Cordley, *Lawrence*, 268; *Kansas City Daily Journal*, Dec. 22, 1864.

20. *DAB*, s.v. "Robinson, Charles."

21. Burton J. Williams, "Quantrill's Raid on Lawrence: A Question of Complicity," *KHQ* 34, no. 2 (Summer 1968): 144–45; Castel, *Frontier State*, 138.

22. Castel, *Frontier State*, 232.

23. *Lawrence Daily Kansas Tribune*, Apr. 12, 1865; *Lawrence Journal*, Apr. 13, 1865.

24. *OR*, 41, 3:548.

25. Bidlack, "Ladd's Description," 120.

26. B. James George, Sr., "The Gregg Biography," LKSHS, 76.

27. *Kansas City Daily Journal*, Aug. 28, 1864.

28. *Lawrence Daily Kansas Tribune*, May 10, 1864.

BIBLIOGRAPHY

Books, pamphlets, and manuscripts

Andreas, A. T. *History of the State of Kansas.* 2 vols. Chicago: A. T. Andreas, 1883.

Birdsall, A. *History of Jackson County, Missouri.* 2d ed. 1881. Reprint. Kansas City, Mo.: Ramfre, 1966.

Blair, Ed. *History of Johnson County, Kansas.* Lawrence: Standard, 1915.

Brown, G. W. *Reminiscences of Gov. R. J. Walker.* Rockford, Ill.: G. W. Brown, 1902.

Brownlee, Richard S. *Gray Ghosts of the Confederacy: Guerrilla Warfare in the West, 1861–1865.* Baton Rouge: Louisiana State Univ. Press, 1958.

Burke, W. S. *Military History of Kansas Regiments During the War for the Suppression of the Great Rebellion.* Leavenworth, Kans.: W. S. Burke, 1870.

Castel, Albert. *A Frontier State at War: Kansas, 1861–1865.* Ithaca, N.Y.: Cornell Univ. Press, 1958.

——— . *General Sterling Price and the Civil War in the West.* Baton Rouge: Louisiana State Univ. Press, 1968.

——— . *William Clarke Quantrill: His Life and Times.* New York: Frederick Fell, 1962.

Connelley, William Elsey. *History of Kansas, State and People.* 5 vols. Chicago: American Historical Society, 1928.

——— . *The Life of Preston B. Plumb, 1837–1891.* Chicago: Brown and Howell, 1913.

——— . *Papers.* Box 13. LKSHS.

——— . *Quantrill and the Border Wars.* 2d ed. 1909. Reprint. New York: Pageant, 1956.

Cordley, Richard. *History of Lawrence, Kansas From the First Settlement to the Close of the Rebellion.* Lawrence: E. F. Caldwell, 1895.

——— . *Pioneer Days in Kansas.* Boston: Pilgrim, 1903.

Douglas County Historical Society Files. Kansas Collection, Spencer Library, University of Kansas, Lawrence.

Douglas County Scrapbook. LKSHS.

Ewing, Thomas, Jr. Private Papers, 1856–1908. LKSHS.

Fellman, Michael. *Inside War: The Guerrilla Conflict in Missouri During the American Civil War.* New York: Oxford Univ. Press, 1989.

Fisher, H. D. *The Gun and the Gospel—early Kansas and Chaplain Fisher.* Chicago: Kenwood, 1896.

Garwood, Darrell. *Crossroads of America: The Story of Kansas City.* New York: W. W. Norton, 1948.

George, B. James, Sr. "The Gregg Biography—Captain William Henry Gregg, Confederate and Quantrillian Officer." LKSHS.

Goodman, Thomas. *A Thrilling Record.* 2d ed. 1868. Reprint. Maryville, Mo.: Rush, 1960.

Gregg, William H. "The Lawrence Massacre." LKSHS.

History of Clay and Platte Counties, Missouri. St. Louis: National, 1885.

Hunt, Elvid. *History of Fort Leavenworth, 1827–1927.* Fort Leavenworth, Kans.: The General Service Schools Press, 1926.

Johnson, Allen, and Dumas Malone, eds. *Dictionary of American Biography.* 23 vols. New York: Scribner's, 1928–31.

Kansas Scrapbook. LKSHS.

Kerby, Robert L. *Kirby Smith's Confederacy: The Trans Mississippi South, 1863–1865.* New York: Columbia Univ. Press, 1972.

Larkin, Lew. *Bingham: Fighting Artist, The Story of Missouri's Immortal Painter, Patriot, Soldier, and Statesman.* St. Louis: State, 1955.

Learned Scrapbook. Kansas Collections, Spencer Library, University of Kansas, Lawrence.

Lowman, H. E. *Narrative of the Lawrence Massacre on the morning of the 21st of August, 1863.* Lawrence, Kans.: State Journal Steam Press, 1864.

Lyon County Scrapbook. LKSHS.

McDonough, James L. *Schofield: Union General in the Civil War and Reconstruction.* Tallahassee: Florida State Univ. Press, 1972.

McReynolds, Edwin C. *Missouri: A History of the Crossroads State.* Norman: Univ. of Oklahoma Press, 1962.

Miller, George. *Missouri's Memorable Decade, 1860–1870: an Historical Sketch Personal—Political—Religious. . . .* Columbia, Mo: E. W. Stephens, 1898.

Monaghan, Jay. *Civil War on the Western Border, 1854–1865.* Boston: Little, Brown, 1955.

Nevins, Allan. *Ordeal of the Union.* 8 vols. New York: Scribner's, 1947–71.

Nichols, Alice. *Bleeding Kansas.* New York: Oxford Univ. Press, 1954.

Pilla, F. L. Letter to "Dear Brother," Sept. 21, 1863. Kansas Collections, Spencer Library, University of Kansas, Lawrence.

Quantrill Scrapbook. LKSHS.

Rice, Martin. *Rural Rhymes, and Talks and Tales of Olden Times.* Kansas City, Mo., 1882.

Ridenour, Peter D. *Autobiography of Peter D. Ridenour with the Genealogies of the Ridenour and Beatty Families.* Kansas City, Mo.: Hudson, 1908.

Riggs, Henry Earle. *Our Pioneer Ancestors.* Ann Arbor, Mich.: N.p., 1942.

Robinson, Charles, and Sara T. D. Private Papers, 1834–1911. LKSHS.

Robinson, Sara T. D. *Kansas: Its Interior and Exterior Life.* Boston: Crosby, Nichols and Co., 1857.

Schofield, John M. *Forty-six Years in the Army.* New York: Century, 1897.

Shea, John C. *Reminiscences of Quantrell's Raid upon the city of Lawrence: Thrilling Narrative of Living Eye Witnesses.* Kansas City, Mo.: Isaac P. Moore, 1879.

Speer, John I. *The Life of Gen. James H. Lane, "The Liberator of Kansas" with Corroborative Incidents of Pioneer History.* Garden City, Kans.: John Speer, 1896.

Starr, Stephen Z. *Jennison's Jayhawkers: A Civil War Cavalry Regiment and its Commander.* Baton Rouge: Louisiana State Univ. Press, 1973.

Walton, George. *Sentinel of the Plains: Fort Leavenworth and the American West.* Englewood Cliffs, N.J.: Prentice-Hall, 1973.

War of the Rebellion: Official Records of the Union and Confederate Armies. 128 vols. Washington, D.C.: Government Printing Office, 1880–1901.

Wilson, Don W. *Governor Charles Robinson of Kansas*. Lawrence: Univ. Press of Kansas, 1975.

Younger, Cole. *The Story of Cole Younger, by Himself*. 1903. Reprint. Provo, Utah: Triton, 1988.

Periodicals

KHC   *Kansas Historical Collections*, 1887–1933
KHQ   *Kansas Historical Quarterly*, 1933–78
MHR   *Missouri Historical Review*
WHQ   *Westport (Missouri) Historical Quarterly*

Barnes, Lela, ed. "An Editor Looks at Early-Day Kansas: The Letters of Charles Monroe Chase." *KHQ* 26, no.2 (Summer 1960): 113–51.

Berneking, Carolyn, ed. "A Look at Early Lawrence: Letters from Robert Gaston Elliott." *KHQ* 43, no. 3 (Autumn 1977): 282–96.

Bidlack, Russell E. "Erastus D. Ladd's Description of the Lawrence Massacre." *KHQ* 29, no. 2 (Summer 1963): 113–21.

Brownlee, Richard S. "The Battle of Pilot Knob, Iron County, Missouri, September 27, 1864. *MHR* 59, no. 1 (Oct. 1964): 1–30.

Caldwell, Martha B. "The Eldridge House." *KHQ* 9, no. 4 (1940): 347–70.

Castel, Albert. "Kansas Jayhawking Raids into Western Missouri in 1861." *MHR* 54, no. 1 (Oct. 1959): 1–11.

Connelley, William E., ed. "The Civil War Diary of John Howard Kitts." *KHC* 14 (1915–18): 318–32.

Conway, Alan, ed. "The Sacking of Lawrence." *KHQ* 24, no. 2 (Summer 1958): 144–50.

Dix, Mrs. R. C. "Quantrill's Raid—An Eyewitness Account." *WHQ* 1, no. 1 (May 1965): 8–11.

Doerschuk, Albert N., ed. "Extracts from War-Time Letters, 1861–1864." *MHR* 23, no. 1 (Oct. 1928): 99–110.

Elliott, R. G. "The Quantrill Raid as Seen from the Eldridge House." *KHC* 2 (1920): 179–96.

Farlow, Joyce, and Louise Barry, eds. "Vincent B. Osborne's Civil War Experiences." *KHQ* 20, no. 2 (May 1952): 108–33.

Gambone, Joseph G. "Economic Relief in Territorial Kansas, 1860–1861." *KHQ* 36, no. 2 (Summer 1970): 149–74.

Gardner, Theodore. "The First Kansas Battery." *KHC* 14 (1915–18): 235–82.

Herklotz, Hildegarde Rose. "Jayhawkers in Missouri, 1858–1863." *MHR* 18 (Oct. 1923): 64–101.

Horton, James Clark. "Peter D. Ridenour and Harlow W. Baker, Two Pioneer Kansas Merchants." *KHC* 10 (1907–8): 589–621.

Hubbard, David. "Reminiscences of the Yeager Raid on the Santa Fe Trail, in 1863." *KHC* 8 (1903–4): 168–71.

Langsdorf, Edgar, ed. "Jim Lane and the Frontier Guard." *KHQ* 9 (Feb. 1940): 13–25.

———. "Letters of Joseph H. Trego, 1857–1864." *KHQ* 19 (Aug. 1951): 287–309.

Lutz, John J. "Quantrill and the Morgan Walker Tragedy." *KHC* 8 (1903–4): 324–31.

McDonough, James L. "And All for Nothing—Early Experiences of John M. Schofield in Missouri." *MHR* 64 (Apr. 1970): 306–21.

McLarty, Vivian Kirkpatrick, ed. "Civil War Letters of Colonel Bazel F. Lazear." *MHR* 44, pt. 2 (July 1950): 387–401.

Martin, George W. "The First Two Years of Kansas." *KHC* 10 (1907–8): 120–48.

Mechem, Kirke. "Letters of Julia Louisa Lovejoy, 1856–1864." *KHQ* 16, no. 2 (1948): 175–211.

Mitchell, W. A. "Historic Linn." *KHC* 16 (1926): 607–57.

Niepman, Ann Davis. "General Orders No. 11 and Border Warfare During the Civil War." *MHR* 66, no. 2 (Jan. 1972): 185–210.

Palmer, Henry E. "The Black Flag Character of the War on the Border." *KHC* 9 (1905–6): 455–66.

Peterson, John M., ed. "Letters of Edward and Sarah Fitch, Lawrence, Kansas, 1855–1863, Part II." *Kansas History* 12, no. 2 (Summer 1989): 78–100.

Speer, John. "The Burning of Osceola, Mo., by Lane, and the Quantrill Massacre Contrasted." *KHC* 6 (1897–1900): 305–12.

"Statement of J. A. Pike." *KHC* 14 (1915–18): 311–18.

Thruston, Ethylene Ballard. "Captain Dick Yeager—Quantrill Man." *WHQ* 4, no. 1 (June 1968): 3–6.

Unrau, William E., ed. "In Pursuit of Quantrill: An Enlisted Man's Response." *KHQ* 39, no. 3 (Autumn 1973): 379–91.

Williams, Burton J. "Quantrill's Raid on Lawrence: A Question of Complicity." *KHQ* 34, no. 2 (Summer 1968): 143–49.

Yost, Genevieve. "History of Lynchings in Kansas." *KHQ* 2, no. 2 (May 1933): 182–219.

Newspapers

Atchison Freedom's Champion 1861–63
Boston (Massachusetts) Daily Advertiser 1863
Boston (Massachusetts) Daily Post 1863
Charleston (South Carolina) Daily Mercury 1863
Council Grove (Kansas) Press 1861–63
Emporia News 1862
Junction City Smoky Hill and Republican Union 1863
Kansas City (Missouri) Daily Western Journal of Commerce 1862–64
Kansas City (Missouri) Weekly Western Journal of Commerce 1863
Lawrence Daily Journal-World 1924, 1939
Lawrence Daily Kansas Tribune 1864–65
Lawrence Herald of Freedom 1855–56
Lawrence Kansas State Journal 1861–65
Lawrence Republican 1861–62
Leavenworth Daily Conservative 1862–63
Leavenworth Daily Times 1861–63
Liberty (Missouri) Tribune 1862
Manhattan (Kansas) Independent 1863
New York Daily Times 1863
Olathe Mirror 1861–62
Oskaloosa Independent 1861–63
(Topeka) Kansas State Record 1863
Wyandotte Commercial Gazette 1862–63

INDEX